THE
KITCHEN WITCH
COMPANION

THE
KITCHEN WITCH
COMPANION

SIMPLE AND SUBLIME
CULINARY MAGIC

PATRICIA TELESCO

CITADEL PRESS
Kensington Publishing Corp.
www.kensingtonbooks.com

Dedicated to my neo-Pagan family everywhere—
if you feed them, they will come!

CITADEL PRESS BOOKS are published by

Kensington Publishing Corp.
850 Third Avenue
New York, NY 10022

All Kensington titles, imprints, and distributed lines are available at special quantity discounts for bulk purchases for sales promotions, premiums, fund-raising, educational, or institutional use. Special book excerpts or customized printings can also be created to fit specific needs. For details, write or phone the office of the Kensington special sales manager: Kensington Publishing Corp., 850 Third Avenue, New York, NY 10022, attn: Special Sales Department; phone 1-800-221-2647.

CITADEL PRESS and the Citadel logo are Reg. U.S. Pat. & TM Off.

First printing: March 2005

10   9   8   7   6   5   4   3   2   1

Printed in the United States of America

Library of Congress Control Number: 2004113766

ISBN 0-8065-2670-X

Contents

CONTENTS

Preface—A Decade to Reflect

A decade ago *A Kitchen Witch's Cookbook* was published as a bold step forward in New Age writing. Rather than create a book that was strewn with time-consuming activities or odd-sounding components, this book tackled an everyday ritual (cooking) and gave it a spiritual dimension. Actually, it might be more accurate to say it honored a latent spirituality that the culinary arts have always embraced. Other than Scott Cunningham's *The Magick in Food*, no other New Age text to date had dealt completely with something so near and dear to everyday life.

That hearth-and-home approach endeared *A Kitchen Witch's Cookbook* to thousands of hungry neo-Pagans (as the saying goes, If you feed them they will come!). Since that time, I have become known as the "world's most famous kitchen witch" and "the Martha Stewart of Paganism." While somewhat humorous, these titles indicate the strength of my love for the kitchen and cooking, and I'd be lying if I didn't say I found the association very flattering.

It is now thirteen years into my career as a writer. It's not surprising to me that historically my most successful books, and the ones most enjoyable to write, have continued the down-home, "keep it simple and sublime" approach. Anywhere possible I sneak in recipes for culinary delights or kitchen craftiness. I can't help it. It's my passion and where I "live." Everything from soup to nuts, every item in the home, holds magical potential. It's that potential, and the excitement about it, that I hope I've successfully and zeal-ously passed along to readers.

In keeping with this tradition, I am thrilled to present *The Kitchen Witch Companion* to you. For everyone who wrote asking for another cookbook, everyone who had recipe ideas, everyone who prepared meals from any of my previous suggestions—this book celebrates *you*! I have kept a diligent log of what people craved in the way of new, magical, and tasty foods, alongside nifty kitchen-witchy helps and hints that you all have generously sup-plied over the years. Whatever I could manage to use in keeping with our topic is included in these pages.

So, get out your oven mitts, wooden spoons, and mixing bowls and prepare to whip up some wonderful, whimsical, and edible magic!

PART I

HOME IS WHERE
THE HEARTH IS

Cooking is at once child's play and adult joy.
And cooking done with care is an act of love.

—CRAIG CLAIBORNE

INTRODUCTION

A dining room table with children's eager, hungry faces around it ceases to be a mere dining room table and becomes an altar.

—SIMEON STRUNSKY

Think, for just a moment, of the wonderful sensation that the smell of freshly baked cookies inspires, or how the aroma of warm bread seems to tempt even the most stalwart of individuals into taking a nibble. Think of those days when your loved ones all gathered around a table for shared food and laughter. When you do, is there a whimsical smile on your face? Do warm memories trickle into your mind? Does your stomach rumble a bit? Certainly so! This is the power of food magic in its most simple, beautiful form.

With this nearly universal human response in mind, it's not surprising to discover that the kitchen has always been a kind of sacred space. In some settings, like China, the stove even had its own indwelling goddess who kept an eye on the family and blessed every meal! Additionally, certain edibles and recipe components were considered real "soul food" that could inspire specific energies when properly prepared and consumed. For example, in

Japan people eat rice on their birthday for luck and wish fulfillment like Americans eat cake! In China people eat apricots to improve prophetic abilities, and in Europe eating goose on Michelmas Day brings prosperity. So, despite our fast-food society, there can be far more meaning to the entire cooking–eating process than simply feeding one's stomach. Now our goal is to satisfy the spirit too!

Don't worry, this doesn't mean you have to go out and take gourmet cooking classes or transform your kitchen into something resembling a magazine picture. The hearth gods and goddesses are a very practical lot, who work with what you have. They do not ask us to do anything beyond our vision or abilities. All these spirits ask is that you open up to the magical potentials and possibilities that are around you every day, especially those in your own home, then let that wonderful energy flow. In other words— from this page forward it's not only okay to play with your food, it's encouraged!

The entire theme of *The Kitchen Witch Companion* is to eat, drink, and make magic! Now before you ask how one can possibly do that by just playing in the pantry, stop for a moment and reflect on family or household traditions. I'm willing to bet that you have several customs with a bit of that special spark in them already. For example, what was your customary Yule dinner and why? What emotions does thinking about this celebration evoke? What do you eat when you're sick, and why? See, there's the magic! There are all kinds of foods and drinks that you already associate with specific feelings, circumstances, or effects. Now all you're going to do is put that association to good use, blending in a little divine blessing and ritualistic overtones to help the process manifest in the best possible way.

In part I of this book, you'll learn all about various hearth deities and how to honor either (or both) in your kitchen's sacred space. You'll also discover the magical potential in common, everyday culinary implements and how to activate that potential for sautéed sorcery, warmed wizardry, and marinated mysticism. This section includes great helps and hints that turn any meal into a magical masterpiece, even if the ingredients come from a box! Perhaps most important, you'll discover the kitchen witch's credo, which takes proverbial "kitchen magic" far beyond the kitchen into every aspect of your life.

Part II is the meaty portion of this book (forgive the pun), filled to overflowing with menu-planning ideas, hints for decoration, recipes, and divine beings from around the world to call upon to bless all your efforts. This section is set up similarly to a normal cookbook in that it's separated by types of culinary adventures. If you want a blissful barbecue or a casserole to take to your coven meeting, simply turn the page, whip up the magic, and take a bite!

Hungry yet? Good—let's get cooking!

FIERY FOLKWAYS, HISTORY, AND LORE

My very first lessons in the art of telling stories took place in the kitchen . . . my mother and three or four of her friends . . . told stories . . . with effortless art and technique. They were natural-born storytellers in the oral tradition.

—PAULE MARSHALL

Come on in and sit for a spell! I have been busy in my kitchen whipping up some magic for your spiritual and physical taste buds to enjoy. Before launching into spell-recipes, however, let's take a moment to talk about your hearth, home, and sacred fires. While you may have never considered cooking as even remotely spiritual, it certainly can be. Consider for a moment how recipes, especially traditional ones, get followed very closely, as if they were a little ritual. Think of how you learned this process, carefully following the patterns provided by a parent or grandparent, and loved the sense of kinship it created. The kitchen was a fun place, a meaningful place . . . a place where the people you cared about came together in the spirit of family.

Even among the ancients the fire was a place that offered comfort. It provided warmth, protection, and a common place to gather and exchange news of the day. When we moved away from living in caves and made actual structures, the fire pit or cooking area was the first to be built, based on the feeling that this represented not simply the heart of the home, but of the entire community. In fact, if you think back to a recent party, you'll notice the kitchen area still has that magnetic appeal. Why is it that everyone gathers there for intimate discussions? Because that's how it has been since our earliest days. We are coming together again around the sacred fire.

Fire Keeping

When there was no more lantern in the kitchen,
The fire got out through the crannies in the stove
And danced in yellow wrigglers on the ceiling
As much at home as if they'd always danced there

—ROBERT FROST

To fully understand the importance and meaningfulness of the modern oven and fireplace, we have to turn back the pages of time to when fire was still a mystery. Perhaps a cave dweller wandered near a lightning strike to discover the warmth and light of the residual fire. Perhaps another person dropped a piece of raw meat or fish into a similar fire and cooking was born. After all, some of humankind's best discoveries came about by sheer happenstance. No matter how it happened, however, our forebears came to revere and treasure this great gift. So much was the case that after we learned how to create fire during Cro-Magnon times, there were often individuals specially chosen in various communities to tend central flames, or the fires of a temple.

FIRE

The Latin word for hearth or fireplace translates as "focus," probably because the fire was the heart of the circle—the tribe's gathering place. And so, too, did the hearth of the home become its focus. You will notice even in modern homes the fireplace, no longer essential for warmth, is still centrally located and is often the place where friends and family gather (complete with mantels that honor ancestors and kinship). This is also why many tables still have candles set upon them. They replace the central fireplace in homes without one.

During the time when people were still hunter-gatherers, groups of about twenty-five traveled the land together. A fire keeper traveled with them. When they reached a destination, the women asked for the fire from the keeper, and in return that man got his night's meal. A little later this custom translated into offering fire from one community to another as a sign of welcome, and into bringing small gifts when visiting someone's home. Those gifts were offerings so as to not offend the hearth god!

As people became more settled and ritualistic, we find fire as part of important social observances. Come spring, for example, all but the matron of certain regions would extinguish their fire. Then, that matron (or other community leader) would bring fire from his or her hearth to rekindle life in the community.

We find remnants of these customs in folklore around the world. In Armenian tradition, you always took fire from your old home when moving to the new one. This flame was then used to kindle the new hearth. Greek people had a very similar custom. Needless to say, if the fire went out between the two places it was thought an ill omen.

All of this seems very domestic, so what of spirituality and religion? Well, Persians had a sacred fire chief, a position noted among mages as a very respected station. The chief would create the altar fires to represent deity and the power of life.

The Persians were certainly not alone in such reverence. Slavonic custom instructs that young ones are never to swear or scream when a fire is being built and lit. This is an insult to the spirit of the fire and is considered very ill mannered. And, of course, even modern Native Americans still call fire "our grandfather"—a title that confers a great deal of respect.

I realize it's hard to find a common place of reverence when we can turn on fire with a simple match or flick of our stove's switches. Modernization has separated us from the sacred flame on many levels. However, at least part of this book's goal is that of reconnecting you with that special regard, and the hearth god or goddess within each of us. One thing that helped me was to remember the first time I got burned by fire. I lit a match and misjudged the burning time. In that moment, my respect for fire grew by leaps and bounds. I began to treat it differently.

If you can remember such a moment, add to that what I've just shared of fire's importance in our communal history. Now go to your stove or fireplace and start a new flame. Do so with honor, respect, and gratitude in your thoughts. Welcome the spirit of fire . . . and begin opening that inner doorway to the heart-flame that is your hearth god or goddess. Get to know him or her a little more intimately. And if you wish, set up a special place in your kitchen or near the fireplace that honors this being (ideas for this can be found in chapter 2).

A Brief Cooking Chronicle

A man finds room in the few square inches of the face for the traits of all his ancestors; for the expression of all his history, and his wants.

—RALPH WALDO EMERSON

As you probably suspected, modern culinary tools and devices would look like magic to our ancestors. The first breads, for example, were cooked on stones heated in a fire. This method was fairly universal, being noted by historians in regions as far separated as Ireland and Mexico. Sometimes people added some type of covering to the stone to keep the heat in and more even. Eventually that led to the idea of a dome-shaped oven, some examples of which were discovered dating back to 5100 B.C.E. in Asia, Egypt, and Mesopotamia.

People continued to use rudimentary systems for thousands of years, but they still managed to achieve some pretty remarkable results. When one reads about the lavish feasts of the Greeks, for example, whose main goal was to establish or reinforce political affiliations, they sound quite palatable. Cheese, breads, olive oil, figs, grapes, lentils, yogurt, cider, wine, olives, phyllo, honey, and seafood were among the primary ingredients for dishes served with lavish flair.

From the spiritual perspective there was hardly any meat at the Greek feasts, because they felt it was wrong to consume an animal that had not first been offered to the gods. Even vegetables

COOKING

In some areas not to cook for your mate, or to abstain from a family meal, is a sign of dissension in the home. One example comes from Tibet where being absent from the table for twenty-four hours implies a huge disagreement. Should this person continue to stay away and eventually undertake a rite called "throwing away the cooking pots," inevitably he will leave home and have to set up another household. With this in mind, it's no surprise that even modern families try to eat around one table (and children are chastised for fighting there).

and fruit were not wholly immune—some being considered more pure than others, and having an indwelling spirit. Thus, it's not surprising that we find accounts that indicate the worship of Dionysus was linked with wine drinking, and the worship of Demeter was linked with baking and eating bread.

The Greeks were not alone in connecting deity to food, or in utilizing it on a religious level. The Hindus forbid eating beef because the cow is sacred to God. Chinese Taoists say that the purpose of cooking is to maintain long life, and so they add special herbs to their meals. Buddhist monks in Japan abstain from eating meat or fish because one tenet of their faith is to limit the taking of life whenever possible. Since even vegetables are alive, none are wasted and eating is a very real sacrament. We'll talk more about what foods were sacred in various cultures, and why, in "Foods of and for the Gods," chapter 2.

Let's look a little more closely at the history of Chinese cuisine, as it reflects some similar resonance to that which we've explored thus far. It is said that the emperor Fu was responsible for teaching people how to cook about twenty centuries before Christ walked the earth. Nonetheless, the art of Chinese cooking really took shape in the Chou Dynasty (1122–249 B.C.E.). The two main forces shaping the culinary arts were the philosophies of Confucianism and Taoism.

Confucianism sees cooking as an art to be enjoyed. In this system good food and good friends are a complementary and beneficial combination to be celebrated. No gathering ever took place without the presence of some type of food.

I was not surprised to discover that Confucius was a great lover of both cooking and good table etiquette. The basic standards he set remain in use among the Chinese today For example, using knives at dinner is a social faux pas, which is why most foods are cut into small pieces during preparation.

Confucius seemed to be a fairly good kitchen witch in that he regarded this art as being dependent on balance and blending. A good chef had to understand the elements of flavor matching, textures, and colors, and how to present them harmoniously. A good kitchen witch must likewise know how to blend her components' energies into a functional whole that still tastes good!

While Confucius was pleasing the eye and palate, Taoists were focusing on hygienic and nourishing methods of food blending and preparation. Their goal was promoting the most healthful, holistic benefits of the food to ensure longevity. They may have been the first to realize that overcooking vegetables often robs them of important vitamins and medicinal value. This awareness combined with a generally low-fat diet may have marked an important health benefit that people today are just beginning to appreciate.

As we consider our history, it would be remiss of me not to mention how the mixing and mingling of cultures affected food styles and tastes. In Sicily around 1000 C.E. there were three distinct cultures mixing and mingling—Latin, Arabic, and Greek. The Sicilian kitchen garden resembled something even a Caliph would appreciate, and many of the foods included spices with ties to Arabia and beyond. All of these herbs had folkloric value. The Arabian spice traders cleverly recognized that the value of a spice was increased if it had magical qualities. And the accumulated lore and beliefs of these Eastern merchants were carried to Europe, and many of them remain in the kitchen witch's Book of Shadows!

But what of the "New World"? The indigenous people of North America used cooking implements made of bone and clay, and other natural materials. Their meals were composed of beans, pumpkin, squash, regional fruits, and whatever meat could be hunted.

Cooking utensils were often pottery or stone. The main meal seemed to be taken at noon when a larger fire would not be necessary (large fires at night could prove dangerous if they attracted the wrong elements). Grinding stones were used to turn corn and other grains into flour. Needless to say this was a painstaking and laborious task.

Natives also knapped flint and obsidian to create sharp-edged tools for butchering meat and cutting other food. Other "kitchen" tools were made from bone and horn.

While all this work makes one weary, we should not overlook the fact that Native Americans considered life to be sacred. The earth was a provider; each animal had an essence and energy. So they were not typically wasteful. When an animal was killed in a hunt, that animal's spirit was thanked for its gift, and as much of the body as possible would be used. What could not be, was given back to nature in gratitude for its providence.

Meanwhile south of the current border, a Mexican legend has it that God attempted to create man from clay, but found no form, then from bark but found no intellectual capacity, and finally from corn, where God found man's spirit. Similar to Sicily, Mexico's foods were influenced by the variety of peoples who wandered through the land. However, one of the oldest cooking traditions, dating back to about 1800 B.C.E., is tied into the Day of the Dead festivities.

Taking place in early November, as do many similar holidays around the world, the Day of the Dead honors the ancestral spirits. In its original form it was likely tied to the worship of an underworld deity ("underworld" meaning simply a place where deceased spirits reside). The Mexicans believed that life and death are part of one another and that every year their loved ones can return in spirit form. So, they prepare all manner of favorite dishes and leave them either at the family table or at the gravesite for the spirits to enjoy, accompanied by pictures of friends and relatives for whom the feast is intended.

On the opposite end of the earth we find the Inuit people inhabiting that region as much as 2,500 years ago. Their life, too, was harsh. They depended heavily on fish, whale, and whatever small game they could find for food. The process undertaken for the hunt included magic charms, songs, and rituals intended to ensure success.

When at last food returned home, it was prepared in a central living area that was constructed with an open skylight to let smoke out. Come the evening this same space became the ground upon which the stories and traditions of the tribe were passed along to children as a kind of cultural classroom. In this I find a charming parallel to early American settings, where the first house in any area became a classroom, and the kitchen table became a child's desk.

Moving forward in more mundane history, an oven that comes closer to being what we would consider efficient appeared in the eighteenth century. It retained heat far better and allowed for some moisture to be introduced into dishes. More important to cooks, however, it didn't have to be cleaned between each use, making it very popular with European bakers. Mind you, it wasn't until the nineteenth century that experiments in convection heat, oil heat, and gas eventually led to replacing wood and coal stoves with the modern cooking appliances many of us use today.

As we've already seen, until this time reverence toward the hearth existed around the world. That respect was expressed in different forms, but it was always present. Only in the past century has spirituality been separated from our tables, our kitchens, and our hearth—something I hope this book will change for you.

Right about now I suspect you're feeling very grateful for your modern oven or microwave (as am I). Knowing what our ancestors could do with what, to our eyes, were very rudimentary tools is pretty humbling. When I cook at a campfire, I often think about them and this history as it helps me understand why the fire, the kitchen, and food has so much associated mythology and lore. Let's take a moment to examine some of that richness so we can bring it home and kindle our own fires with it!

Cooking Beliefs, Folklore, and Practices

Live your beliefs and you can turn
the world around.

—HENRY DAVID THOREAU

As we've begun to explore, there's a wealth of mythology and lore surrounding our hearthside, be it a fireplace, a grill, or a kitchen stove. The folklore of the pantry, however, proved a little more complicated to include here since much of it focused on specific foods or beverages. Because I wanted to keep those beliefs and share them in conjunction with various recipes in part 2, I won't go into detail about specific food groups at this time. Rather, I'd first like to share superstitions surrounding the kitchen, then take you on a global tour that provides some unique cultural feelings about fire, food, and kitchen witchery.

Kitchen Superstitions

One might wonder how superstition and magic link together. From what I've seen, such folk beliefs were a repository for traditional practices when such practices were not otherwise safe. If we call something a custom (like blowing out birthday candles) no one thinks twice, but if we call such an action a spell or magic—some folks get their proverbial knickers in a twist. Thus, the wise homemaker utilized the safety net of superstitious action to keep some ancient symbols and methods alive.

With that in mind, consider too how much power resides in a folk belief that was held dear to thousands of people, over hundreds of years (and often much longer). We may not remember the reason for the custom, and may not even recognize its symbolic value, but we enact it nonetheless. It has become a habit with which we're comfortable, and one that has meaning, like knocking on wood for luck. Once people worshipped the trees and used them in healing. That ancient root gave birth to the modern action.

Here are just a few superstitions that surround the kitchen:

- To ensure that bread rises and brews age properly, prepare them during the waxing to full moon (modern witches still utilize lunar symbolism to support their magic—the waxing-to-full moon bringing similar "fullness").

- Should your apron fall off in the kitchen it means someone is thinking about you. Since many of us no longer wear aprons—perhaps this could be applied to a button coming undone or a shoe untied.

- If you mix up the salt and sugar accidentally it implies better fortune awaits. Thus a blend of salt and sugar could be considered fortunate components in our pantry magic.

- Never sit on a kitchen table if you hope to be married (I suspect Miss Manners had something else to say about this!).

- If your hearth fires pop, look at the cinders for shapes and interpret them similarly to how you might read tea leaves. Note that there are many foods that were used for divination, too, and those will be the components to which we look for psychic insight.

- It's unlucky to put a pair of shoes or boots on a table. This portends a fight in the home (probably over the placement of the apparel). Oddly, however, if a woman's child puts shoes on the table it signifies a future sibling.

- In Hindu tradition the kitchen is maintained with diligence due a temple. You do not wear shoes in the kitchen as it angers the gods. Before eating any food, people sprinkle water around the plates to honor the ancestors, and they never sweep the kitchen floor after sunset lest Lakshmi (the goddess of good fortune) be swept away. If someone forgets any of these things the best way to avert the unpleasantness

FOLKLORE

Folklore is often passed along by oral tradition, and it helps define our cultures and build social identity. History reveals a rich body of folklore about food. For example, the story of Jack and the beanstalk is a folkloric metaphor based on Old World beliefs that beans could house the souls of the dead. Eating one could lead to possession. So when Jack planted his magic bean, he unwittingly opened the door between the worlds (which is what ultimately necessitated cutting down the stalk).

is to pray as follows: "In the tips of the fingers resides Lakshmi; in the middle, Sarasvati; in the palm of the hand resides Parvati; looking at my hands, I begin my day."

- It is very fortunate to see a spider in the kitchen—but it must never be killed or it halts your prosperity (i.e., If you would to live and thrive, let the spider stay alive!).

- Come Chinese New Year it's customary to make sure the kitchen is spotless so that it will please the kitchen god. This being watches the family and reports to heaven on their comings and goings during this time of year. Thus, the statue of the god gets an offering of honey so his words will only be sweet (or his mouth will be stuck shut!).

- On Yule it's an Irish custom to make up the kitchen table once again after dinner leaving out milk and a loaf of bread. The door is left open so wandering travelers will not want. So doing keeps providence in the home.

- In some English stories there are house fairies called Hobs. If you leave out sweet milk for them, they'll protect your kitchen.

- If you're having trouble lighting your pilot or a fire, look to see if the sun's rays are on that region. If so, the fire will not light until the sun is gone (because fire originally was stolen from the sun).

- If you want to help with cooking or the night's fires, always ask first. Not doing so insults the hearth god or goddess of that home and causes problems with friendships. It's also a good idea to bring a small gift to appease this being (while you give it to the homeowner, the meaning still remains).
- A new broom for your kitchen should not be bought in May or it will cause disruptions in the family.

I realize this is but a small sampling of the world's folk beliefs, but these superstitions give you a starting point. I encourage you to look to actions your parents or grandparents did routinely around the home for luck, health, peace, joy, and protection. All of those little customs are part of the kitchen witch's toolbox, and all the more meaningful because they come from your lineage.

Myth and Meaning

As with folklore, the world is abundant with stories and beliefs surrounding food, eating, and the hearth. I share these with you in the hopes that you will see the flickers of magic that tie them all together.

India

In India vegetarianism ties into the practice of Ayurveda, a sacred system of wholeness in body and spirit. The people believe that flesh is "dead" food and thus is missing all the vital energy that could otherwise improve one's spiritual and mental state. They also feel that what an animal experiences just before its death is passed along in the meat not only in chemicals but energy imprints that are not healthy. Finally, in watching carnivores it's been determined that they breathe more quickly than herbivores, and the slower breath is a central key to meditative practices.

Hawaii

In Hawaii there was an ancient religion called Aikapu in which men and women's labor in cooking and food was divided. Eating was a sacred religious experience that enabled one to commune with deity. Thus the entire process of preparing and eating food was laden with ritual.

This faith required female believers to abstain from coconut, banana, pig, and red fish, all of which were considered sacred to the gods who governed men's work. These deities were Ku (a war God), Kanaloa (ocean God), Lono (agricultural), and Ku'ulakai (fishing). In mythology the first announcement of this custom came with a question. The women asked: "If we give up these foods, it means men will always cook?" The reply from the gods was a hearty "Yes." It seems the women were likewise amenable to this agreement since it also meant they would never be offered as sacrifices!

Ireland

In Irish mythology we find talk of the Salmon of Knowledge that a certain poet and druid named Finneigeas tried to catch for seven years. Finneigeas heard a prophecy that wisdom would be granted to whoever caught and ate the fish, which was golden in color and very elusive. Hundreds of warriors and fishermen tried to capture it but failed.

Finneigeas has a companion by the name of Fionn. During his time with the druid Fionn watched Finneigeas try and try to capture the fish. Each time he avoided the fish's eyes. To stare into them would bring a deep sleep. Once he was not so careful and Fionn awoke him before the fish completely swam away.

At long last Finneigeas achieved his goal. He asked Fionn to build a fire and cook the fish, but promise not to eat even one mouthful. Fionn, being a faithful helpmate, began to do so. A drop of oil landed on his thumb and hurt mightily. Fionn put his thumb in his mouth, thinking nothing of it.

When the fish was done, he brought it to Finneigeas who noticed something about the lad seemed different. He asked about the fish. Fionn told him that he hadn't eaten any of it, but then he remembered the burned thumb and explained. Thus it was that faithful Fionn gained the wisdom of the Salmon, all thanks to a cooking accident!

Scotland

The Scottish avoid singing while baking (especially bread) as it's a bad omen. Make certain only one person places the bread in the oven unless you want a quarrel to erupt. Similarly, break the bread instead of slicing it as this protects your prosperity and kinship. Should you have salt nearby, and want to improve the bonds between you and another, sprinkle some on that fresh bread. Salt not only represents kinship here but the wish of prosperity and a protective charm for children.

Germany

German mythology tells of a group of beings similar to dwarves who were called the Moss People. Moss People are small, looking old but no larger than a three-year-old human. Their clothing is made of moss. Of the lot, female Moss People are much more friendly. You can tell females apart by their green and red clothing and hats. Many times, the women of the Moss People will ask someone for something to eat. If you provide it, they will always return the favor in some way. Perhaps they will wash your kitchen pots, or give you good advice. They also love to bake and will leave little bits of dough for someone they favor. Not to eat this is a high offense, resulting in all manner of mischief and misfortune.

Greece

Greek mythology is ripe for the kitchen witch's picking. First let's consider Hestia, a goddess whose job was to tend the domestic hearth. Her importance to this culture is indicated by the fact that she was the firstborn of six Olympians. In Greek culture, she represented a very important social duty—that of hospitality in a gentle and wise manner. Unlike many of the Greek gods, hers was not a lavish life, but rather one focused on the home, in which any fire was her proverbial altar.

I must confess that this is what I truly love about Hestia. I get the feeling she was a goddess for everyday people, especially those who tended the kitchens and fires. Her focus on hospitality is also well within the kitchen witch's domain, in that those you welcome into your sacred space should feel . . . well, at home!

People believed that Hestia protected their happiness and security. She presided over any fire offerings, and it was common to hear prayers to her at every meal. Let us consider this Homeretic hymn as an example:

> Hestia, you who tend the holy house of the lord Apollo, the Far-shooter at goodly Pytho, with soft oil dripping ever from your locks, come now into this house, come, having one mind with Zeus the all-wise—draw near, and withal bestow grace upon my song.

Or this Orphic hymn:

> Daughter of Kronos, venerable guardian of the hearth, we honor you. You protect the foundation of every house of Gods or men. Your beauty and laughter inspire trust. Give us health. Help us discover the necessity of hospitality. Teach us patience.

Considering this type of respect, it's not surprising to find that people worshipped Hestia daily. She welcomed new children to the hearth. She received family offerings and libations, any new public hearth was dedicated to her, and the fires of her temple were never allowed to go out. We will be revisiting her in chapter 2 when I cover the possibility of dedicating your kitchen to a particular god or goddess.

Another version of Hestia in Rome was Vesta, a name that means "shining." This figure ruled over all religious fires. Her temple virgins held tremendous power. They were the only female priests in Rome and were selected from distinguished families to serve the temple for thirty years. Unlike a single woman, the virgins could own property and write legal documents. No one was allowed to harm them, and a person sentenced to death would be pardoned if he met one on the way to his execution. Here is one of her hymns written by Orpheus:

> *Daughter of Saturn, venerable dame,*
> *The seat containing of unweary'd flame;*
>
> *In sacred rites these ministers are thine,*
> *Mystics much-blessed, holy and divine*
> *In thee, the Gods have fix'd place,*
> *Strong, stable, basis of the mortal race:*
> *Eternal, much-form'd ever-florid queen,*
> *Laughing and blessed, and of lovely mien;*
>
> *Accept these rites, accord each just desire,*
> *And gentle health, and needful good inspire*

While on the surface Vesta seems far removed from the warm, hearthside approach Hestia personified, nearly every Roman household honored her. A bit of this more intimate nature was implied in the declaration that was made when a girl was chosen to enter Vesta's service: *"I take you, you shall be the priestess of Vesta and you shall fulfill the sacred rites for the safety of the Roman people."* This charge indicates that Vesta was, indeed, the protectress of every home.

England

The making of butter is surrounded by magic. People believed that fairies could sneak into the dairy and enchant the cream if they wished mischief. In particular, they were blamed for preventing it from turning to butter, and a number of the charms we've discovered thus far were used to nullify their power.

First, it's best that the churn be made of rowan wood (or minimally has a rowan handle) in order to protect the whole mechanism against fairy tampering. Before starting a recipe the cook might toss a handful of salt onto the fire to scare away any evil or even whimsical influences. The Irish had a slight variation on this. They put smoking turf under the churn as a purifier. And should the cook still feel a little uncertain of the protective power he or she invoked, they might add three hairs from a black cat's tail and a silver coin into the blend (yuck!).

Another "fix" was that of plunging a red-hot poker into the cream when the butter would not come. The symbolism here was that of burning out evil. And all the while you might hear a maid whispering incantations to herself such as:

> Churn, butter, dash
> Cow's gone to the marsh
> Peter stands at the toll-gate
> Begging butter for his cake,
> Come, butter, come!

China

Similar to Japanese practice, China, too, had a residential kitchen god by the name of Tsao-Wang (who also presided over the hearth). Tsao-Wang is diligent in his reports of the family and their behavior to the heavenly jade emperor. In this setting the deity is represented on paper in a small wooden temple just over the stove or in some other southward-facing region of the kitchen. An image of his wife is set beside him to watch over women's stayings and goings.

Each morning the family makes an offering of joss sticks to the god, and on the twenty-fourth day of the twelfth month (just prior to his making a report) the image gets sweets and straw (which is for the god's horse). At the end of the day Tsao-Wang's image is taken down and burned with pine needles and firecrackers, which is how the god ascends. A new image of the god goes up on the new year, which is when he returns to the home.

Afterthought

By now I'm fairly certain you're beginning to see the links among myth, folklore, superstition, and the kitchen magic many still practice today. Our ancestors, being pressed for time and facing harsh lives, made do with what they had. They made sense of the world in a way that was meaningful considering their culture and era, and most important they didn't separate spirituality from daily life. It was part of each person, each moment, and each kitchen. So, let's move on now to making the changes necessary to transform your ho-hum pantry into a perfect sacred space to whip up some magic.

Stir It Up: Mundane and Magical Preparations

*And, indeed, is there not something holy about a
great kitchen? The scoured gleam of row upon row
of metal vessels dangling from hooks or reposing on
their shelves till needed with the air of so many
chalices waiting for the celebration of the sacrament
of food. And the range . . . like an altar, yes, before
which my mother bowed in perpetual homage, a
fringe of sweat upon her upper lip and the fire
glowing on her cheeks.*

—ANGELA CARTER

With the foundation of the past building a bridge to inspire the future of kitchen witchery, the next step is thinking about the basics. What tools do you need to practice this art? Do you have to have any special training? Where exactly does one begin?

First, relax. I absolutely promise nothing here will require that your kitchen or home suddenly transform into an image from a fancy home decor book. Mine certainly doesn't look that way (three kids, two dogs, three cats, two lizards, one husband—do the math!). Kitchen witches also aren't some elite group who require an entrance exam to "qualify" for practice! Really, the only thing you need to know is that this approach to magic calls to you, makes sense to you, and fulfills your role as a spiritual adviser in your home life.

The Kitchen Witch's Credo

I'm betting some of you have already posed the question: But how do I know if kitchen witchery "calls" to me? To be honest, I kind of stumbled into the tradition quite unwittingly and only found a name for it many years later. That need not be the case for you.

There are, of course, some telltale signs that kitchen witchery is in your heart. Delighting in puttering in the pantry is but one of them. I certainly know some kitchen witches who aren't exactly domestic gods or goddesses—some aren't great at cooking, cleaning, or staying within a budget. Nonetheless, all have a strong love of their sacred space of home and a very protective streak when it comes to maintaining an ambiance of peace and love there. Beyond that consider the Kitchen Witch's Credo (see page 28) as a good starting point for self-examination.

Let's take a minute to consider some of these points a little more closely. Our society in general tends to seek out complexity even when simplicity would do twice as well. The kitchen witch is just the opposite. He or she thrives on makeshift, "fly by the seat of your broomstick" components and incantations. If it's within arm's reach—it's fair game as long as it's meaningful to the task at hand. Because such vision-driven tradition begins at your own hearth, it is not surprising that all these efforts would reflect your ideals in a remarkable way.

THE KITCHEN WITCH'S CREDO

- Simplicity, creativity, and personalization equate to power and manifestation.
- Life is a ritual and act of worship.
- The three keynotes of the kitchen witch are functionality, finesse, and fun.
- Kitchen witches blend spirituality and magic with everyday life.
- Kitchen witchery always reflects your own principles.
- Humor is good soul food (laugh once a day, it's good for you).
- Kitchen witches reconnect with the hearth within (and/or the hearth goddess).
- A kitchen witch's home is his or her castle and sacred space.
- Attitude is everything.
- The kitchen witch is wise and frugal. If something can be useful in at least three spell recipes—buy it.
- Fancy isn't better—in fact it often distracts from the goal.
- Honor, respect and gratitude are the tripod on which our lives rest.
- There is nothing on this earth that cannot be used for magic.

And last, but certainly not least:

- You are what you eat—so eat well!

It's pretty easy to see how creativity and personalization both fit into the simplicity equation. You have to look at things differently—consider what they mean to you and their daily functions. For example, when I look at a microwave I think about "fast food." A microwave speeds up the cooking process. So, magically speaking, if you use it as part of a spell-recipe, the symbolic value would be to cook up the magic (the manifestation) more quickly.

KITCHEN WITCH'S SPICE CABINET

Plant stems, spices, seeds, flowers, and bark have had symbolic value in people's homes for a very long time. If we look only at North American tradition, the following herbs in your cupboard could speak volumes to those who knew their meaning:

Basil: a royal demeanor

Caraway: protection against malicious witchery, but also an herb of hospitality and love

Cinnamon: sacredness

Coriander: love

Fennel: preserving youthful outlooks and bolstering courage

Ginger: health

Oregano: happiness

Rosemary: devotion and remembrance

Sage: wisdom and redemption

Thyme: banishing nightmares

The idea of life being your ritual and act of worship also ties into simplicity. Let's face it. Most people don't have time for a ritual that takes several hours to prepare and enact. They're busy juggling 101 other things and figuring out how to add yet one more thing into the multitasking equation. It's very important that we get away from the idea that fancy equals more power. To my thinking, the more you're trying to remember to do, the less you're focusing on your goal! This is also why blending your spirituality with daily tasks is so important. No one ever said you had to stop and switch hats, saying—"Okay I'm magical now!" Your attitude—the way you approach each moment of living—is what really counts here.

Functionality, finesse, and fun work into this program beautifully.

Simplicity also implies that whatever you choose to do should function for your purpose. Doing it with *finesse* is, well, the fun part. I love making a sinfully simple, magical dish and having people rave over it as if I slaved all day. Kitchen witches also love putting their personal signature on everything they do or create— that, too, is finesse! And of course *fun* covers the humorous aspect. My mother taught me that laughter was a necessary coping mechanism. Too many people are wrapped up in gloom and doom and forget to celebrate each moment. You can't get them back, folks. Celebrate the here-and-now, *now*.

What of frugality? Now I'm not saying you have to nickel-and-dime yourself to death, but I do not believe that our spiritual progress should be measured by the size of our pocketbooks either. Once you understand and accept that *you are the magic*, all else is window dressing. This is where seeing yourself and your space as truly sacred come into play. We're not quite used to the idea that we are the priest or priestess of our lives. Kitchen witchery brings that idea into your heart and into your home every single day.

Honor, respect, and gratitude may sound rather lofty, but they're a very important foundation for the kitchen witch (and really for any positive spiritual path)—right up there with courtesy in my book. If we honor the sacredness of all things, we won't be likely to abuse our arts. If we respect ourselves and others, we won't be tempted to do anything that goes against personal principles and ideals, or show intolerance toward those whom other people hold dear. Gratitude, however, is the key that makes this trinity work. I have seen so many neo-Pagans enact special rituals or spells, and when they finally manifest they forget to say thank you. Thank yourself, thank Spirit, thank the universe. A heart full of gratitude is also one ready to both give and receive.

Finally, and perhaps most significantly to this kitchen witch— You are what you eat! Think for a moment about the images, expectations, or ideals that you've swallowed (and in some cases got indigestion). When we're talking about magical food, we can't forget that we're multidimensional beings (body, mind, spirit). Whatever we internalize in energy and foods should be good for us, and not cause a nasty bout of emotional, mental, spiritual, or physical gas. So, as you go through this book I encourage you to think very carefully about what you're blending together and why. Make sure that whatever you put on your serving platter meets the needs of body, mind, and soul equally, meaningfully, and flavorfully.

The Sacred Pantry and Beyond

If you can organize your kitchen, you can organize your life.

—Louis Parrish

If you're still reading, it's fairly safe to assume that you've made the choice to venture forward and see what awaits you in kitchen magic, or that you simply found a name for what you were already doing quite happily. Welcome to my world! Forgive me if I seem to gush, but I believe you're going to love this path and be delighted with the flexibility and responsiveness of your choice. In nearly twenty years I've never found kitchen magic to be dull, uneventful, or a waste of time and energy. Nonetheless, I'd like to remind you that my approach to the hearth and yours might be extremely different. We're two different people with different visions of our spirituality. What I'm sharing with you, therefore, are simply some good helps and hints to which you should bring an equal quantity of your personal vision, creativity, and love.

Step one in kitchen witchery (if there is a "first" step, per se) is to begin seeing your home, and especially your kitchen, in a different light. From this point forward this isn't just a place where you hang

Religion and Mealtime

Religion has often shaped our eating habits. For example, the Puritans had to prepare their meals on Saturday for Sunday because of a prohibition against working on the Sabbath. Another illustration comes from Polish American customs where people are often greeted with the phrase "guest in the home, God in the home" followed very shortly thereafter by "put another chair at the table!" In this case, deity gets involved in hospitality.

Perhaps the strongest remaining example of religion's influence on our eating and dining customs is that of prayer before meals. This tradition most likely started during the time when people still thanked the spirit of the animal for giving of its life and sustenance to nourish the family. Slowly the tradition transformed to reflect each family's culture and religious persuasion. In Europe, for example, it wasn't uncommon to pray before and after the meal. In Arabia the diners say a short prayer that begins "in God's name" and adds just prior to the first bite "praise be to God."

Where religion was quiet, hospitality traditions stepped in. Thus the French wish eaters, bon appetít (good appetite), Germans say *prost mablzeit* (may your dinner be beneficial), and in Portugal a stranger happening by one's dinner table is greeted with a phrase that means "Have you been served?" Most people politely decline and wish the homeowner profit.

your hat. It's about to become a magical work space, one where both elemental and sacred energies will dance and play together. Going back to "attitude is everything" when you're going to be using your personal space for spiritual goals, remember to approach it differently—remember to treat it like your personal church.

Now, this doesn't mean you shouldn't have fun. Nor does it

mean everything has to be pristine. However, I do think your over-all demeanor and thoughtfulness counts for a lot. I also prefer a neat working area over a cluttered one. (Clutter seems to mess up the flow of energy somehow, if only by being distracting. After all, how often do you see a messy church or temple?)

Another important shift in your attitude comes down to aware-ness. Magic is within and without. It's part of everything and every moment if we allow it to be. But like many things in life, we have to teach ourselves to let go and let it flow! There are dozens of opportunities to weave positive energy into your life every day if you keep your eyes open and start looking at potentials. To give you an example from my own home at the time of this writing, my kids have been down with a nasty cold. So every day I've been smudging the house with sage to decrease negative energies. Better still, sage has some natural antibacterial properties! In this way proven herbal attributes blend with spiritual goals beautifully, and without taking any extra time.

Awareness doesn't stop at your kitchen threshold, though. It's something that should be keyed in no matter where you are or what you're doing. Sometimes people get hooked on the title "kitchen witch," and don't realize that magic is flexible and spon-taneous enough to extend far beyond that one space. It is, in fact, as much of a philosophy for living as it is a practice. From that perspective the goal is to let magical thoughts turn to action nat-urally. And the more you do so, the easier it gets.

Let me give you an illustration. What about when you do the laundry? This isn't exactly a culinary exploit, but it can benefit from kitchen witchery. If there's been a lot of tension at home, add some lemon rind to the wash water to purify the clothing. Then toss a bundle of herbs in an old stocking when you dry them to charge the items with positive energy. A blend of bay, cinna-mon, ginger, and thyme might do the trick to bring vitality, strength, and insight.

Or what about lightbulbs? We turn them on and off all day long for various things. Why not add a dab of a specially prepared herbal tincture (according to the needed energy) to each lightbulb in various rooms? That way every time you turn on the light—you're also "turning on" the magic you've placed there. The warmth of the light simply heats it up (activates it). To that basic process you could also add a short incantation like

> *With the turn of a switch* [turn the light switch]
>> *And the casting of light*
>>> *Let my magic take to flight!*

See how easy that is? Okay, so it's not classical poetry. If we remember the rule of KISS—hey, this works, and it's really easy to memorize.

I bet if you stop for a moment and ponder, you can come up with ways to express the inner kitchen witch in every room, your car, your office, hotel rooms, in hobbies, and so forth. Here are just a few more examples to get your creative juices flowing:

- Stuff magically charged herb sachets in your drawers to charge the clothing, and hang one filled with strong aromatics in the shower so you can energize yourself before other chores or your job.

- Write your worries on a piece of toilet paper and flush them neatly away. (Warning—if you have a septic system, ignore this idea. All that negativity would remain in the system.)

- If you have a fireplace, teach your children how to observe the flames as they dance. Make it like a Sunday-night movie where everyone shares what they see. Also, if your children have worries, they can write them down, burn the paper in the fire, and let the smoke carry the pressures away!

- When you're feeling a bit flighty, go to the cellar and sit down (it's the area in your home that's within the Mother's soils).

- Similarly when you feel out of touch with Spirit, go to the highest point you can safely reach in your house for meditation, prayer, or whatever feels right.

- To inspire change, open windows or doors to welcome that new energy.

- If the overall energy in your home seems "off," consider moving a few things around to where they feel "right" and then cleaning afterward. Also burn some refreshing incense. This is a very rudimentary form of feng shui.

- Create an herbal travel charm for your car and put it in the trunk or glove compartment. You could include one herb from each element in your bundles. For example, cedar—fire, lemon—water, wheat—earth, marjoram—air. This blend respectively provides protection, love, providence, and happiness.

- Make another charm like this last one that you can tuck in your suitcases for safe and uncomplicated airline trips.

- Consider assembling a small portable kitchen witch's kit for when you're away from home. Include the herbs you use most often, a candle, a fire-safe container in which to burn things, and anything else you can think of that's absolutely necessary to your craft. Put this in a safe box that you ship in *checked* luggage (you may find you have trouble with carry-on due to security protocols).

- Bring decorative items to the office that have elemental correspondences and put them as close to that direction as possible. Most folk won't look twice at something that appears to be a knickknack.

- Make a sleep sachet for your bedroom out of pantry herbs like chamomile, thyme, mint, and rosemary (all used to encourage a good night's sleep).

- Assemble some potpourri for your dining room that includes lavender, gardenia, and violet. These three herbs inspire peace (to keep folks from arguing at the dinner table).

- To one cup of cornstarch add a teaspoon each of marjoram (joy), nutmeg (health), lemon rind (love), and thyme (purification). Sprinkle this into your rugs just before running the vacuum. The thyme takes out any negativity, and the other herbs restore positive vibrations.

I could go on, but this should have given you the general feel for how kitchen magic certainly isn't limited to your kitchen!

Beyond this, you can certainly choose to create more formal sacred space in the area where you're working. For the most part pantry magic is considered a "low" art due to its simplicity (roughly translated this means that mischievous spirits are more attracted to things with a bigger "kick" than the average energy levels that kitchen witchery utilizes). So, formal sacred space isn't a necessity here, but it can be helpful. In particular it helps keep out stray energies from those folks who have no idea what kind of vibes they are broadcasting. It also negates any residual energy patterns that might cause your magic to go awry. If you think of sacred space as a plug in your sink, once you put it in place nothing comes up or down that drain until that plug gets moved (which is what you'll do when you release your spell or ritual to do its work).

Some people reading these pages already know how to create sacred space. For those who do not, however, I'd like to take a moment to share a simple approach that's suited to your hearth. To begin, try to imagine a bubble that extends to every doorway in your line of sight (note that this bubble is below and above you too). The bubble comes from light energy—namely the interplay of the four elemental powers working together. To accomplish the desired result, it's recommended you begin in the east, requesting the assistance of air with an invocation such as:

> *Powers of the air, on whose winds the aroma of magic*
> *float*
> *Come and join me in this sacred kitchen and bless my*
> *efforts*
> *With the gift of effective communication*

Continue this way, turning to the south, west, and north, respectively, while saying something like:

> *Powers of the fire, whose embers cook the magic to*
> *perfection*
> *Come and join me in this sacred kitchen and bless my*
> *efforts*
> *With the gift of health*
>
> *Powers of the water, whose drops quench spiritual*
> *thirst*
> *Come join me in this sacred kitchen and bless my*
> *efforts*
> *With the gift of love.*
>
> *Powers of the earth, whose soils nurture nature's*
> *bounty for the table*
> *Come and join me in this sacred kitchen and bless my*
> *efforts*
> *With the gift of Security*
>
> *So be it.*

Note that as you turn toward each area you should keep a strong visualization of the "bubble" in that region forming up and joining with the rest. If it helps, use different colors of light for each element in your mind's eye—air being yellow, fire—red or orange, water—blue or purple, and earth—brown or green.

When you're done, go ahead and create whatever concoctions you'd planned for today within that safe sphere. Once your work is completed, you can say farewell to the four powers, and thank them for their assistance in whatever manner you feel fitting. Here's one example:

> Earth, thank you for your sustenance
> Water, thank you for your creativity
> Fire, thank you for your passion
> Air, thank you for your motivation
> Move out now from my sacred hearth and bless all
>   those you encounter along the way with the gentle
>   energies created here today. Merry part!

As an aside, you may want to combine the creation of sacred space with any work you plan on doing with a deity, which we will be discussing later in this chapter.

Have Pot Holder, Will Travel—Tools of the Trade

> A determined soul will do more with a rusty monkey
> wrench than a loafer will accomplish with all the tools
> in a machine shop.
>
> —ROBERT HUGHES

No matter your craft, it's always good to have a feel for your media and tools. As one might expect, the kitchen witch's primary tools and components reside right in his or her own kitchen. Your favorite wooden spoon becomes a wand, a kitchen knife transforms into an athame, a coffee cup becomes a chalice, and a pot becomes a cauldron! What's really wonderful is that since you use these items all the time, they're already saturated with your energy patterns, which in turn will support your magic.

The thing to remember here is that when you're using "mundane" items for spiritual goals, treat them with the proper respect. Cleanse them, charge them, and bless them for the tasks at hand.

Tools

Even though the Byzantines were using very small forks as early as 100 C.E., it wasn't really until the eleventh century that Italian-designed two-prong forks appeared, and many English homes had them around the 1500s, but they were rarely used. It seems there was an odd stigma associated with this utensil; people thought that somehow it was healthier and more luck enhancing to eat meat with one's fingers. Even in the 1800s sailors were forbidden to use forks, as doing so was regarded as effeminate.

Another tool, the spoon, was used regularly in cooking by primitive cave dwellers. However it wasn't until the seventeenth century that it actually joined the fork and knife on a dinner table as a common utensil.

These actions in themselves help you to think about each of those items differently—as having a real astral presence and potential for designing the energy you desire.

Helpful Hints for Cleansing, Charging, and Blessing

- *Cleansing:* Most common household items can be cleansed using plain old soap and water! Alternatives include lemon juice, smudging with sage or cedar incense (a burning bay leaf will also work), and sprinkling with salt or saltwater.

- *Charging:* Just like a car battery, our tools periodically can use a boost of energy to help them fulfill their function in our sacred space. Exactly how you go about charging will depend on the final purpose of that item. Something that's being used for more intuitive energies can be left in the light of a waxing to full moon. Something that's being used for more logical, mundane goals can be left in sunlight. Or, you can visualize the item being filled with a sparkling light whose hue supports your magical goal (like red for love and blue for peace and joy).

- *Blessing:* Historically speaking blessing seems to have been commonly done with a laying on of hands and a prayer or incantation. For those of you planning to work with deity, a prayer makes perfect sense. For those who wish to simply invite universal favor and elemental energies, an incantation is more practicable. Again, your words need not be fancy, just let them come from your heart. Intention is everything.

When you're already in that mental space, take a few minutes and look around your kitchen. Make a list of tools, ingredients, and so forth, that you have on hand. Afterward, next to each one write down what comes to mind magically about these items. In other words, if you bundle together each item's mundane applications with personal beliefs, what would the metaphysical application of that item become? For example, you use your refrigerator to keep things cold or to cool things down. Metaphysically this could translate into cooling a heated temper. Likewise, when something freezes, its molecules slow, so metaphysically your freezer could be used as a tool for slowing down a situation or halting negativity.

Here are more examples for your consideration. However, I cannot stress enough that if something has a different meaning to you—that meaning is the one you should apply in your kitchen magic.

- *Toaster:* gentle warming of emotions
- *Oven:* a womb or goddess symbol
- *Tea kettle:* the whistle announces energy's movement
- *Blender:* whipping magic into proper proportions

- *Food processor:* transformational energy
- *Coffee grinder:* breaking things down to a simple, usable form
- *Coffeepot:* power, awareness, alertness
- *Food storage containers:* preserving a specific type of energy
- *Dish soap:* cleansing (note that this meaning may vary depending on the name of the brand you use)
- *Straining spoon:* getting rid of those things you don't need or filtering energies to determine what's best for you
- *Paper plate:* ease and socialization
- *Trivet:* protection, especially from fiery energy (like anger or overt passion)
- *Salad dressing:* finding the beauty and flavor in simple things
- *Can opener:* opportunity
- *Rolling pin:* smoothing out a bumpy situation
- *Yeast:* increasing energy or lifting heaviness
- *Molasses:* sticking to a goal or ideal (peanut butter works, too)
- *Tea:* comfort, relaxation
- *Butter:* getting on someone's good side (butter them up)
- *Oil:* smoothing things over; release and liberation
- *Sugar:* life's sweet things

Once you've finished this exercise, take the whole concept one step further. Move around your whole house with that expectant, appreciative eye. Make another list. Remember that there's nothing on this planet that cannot be used for your kitchen magic if it makes sense to you. For example, the telephone represents communication, the couch—rest and relaxation. Doors are openings through which energy can move (or that can keep energy away). Curtains symbolize privacy.

I should warn you now, though, that making these associations can become quite addictive. Before you know it you'll be wandering through supermarkets saying to yourself, "Ya know, that would make a great component for a spell!" when you look at products. When that happens, pat yourself on the back—it has become wholly natural for you to see the metaphysical potential in anything and everything you encounter.

Food of and for the Gods?

You are interested in the kitchen of the world—you want to find out what is cooking, who has a finger in the pie, and who will burn his finger.

—JULIANA, QUEEN OF THE NETHERLANDS

It would be remiss of me not to take a little time and space to discuss a deity's role in a kitchen witch's life. Now, you need not be a deist to be a kitchen witch. Some people use magic simply as a methodology as opposed to an ideology or a religion. However, in looking at the history we've already discussed it's obvious that pantry or hearth gods and goddesses were very important to our ancestors. So, for those kitchen witches seeking closer union with Spirit, your cooking surface now becomes an altar!

But let me back up just a bit. The first thing I want to share with you is that the kitchen witch's role is one of co-creator with the divine. You are god or goddess. Each individual carries a unique spark, a piece of eternity in his or her soul. While our world has changed, our need to have a spiritual touchstone has not. As life's pace has hastened and responsibilities grown to where it seems like there's very little room for god or goddess left, this being remains ready to become part of our daily lives if we but open the door both within and without.

SALT DOUGH INSTRUCTIONS

The basic proportion for salt dough is 1 cup flour, ½ cup salt, and ¼ cup water. Knead this together, adding whatever food coloring you wish to portions of it. Salt dough will harden on its own if left to dry, or you can hasten the process by placing it in a low temperature oven (about 225 degrees F.).

How does one go about picking a divinity suited to hearth and home? Well you could consider various food groups—like Asnan the Mesopotamian goddess of grain, or those who preside over nourishment like Durga of the Hindu pantheon. Vegetarians might seek out someone like Pan, the Greek vegetation god, while carnivores might honor a hunting image like Zagreus, the pre-Hellenic god of hunting and a chief god of Orphic tradition. Alternatively one might look to the attributes of various beings for those things that your home most needs—such as gods of health, peace, joy, and providence.

What's important here is that whomever you choose is a persona toward whom you feel drawn, and also one you're willing to honor in some way in your sacred space. Here's a list of some potential hearth gods or goddesses.

Agnayi or Agni: Hindu goddess and god of fire
Albina: Greek goddess of barley
Anat: Canaanite goddess of love and fertility
Anna Perenna: Roman goddess of the year and providence
Aradia: Italian witch goddess
Ashnan: Babylonian goddess of grain
Baldur: Scandinavian god of wisdom and all good things
Bannik: Slavonic god of the home

Benten: Japanese goddess of love, luck, and good fortune

Berchta: Teutonic goddess of marriage

Buddhi: Hindu goddess of prosperity

Ceres: Roman corn goddess

Cerridwen: Celtic mother figure and grain goddess

Chicomecoatz: Aztec maize goddess of rural abundance

Concordia: Roman goddess of peace and harmony

Dugnai: Slavic house and bread goddess

Ekadzati: Tibetan goddess of wisdom and the mystical arts

Erce: Old English goddess of blessings

Fornax: Roman goddess of ovens

Fuchi: Japanese fire goddess

Ganymede: Greek bearer of the cup of hospitality

Gibil: Bablyonian fire god

Hastsechogan: Navajo home god and protector

Hebe: Greek cupbearer

Hehsui-no-kami: Japanese kitchen goddess

Hermes: Greek god of communication

Hestia: Greek goddess of home and hearth

Huixtocihuatl: Aztec salt goddess

Ida: Hindu goddess of fire and devotion

Ivenopae: Indonesian mother of rice

Kedesh: Syrian goddess of health and life

Lakshmi: Hindu goddess of good fortune and plenty

Li: Chinese goddess of nourishing fire

Mama Occlo: Inca goddess of domestic arts

Nusku: Babylonian fire god who also oversaw matters of justice

Ogetsu-hime-no-kami: Japanese goddess of food

Okitsu-hime: Japanese kitchen goddess

Ops: Roman goddess of the earth, fertility, and wealth

Pukkeenegak: Eskimo provider of food and clothing

Samkhat: Babylonian goddess of joy

Saule: Slavic goddess of the sun, hearth fire, and domestic arts

Tamon: Japanese god of good fortune

Tao Quan: Vietnamese Three Kitchen Gods, who are present in the kitchen of every home

Tsao Wang: Chinese kitchen god who watches over moral conduct in the home

Vasudhara: Hindu goddess of abundance

Vesta: Roman goddess of domestic fires

Vulcan: Roman god of the fire and the forge

Yabune: Japanese god who watches over the household

Once you choose a deity for your pantry, the next thing to consider is how best to represent this being. Statuary is but one idea that's certainly fast, but also rather expensive. More in keeping with kitchen witchery, you might wish to create your god or goddess out of salt dough, or perhaps a corn-and-herb bundle, reminiscent of early American decor.

Once purchased or devised, the image of your god or goddess should be placed somewhere you can see it regularly, especially when working kitchen magic. Don't forget to give him or her suitable offerings of whatever wonders you're whipping up, and welcome them into your sacred pantry daily. The kitchen god or goddess isn't pushy or presumptuous and will treat your home with the same respect as you'd wish from any other guest.

A FLICK OF THE WAND: PUTTING IT ALL TOGETHER

There is no event greater in life than the appearance of new persons about our hearth, except it be the progress of the character which draws them.

—RALPH WALDO EMERSON

With the basic ideals of kitchen witchery firmly in one hand, and your cookbooks and wooden spoon eagerly poised in the other, the next step is putting all this information together into functional, magical, and tasty meals. Now, if you don't consider yourself much of a cook, fear not! As I've emphasized, kitchen witchery is about intention. You don't have to create elaborate dishes to fill them with love, peace, joy, health, or whatever else you feel your home needs. In fact, I firmly believe that even pre-made meals can accept magical energy into them if you choose them with care and bless them before serving. Yes, even macaroni and cheese or TV dinners qualify. So when life's hectic pace leaves you grabbing for drive-through burgers or canned soup, just remember to sprinkle in a focused prayer or incantation so you can still internalize good vibrations.

Having said that, the quality of the energy isn't exactly the same in fast foods (at least not to me) as it is in a home-cooked meal. There is something special about food that's made with intention from start to finish—ingredients chosen with care, blended with magical words, warmed with love, and served out with joy. And for those of you with a passion for cooking, it's only doubly so. I remember intimately watching my mother make roast beef, and Dad designing his favorite cookies. There was real joy in those foods, and you could taste the love in every bite. Now, Mom and Dad weren't neo-Pagans, but that didn't matter. The pure pleasure they found in making these foods translated into what the family felt and tasted just the same. It can be this way for everything you create in the sacred kitchen.

Menu Planning

If I actually ran the world, I'd do it from the kitchen.
It's not anything deliberate or a statement or anything,
that's just how I understand things. It's arranged along
informal lines.

—Jamaica Kincaid

Whether you're making one dish or twenty, good magic depends on the symbolic value of the chosen food and how you put it together. But it's easier to take things one step at a time, starting with your ingredients. Though you'll be seeing a lot of information about the metaphysical value of herbs, vegetables, fruits, meats, and so forth in this book, it would be very helpful to pick up at least one resource book for your kitchen magic. I have two that I think you may like. They are *Nectar and Ambrosia* by Tamra Andrews and *Cornucopia* by Annie Lise Roberts. Additionally Scott

Menu

Novalis (German Romantic poet) once said, "Dinner itself is like a curve: It starts off with the lightest courses then rises to the heavier and concludes with light courses again." According to expert meal planners, the best meals are akin to a well-orchestrated play where the plot progresses normally in flavor and texture to a high point. At lavish feasts the menu was printed so guests could determine how much to eat at each course.

The first menus appeared in Greece and Rome on tablets, but they seemed to be an individual's custom versus that of an entire nation. It wasn't really until the nineteenth century that menus came into popular use. Typically the first course consisted of soups and sometimes vegetables or other small side dishes, the second of the fanciest dish with salads and breads, and the third of sweets and fruit.

Cunningham's *The Magick in Food* and any good dictionary of symbols would prove very useful. I am the first to want to avoid extra expenditures; however, having good references on hand is incredibly helpful, especially when you just can't seem to think of the right ingredients to get the job done. Besides, there's nothing that says you can't buy these books secondhand.

Ingredients

For magical purposes, start thinking of your ingredients as potential spell components. In this process, as you choose and blend ingredients you're not only seeking the right flavor, but also the perfect balance of energies that will achieve your goals. But how exactly do you choose correctly and still manage to have the recipe come out right?

Well, first off, never eliminate a necessary ingredient in a recipe.

ABBREVIATED SUBSTITUTIONS LIST

Allspice, 1 teaspoon	½ teaspoon cinnamon plus ½ teaspoon ginger or cloves
Baking powder, 1 teaspoon	¼ teaspoon baking soda and ½ teaspoon cream of tartar
Beer	Broth (any type)
Brown sugar, 1 cup	1 cup white sugar blended with 1 teaspoon molasses
Chervil	Dry parsley plus a hint of sage
Condensed milk	1 cup of evaporated milk with 1¼ cups of sugar
Corn syrup	Honey
Cream, 1 cup	3 tablespoons butter plus ⅞ cup milk
Goat cheese	Feta
Honey, 1 cup	1¼ cup sugar plus ¼ cup water
Ketchup, 1 cup	1 cup tomato sauce, ½ cup sugar, 2 tablespoons vinegar
Leeks	Shallots or scallions
Lemon juice, 2 teaspoons	1 teaspoon vinegar
Mushrooms	Cubed tofu
Saffron	Turmeric
Soy sauce	Teriyaki sauce or salt and water
Wine	Fruit juice or broth

This is especially true with baking, which requires very careful measurements and timing (as opposed to cooking, which is a little more forgiving of tinkering). For example, unless you're doing flat bread, yeast is essential to making bread rise (and it also nicely symbolizes "rising" energy). On the other hand, you can often replace sour cream with yogurt, allspice with cinnamon and ginger, and wine with juice (and vice versa) without any negative effect on a dish. When you're not really sure about substitutions, refer to a good culinary website. Some of my favorites include:

www.cook-books.com
foodnetwork.com
www.cooksrecipes.com
eat.epicurious.com
www.cookingclub.com

I use the last two most frequently, the cookingclub.com having an interactive community to whom you can pose those nagging questions to which you only learn the answers by experience.

Second, bear in mind that not every single ingredient in your recipe has to have magical meaning. Those that do not (i.e., you've determined to simply use them as a normal ingredient vs. a component) become neutral, simply mingling and mixing with the whole. Now here's the neat part. If you've designed your spell recipe correctly, even the neutral components hold the completed energy for manifestation. This works very similarly to Bach's flower essences in that the energy pattern of one well-charged and chosen component imprints itself on the whole (if that's your intention).

With those two "rules" as a foundation—you can either choose a recipe with at least one main ingredient that matches your goals metaphysically, or create a recipe that includes one or more symbolically correct components. Personally, the former is easier for me. Besides saving time and ensuring some level of success taste-wise, there's still plenty of room to increase the potential manifesting power of the dish during the cooking and serving time. So, for example, if you're hoping to inspire health, then look for a dish in which chicken is the main ingredient (since many people associate chicken, or chicken soup, with recovery).

Also, after I've used a recipe more than once, I find the concepts it provides often spill over into more spontaneous dishes (which is

MAGICKAL FOOD FUNCTIONS

For your reference, here's a short list of food functions as prescribed by the ancients (often thanks to a god or goddess to whom the food was sacred).

Love charms	apple, apricot, asparagus, fish, honey, lettuce, lemon and lime
Longevity	apple, cherry, dates, eggs, grapes, milk, pears, peaches, pine nuts, salt, yogurt
Renewal	almond, asparagus, banana, beans, blueberry, coconut, corn, cucumber, fig, grain, mango, orange, pork, potato, rice, wine
Underworld (food of the dead)	cake, eggs, fig, garlic, onion, celery, pomegranate, sunflower seed, wine
Medicinal	apple, bamboo shoot, cabbage, cheese, garlic, honey, lemon, pepper, strawberry, tomato, yogurt
Purification	beef, blackberry, cherry, lamb, citron, lime, pear, water

where many cooks make their best discoveries). In other words, for those of you who feel a little iffy in the kitchen, this is a good way to make great meals and improve your skills at the same time. For accomplished cooks—it's another way to keep your creative juices flowing and learn new tricks.

Additives

Additives become a very handy kitchen witch's tool because many recipes' flavors won't be harmed by a dash or a dab of a magically charged ingredient. Take teas as a good example. If you combine edible herbs briefly with warm water, then strain, charge, and bless that blend, you can add a half teaspoon to nearly anything without consequence. In similar manner, bless herbs like oregano, basil, and thyme for casseroles, marinades, sauces, and soups.

For longevity you can make a thematic tincture out of herbs by mixing 4 ounces alcohol with 2 ounces of herbs and 2 ounces of water. Steep and strain. The tincture remains fully charged with your intention until it turns cloudy, at which point you should dispose of it. The cloudiness indicates that the blend is too old to be used, and its magic has likewise "turned."

Cooking Process

When she goes about her kitchen duties, chopping, carving, mixing, whisking, she moves with the grace and precision of a ballet dancer, her fingers plying the food with the dexterity of a croupier.

—CRAIG CLAIBORNE

Okay now let's get to the ritual of cooking. Since you already tend to follow the same basic routine for a recipe, there's a pattern and rhythm to your cooking. All that needs to be added is intention and a few meaningful touches—before you know it, there's the magic!

Now, what exactly can you bring to this process to help the energy along? All kinds of sensual cues. Whenever you express your goals with sights, sounds, scents, and so forth, the results typically improve. Why? Because human beings experience and interpret the world through the senses. Add to that the axiom of "as without, so within . . . as within, so without" and you begin to see how sensual cues can resonate spiritually, each one building on the other to create a more complete pattern for your magical energy to follow.

How about choosing your components or central food item for their color value? This is especially helpful if you don't seem to

COLOR CORRESPONDENCES

Black	sleep, solitude, rest, and turning negativity
Blue	thoughtfulness, health, happiness, water energy
Brown	grounding, earth energy
Green	belief, growth, slow but steady change, prosperity, earth energy
Orange	kindness, charity, ingathering, emotional warmth, fire energy
Pink	friendship, social occasions, upbeat attitudes, wholeness
Purple	spirituality, psychic energy, dedication, awareness, water energy
Red	bravery, vigor, health, fire energy
White	purity, cleansing, safety, innocence, air or spirit energy
Yellow	foresight, adventure, movement, inventiveness, communication, air energy

have an ingredient that exactly matches your goal. So, rather than depend on a strict metaphysical value, you can look to the color correspondence instead. Say you're looking for something to make you feel better and you happen to have pink grapefruit—pink's a good mood lifter (being "in the pink") and it also promotes self-love, so that would be one option. Refer to the color chart in this chapter for basic energies, but remember to trust your instincts. Color is another thing that often has very personal meanings, and it's those meanings/applications to which you should apply the energies.

What about hearing? Well, some food makes noise—popcorn comes to mind as does the sizzle of steaks. However, I think that while most kitchen witches enjoy those sounds, they're not quite as inspiring as music. I keep a variety of my favorite New Age CDs handy for when I'm puttering in the pantry, choosing them according to how they make me feel. For example, if the music is quiet and somewhat meditative, I might play it for a dish aimed at restoring peace and harmony. Oh, and don't restrict yourself to just spiritually oriented music. There are a lot of artists whose music I find quite inspiring—like playing "Where My Heart Will Take Me" (the theme song from *Enterprise*) when I'm creating a dish for hopefulness, or one focused on my spiritual path.

The sense of hearing might also be appeased through the use of incantations, chants, mantras, and other verbalizations. Above and beyond the sensual element, words are thoughts uttered outwardly. Since the ability to make and change reality begins in your thoughts, bringing them into verbal form actually increases one's focus and sends the vibrations of each word out on the winds!

For the sense of smell, the aroma of what you're making certainly counts for a lot. However, you can also potentially choose some of your components for their aromatherapy effects, or perhaps make a simmering potpourri for this purpose. Note that aromatherapy attributes are sometimes slightly different from the metaphysical correspondence, more than likely because it's intended to create a subtle influence. Here are some examples:

Apple: choices, clever approaches
Basil: keeping the peace at home
Chamomile: cooling heated tempers, relaxation
Clove: protection
Fennel: strength and renewal
Ginger: zeal
Mint: decreasing negativity
Nutmeg: psychism

SCENT

While we might adore the smell of good food cooking, there were historical situations in which a good hostess would try to keep those scents neatly under wrap. Starting in Greece, certain wines were so highly regarded as to take priority over the food, and nothing would be placed too close to them that would interfere with the wine's aroma. A French tutorial on manners from the 1700s instructs that one should not smell the meat too closely (it was considered rude), and in the old Paris apartments the kitchens were placed away from social rooms so that guests would not be bothered by the household workings that the smell of cooking food suggested.

Rosemary: health
Sage: cleansing
Vanilla: increased energy, perspectives

You can find more ideas along these lines in a good aromatherapy book that focuses on the emotional impact of the fragrances as well as the physical. In particular, *The Fragrant Mind: Aromatherapy for Personality, Mind, Mood, and Emotion* by Valerie Ann Worwood can serve the kitchen witch very well.

Let's look at some other specifics. While this isn't exactly a sensual cue, what about using numerology to support your spell recipes? You can accomplish this in several ways. For example, you could stir something a symbolic number of times (perhaps chanting as you do so), or perhaps create a recipe with a symbolic number of ingredients. Or, you might add a specific number of drops of an energized tincture, or present a meal with a symbolic number of dishes.

If you're unfamiliar with the metaphysical value of various numbers, here's a reference list to get you started:

Numerology for Kitchen Witches

- *One:* Unity, accord, attention. Also the self and now (current situations, not future ones). One item that's completely focused on a specific type of energy.
- *Two:* Choices, a crossroads. Also symmetry and balance.
- *Three:* Body-mind-spirit equation. Fortitude. A great number for kitchen witches (after all, three's a charm!).
- *Four:* Earth energy, foundation, security. Financial matters and mundane issues.
- *Five:* Psychic abilities, insight. Adaptability.
- *Six:* Tenacity. Completing what you start with a flair.
- *Seven:* Lunar energy. Diversity and inner vision. Healing.
- *Eight:* Command, logic (a double earth number). Personal change.
- *Nine:* Karma, the law of three, giving of yourself to others
- *Ten:* Completion. The rational balance to five.

Other Touches

Besides the sensual dimension there are some nice other touches that you might want to bring to your cooking ritual. For example, consider opening your curtains so there's lots of natural light by which to work. The sun is an ancient symbol of blessing, so why not celebrate that while cooking? Also try stirring your food clockwise for increased/positive energy or counterclockwise to decrease or banish energy. Or, brew and bake during a waxing moon to make sure your dish comes out just right.

Speaking of the moon, if your need isn't too pressing you can consider waiting until an auspicious astrological time to prepare your magical dishes. While this isn't a necessity, it's certainly an element on which many ancient mages relied to help their magic manifest more effectively.

Service with a Smile

Every day use your magic to be of service to others.

—Marcia Wieder

Once your dishes are completed, the next step is serving and eating them. Now, since this is a magical ritual, let's not leave these two steps out of the kitchen witch's knack for flair. Think about ways to make your presentation just as beautiful and meaningful as every other step to this point.

Platters and Plates and Napkins, *Oh My*!

Thanks to the wonders of partyware, you have a lot of options from which to choose your serving surfaces. Just yesterday I was at a large supermarket and remarked at what a large variety of decorative plates, cups, and napkins were available. The patterns included a sun, moon, and stars motif, and a classical female image (goddess-like); colors were equally diverse. And while paper may seem rather informal, the heavier quality pieces not only stand up to a full meal, but keep cleanup time to a minimum. So, when you don't have anything at home that seems to suit your goal or the meal itself, consider buying appropriate paper products.

Other similar items to look at while you're planning the look of your table include the tablecloth, place mats, and hotplates (or trivets). Tablecloths were first used in ancient Rome. Their popularity grew outward from that point to the point where they became very expressive of the community (or household) for which they were created. So much was the case that the phrase "to share of cloth" came to mean being treated equally at someone's table to family or nobility. The most lavish tables were covered with linen, sometimes several layers (the more layers, the more prosperity you were exhibiting to onlookers).

The first "place mats" were long pieces of cloth that edged a formal table and were meant to collect bits of dirt or dropped food. These slowly evolved into the individual mats many of us use today.

What of napkins? Well, for a while the tablecloth functioned as a napkin, too. In ancient Rome people often used a napkin-like piece of cloth to bundle up small remnants of food for taking home after a feast. At the medieval table, diners draped large, bath-towel-size napkins over one shoulder. In the 1700s people tucked their napkins at the front to protect lacy garments, and come the nineteenth century cloths as much as a full square yard in size were placed neatly in one's lap (to wear such a cloth around your neck was bad manners!).

I find the symbolism wrapped up in these various cloths very interesting in that it resonates with our arts. We can be quite clever about using this symbolism. Thankfully, the thrifty witch need not use yards and yards of fabric for his or her table-linen projects. Secondhand stores and family-style discount shops often have inexpensive tablecloths too. Remember, it's not about making your spiritual creations more expensive, but rather more expressive! You want to slowly make your entire environment into a reflection of, and support system for, your spiritual goals.

Centerpieces and Favors

When time allows, it's fun to make silk flower arrangements and little favors for the mystical table. It seems that our ancestors enjoyed similar pursuits. In France, Germany, and Italy feathers, silk flowers, and other handmade artificial items were actually preferred as centerpieces over fresh flowers, which were regarded as somewhat common until the nineteenth century. No matter your preference, however, there's no question that a clever centerpiece can act as a lovely transmitter or a decorative adjunct to the energy you're slowly building through overall ambiance. If you're working with live flowers or potpourri, this is yet another way to add the symbolic value of aromas to the environment.

Just as with your other touches, think about the season or the theme of your magic. Find eye-pleasing items to assemble and put out as centerpieces. Try to keep these low so people can see each other across them, unless you can place the piece at one end of the table where it won't hinder anyone's view. This is important because the ability to connect visually with other diners at the table is part of the magic of kinship. Large bulky items in the middle of a group of people can really disrupt the flow of energy.

The history of party favors is a little more elusive. We find English notations of party favors made from lace and ribbon in the sixteenth and seventeenth centuries, especially for Valentine's celebrations. The connection of favors with matters of the heart doesn't end there either. Malaysian weddings feature decorated eggs for guests; Italians prepare hard-shelled candy or marzipan; orange blossoms adorn each plate in Spanish nuptials; and Middle Eastern custom dictates that each guest receive five almonds, which represent health, joy, prosperity, fertility, and long life.

As you can see, favors and their symbolic value depended heavily on historical, cultural, and religious backgrounds, which makes their inclusion here a perfect "kitchen witch's companion." For example, say you're putting together a Spring Celebration meal, why not bundle up some flowering seeds for your guest's garden as a favor? In fall, how about making small bottles of cider vinegar for each guest to enjoy? When creating a dish for peace, blue mints might be a good choice to encourage communication, and when laying out a meal for love, try using violet gum for a favor—it will make your words and emotions sweet!

Presentation

Presentation counts for a lot in kitchen magic, especially if you feel you're missing some symbolic dimensions elsewhere in the dish or cooking process. We can take a cue from cooks in the Middle Ages when we're thinking about presentation. At this time there was something called a *soteltie*, which related to the meal's presentation and took one of two forms. The first was a brief theatrical production or some type of entertainment that took place between courses to give guests a chance to digest their food before the next appeared. This production typically related to the occasion for the feast (much as ritual theater might relate to the reason for a Circle).

The second type of soteltie was an elaborate dish of some sort (that often related to the entertainment). If you wondered where the lyrics "four and twenty blackbirds baked in a pie" originated—now you can make an educated guess! The more amazing the solteltie, the more impressive the skill of the chef, and the more honor was due to the household. It's worthy to note that some of the edible sotelties took wonderful pagan forms, which is what really interested this kitchen witch. A description of one meal from the 1500s included a sugar Diana poised with a moon and her dogs, five nymphs, Hercules on his lion, and three unnamed goddesses. These figures would eventually become the last remove, or dessert—a word that evolved from the French term *deservie* (to clear). Dessert was meant to clear the pallet.

Now, I realize that most of us don't have time to prepare elaborately decorated items for our table. But the modern kitchen witch can add exciting touches to meals and desserts without too much fuss. One example that comes immediately to mind are the premade cake decorations sold at local supermarkets and party shops. Those come in an assortment of shapes that you can, in turn, pattern into something magical. Another example more suitable for cooking than for baking is a flavor injector. While normally used to marinate meats, this device can be filled with a thick gravy, which you can then squeeze out on whatever meat you're serving—making a meaningful symbol on each serving as you go.

Speaking of symbols, you can also create these simply by placing various items on the plate in an inventive manner. When my kids are sad, I make slices of hot dogs into a happy face using both the slices and ketchup to create a fun visual. Where's the magic? Well, it's certainly in my intention, and it's also in the red color of the ketchup (love), and the manner it was applied to the plate (clockwise for positive energy to replace the blues!). This is a very simple example, but it's one from which you should be able to get some neat ideas of your own. Think of foods that are easily manipulated (mashed potatoes, slices of meat that you can carve into patterns, etc.) as a starting point and before you know it you'll be serving out images of your magical goals.

Prayer or Moment of Communing

While the custom of prayer seems to have been somewhat displaced in our drive-through society, I think that there are many reasons to consider including it as a kitchen witch's companion. First, one must disengage from the typical image of prayer from a Christian context and consider it in a more global view. In Japan, for example, on certain special occasions guests are called together, asked to be seated, and the host explains the symbolic value of the food, burns incense, then chants the prayers. In Jewish custom prayer ends the meal rather than starts it. Native Americans take a bit of the meal and burn it with prayers before eating (most likely as an offering of thanks to the creature being consumed), and the ancient Greeks offered libations of wine before eating, and sang a hymn before drinking. Notice anything familiar—chanting, incense, offerings, libations? All of these elements can be seen in modern Wiccan rites.

Here are some examples of prayers meant to bless one's home:

Celtic

The Sacred Three
My fortress be
Encircling me
Come and be round
My hearth and my home.

Polish

Bless this family with
A light in the window when the way is dark
With a warm lace by the hearth when the world is cold
With a welcome smile when the road gets too long
Make this a haven of love when the day ends
For our blessings and our home we give thanks.

Eskimo

The lands around my dwelling
Are more beautiful from the day
When it is given to me to see
Faces I have never seen before.
All is more beautiful,
All is more beautiful,
And life is thankfulness.
These guests of mine
Make my house grand.

Gaelic

God's power guide us
God's might uphold us,
God's eyes watch over us;
God's ear hear us,
God's word give us speech,
God's hand guard us,
God's way lie before us,
God's shield shelter us,
God's host secure us.

Scottish

If there is righteousness in the heart,
There will be beauty in the character.
If there is beauty in the character,
There will be harmony in the home.
If there is harmony in the home,
There will be order in the nation.
If there is order in the nation,
There will be peace in the world.

For those kitchen witches who have chosen to adopt a hearth god or goddess, the element of prayer is doubly important because it offers another opportunity to honor that being. In this case, any libation or offering would be of something sacred to the god or goddess. The incense might be chosen from an aromatic known to please him or her, and of course the deity would be addressed by name in the prayer. Here's a small excerpt from the "Hymn to Ishtar" that gives you a feel for the way our ancestors did it in 1600 B.C.E.:

The goddess—with her there is counsel.
The fate of everything she holds in her hand.
At her glance there is created joy,

Power, magnificence, the protecting deity and
guardian spirit.
She dwells in, she pays heed to compassion and
friendliness.
Besides, agreeableness she truly possesses.
Be it slave, unattached girl, or mother, she preserves
(her).
One calls on her; among women one names her
name.
Who—to her greatness who can be equal?
Strong, exalted, splendid are her decrees.
Ishtar—to her greatness who can be equal?
Strong, exalted, splendid are her decrees.

You can see here that the prayer uplifts Ishtar and states her attributes. By so doing, the person offering the prayer invoked those blessings on himself or herself and those in attendance.

If you don't feel comfortable with the idea of mealtime prayers to bless your food and encourage the positive internalization of the energy you've created, an alternative is to have a moment of silent meditation before eating. This can provide you with time to hone your resolve, focus your energies one last time, and welcome the magic. Finally, eat with thankfulness. Gratitude is positive energy that helps process the patterns you've created and manifest them in reality.

Cleanup and Kinship

One may have a blazing hearth in one's soul and yet
no one ever come to sit by it. Passersby see only a
wisp of smoke from the chimney and continue on
the way.

—VINCENT VAN GOGH

CLEANUP RITUALS

It seems it wasn't only cooking and eating that became ritualized but also the manner of cleanup. For one thing, taking away a guest's plate before he was finished was not only rude but sometimes considered a bad omen. That's why the Chinese rest their chopsticks on top of the bowl when they're finished eating—this way a host can tell when to clear the table. By comparison orthodox Hindus all finish their meals, release their plates (which have been held in one hand throughout the meal), and rise together. This is based on the belief that to lose contact with one's food creates impurities.

In Greek and Roman society, drinking more than one sip of wine together always happened after the tables were cleared and people had a moment to freshen up. In ancient Egypt, one recited an ending prayer and rose to signal a meal's completion, and in the 1800s in Europe it was mandatory that a table be cleared of dishes and any crumbs from the meal before dessert could be served.

Cleanup and after-meal fellowship bring closure to your cooking ritual. Just like a regular rite that needs a solid opening, body, and closing, kitchen magic benefits from having something to tie up all the loose ends. Since you have to clean up anyway, there's no reason not to accomplish two things at once.

Now how does a magical cleanup project differ from an ordinary one? Well, as much as you're probably growing weary of the words—intention and thoughtfulness! The way you approach the chore makes a huge difference in the result and the way that space feels afterward. It's remarkable that as each spice or ingredient gets neatly put away, there's a slight shift in the air. To encourage that shift a little more, try adding a little lemon juice to the wash water for counters and the stove as a purifier. You might also move around your kitchen counterclockwise to symbolically "unwind" the energy you built and return the space to normal. This would also be the time to dismiss any forces you've called upon to protect and empower your sacred space. An example of doing this is provided in chapter 2.

After all that, sit down . . . kick back your heels, and relax by yourself or with your family and friends. Now's the time to revel in the special energy you've created, especially the lingering vibrations of love, peace, harmony, and kinship that hover as sure as the last aromatic breezes from your meal. Cheers!

PART II

SAVORY
SPELL-RECIPES

Cooking is like love. It should be entered into with abandon or not at all.

—HARRIET VAN HORNE

Noncooks think it's silly to invest two hours' work in two minutes' enjoyment; but if cooking is evanescent, well, so is the ballet.

—JULIA CHILD

BARBECUES
AND BLESSED BE'S

Hana: What on Earth is a "barbecue"?
Hel: A primitive tribal ritual featuring paper plates,
*   elbows, flying insects, encrusted meat, hush*
*   puppies, and beer.*
Hana: I daren't ask what a "hush puppy" is.
Hel: Don't.

—TREVANIAN, FROM THE NOVEL *SHIBUMI*

From the time snow melts in western New York until it flies again, and often in between, I can be found merrily playing in my backyard at the grill—trying new dishes or cooking up old favorites. But it wasn't always like that. My grilling efforts began like those of most folks who simply want to enjoy the amazing taste of a fresh-grilled hot dog, corn on the cob, or steak during a summer outing. That was my first mistake. I fell hopelessly head-over-heels in love with both the challenges and results obtained from outdoor cooking.

BARBECUE DEFINED

The word *barbecue* comes from the Spanish term *barbacoa*, descriptive of a surface on which food could be roasted or dried for preserving. The barbecues of the 1700s (which is when the word came into popular use) were made from wood, but they had nothing to do with cooking. They were in fact sleeping and storage frames. A hundred years later, the word was being applied to a cooking apparatus, and then finally a whole food style!

Barbecues were more popular in areas where the weather was hospitable, but also showed strong adherents among people to whom hunting was an important ritual. The sharing of meat became a moment of excitement, pride, and generosity. So it wasn't uncommon for a small fire to be built right at the site of a successful hunt, and a fresh-fired meal prepared and enjoyed.

I started tinkering—trying new marinades and sauces derived from scratch. As the experimental process continued it had an unusual and unforeseen side effect. Friends started arriving unannounced at my door saying "Hey, I've got this slab of meat . . . where's the marinade?"—every summer weekend! So often was this the case that it became a ritual of sorts; everyone jokingly called it my "fire festival." The fact is, however, that while it has no fixed date or time, barbecuing has indeed become a very meaningful magical festival to me.

Grilling at our home is a time to celebrate kinship and culinary creativity. It's an experience that begs to be shared. In those moments beneath an open sky everyone who shows up gets a sense of oneness with our ancestors and realizes how they must have felt huddled around their community fires for warmth, fellowship, and of course—dinner! Like these people I find myself drawn to the welcoming light, its heat, and the tempting smells of the fire, and find I want everyone to join me, including you. Thus this chapter is my celebration of an art that I love, and one that I trust will inspire, refresh, and guide your outdoor culinary extravaganzas as well as your spiritual pursuits! Blessed Be!

Grilling Options

As long as mixed grills and combination salads are popular, anthologies will undoubtedly continue in favor.

—Elizabeth Janeway

In this chapter I'll be sharing with you some ideas for sauces and marinades that can be utilized for grilling or other culinary efforts. For now, however, I'd like to talk about types of grilling and their advantages so that you can choose what's best for your menu.

Charcoal grills burn hot, so its easier to sear meat to seal in juices. Symbolically you can also "seal in" the magic of whatever energies were in your marinade this way. It's also easier to smoke meats using charcoal. Gas is very convenient and even allows food energies to mix and mingle evenly. Wood grilling is tricky because it's somewhat unpredictable. Some pieces of wood may pop and spark due to interior water. However, a wood fire offers a naturally smoky effect and richness of flavor, and you can sometime choose the type of wood to match your spiritual goals.

There are two basic methods of cooking food on the grill: firing it directly or indirectly. Indirect heat is best for delicate foods or those that need a longer cooking time (like flaky fish and thick cuts of meat, respectively). To create indirect heat on charcoal, leave a space in the center of the briquettes. Once they're hot, put ½ cup of water in a fireproof pan in the middle of the briquettes. The food goes on the grill over the pan, and you'll need to add more briquettes adjacent to the pan about every forty-five minutes. It's a little easier to create indirect heat on a two-burner gas grill since you can preheat the whole thing, then turn off one burner (or turn it to low) so one side will be cooler. Alternatively, on a single-rack grill you can cover the grill with a double thickness of foil to diffuse the heat.

For direct heat, place the cooking rack right over the hot coals. This is a forthright method that applies the fire's energy with greater intensity. The only trick is to watch the overall heat with which you're working. If using charcoal, wait until about three-quarters of the coals exhibit a light coating of ash (this equals a medium heat, whereas if you can see a red glow through the ash, it's the equivalent of high heat). Another way to determine whether the coals are ready is to very carefully hold your hand over the heat at the cooking height. If you have to pull your hand away after two seconds, it's a high heat . . . after five seconds it's a low heat (relatively speaking).

Whether grilling directly or not, adding wood chips and chunks can result in marvelous flavor for your food. In ancient times the smoke of a sacred fire was said to bear one's wishes and prayers to heaven. In this case, it will also carry your energy and flavor into the food. Soak mesquite, alder, hickory, wild cherry, apple, maple, or pecan chips for one hour before scattering over the hot coals. Note that you need not use only water to soak the chips. Other options include wine or even whiskey, like Jack Daniels. For safety, poultry should be smoked until it reaches an internal temperature of 180 degrees F., beef and lamb to about 150 degrees F., and pork to about 165 degrees F. Eat the cooked food within four days or freeze it immediately after cooking for future use.

BARBECUE TIPS, HELPS, HINTS

- When cooking with wooden skewers soak them for an hour in water before use. These are best used for fruit, vegetables, and fish. You can also soak them in wine or juice to bring more flavor to the food (remember to coordinate your choice with your magical goals).
- Look for metal skewers that are flat or square so it's easier to turn food. These are best for meat.
- If basting with a sweet sauce, be especially careful, since they can cause flare-ups. Apply them carefully and watch resulting flames.
- Be aware that grilling times in any book, including this one, have to be adjusted for the weather outside. When it's cold, you'll need more coals or a higher flame, and grilling takes longer. Wind makes a very hot fire, and humidity will slow your cooking time.
- Remember that charcoal briquettes burn cooler than hardwood.
- For safety, always marinate your foods in the refrigerator and do not reuse the marinade. Magically speaking, marinade saturates the food with a specific energy before cooking it.
- Move the food around on your grill for the most even results.
- Pierce the food as little as possible. The more you do, the more juices will be lost (and symbolically you want to release the energy of the food into *you*, not the fire).

Lusty Lobster

As is the case with most shellfish, lobster is associated with sexuality and passion. In Japan, it has the additional correspondence of the longevity of a happy event (like marriage). Thus the following dish is ideally suited to the pursuit of pleasure, thanks to the addition of fennel, which provides physical endurance, and orange for the loving touch.

Sauce

- 5 tablespoons olive oil
- 3 tablespoons white wine vinegar
- 1 tablespoon plus 2 teaspoons soy sauce
- 2 teaspoons minced peeled fresh ginger
- 2 teaspoons sugar (optional)
- 3 mandarin oranges, seeded
- 1 medium fennel bulb, trimmed and cut into matchstick-size strips
- ½ medium red onion, thinly sliced
- Salt and pepper to taste

Preparations

Lay out your partner's favorite outfit and dab it with a bit of sexy perfume or cologne, saying: *"The gift of food is the gift of desire, raise our passions ever higher!"* Dress after you've finished preparing the food, remembering that you're "putting on the magic" with your clothing.

To Make the Sauce

In a medium bowl, whisk 2 tablespoons of the oil, vinegar, 2 teaspoons of the soy sauce, ginger, and sugar. Cut peel and white pith from mandarin oranges; discard. Hold oranges over bowl to catch juices, cut between membranes to release segments into bowl. Add fennel and onion; toss gently. Season with salt and pepper. Chill for 1–3 hours before dinner. In the meantime prepare the lobster.

LOBSTER

2 tablespoons olive oil	2 garlic cloves, minced
2 tablespoons butter	4 medium-size lobster tails
3 tablespoons fresh chopped chives	salt and pepper to taste

 Prepare barbecue (medium-high heat). Mix oil, butter, chives, and garlic in a non-aluminum pan and simmer. Turn tails into oil mixture to coat. Sprinkle with salt and pepper. Place lobster tails, meat side down, on grill. Grill 3 minutes. Turn over; grill until meat is opaque in center (about 5 minutes). Serve with sauce over top or on the side. As you're turning, it's a good time to recite your incantation again to strengthen the magic.

Enchantment Pork with Mango (for Love)

According to history, Buddha used a mango grove as a place for meditation. In this region of the world, the best magicians used this fruit as part of love potions. Even today Hindu people use mango leaves to represent happiness, and they sometimes hold weddings beneath the bows of the tree. When combined with pork—a food sacred to Carnea the Roman goddess of our human needs and a symbol of abundance in China— mango makes a wonderful dish to inspire an abundance of warm, joyful, and loving feelings between two or more people.

MANGO TOPPING

1 mango, peeled and coarsely chopped	1 tablespoon chopped fresh jalapeño (including seeds)
¼ cup fresh lime juice	1 teaspoon salt, or to taste
1 large garlic clove	

 Puree mango, lime juice, garlic, jalapeño, and salt in a blender. Set aside.

PORK

1 tablespoon anise seeds	1 ½ teaspoons salt
1 teaspoon cardamom	1 ½ teaspoons brown sugar
1 teaspoon lemon or orange rind, grated	3 tablespoons olive oil
¾ teaspoon black peppercorns	4 (¾-inch-thick) loin pork chops, trimmed

PREPARATIONS

Love is gentle, and should not overwhelm your guests. Therefore place some pink candles (the color of friendly love) around the dining room table and have a rye bread with dill dip for munching on before dinner. Dill provides protection for your efforts as well as a little luck and kinship!

Use a food processor or blender to make a fine meal out of the anise, cardamom, lemon or orange, peppercorns, and salt and sugar. Stir in the olive oil. Prepare charcoal grill (do not spread charcoal out to edges of grill). Brush both sides of pork with spice rub. As you do, try adding an incantation like:

> Rub a dub dub
> Bless this good grub
> With love and bliss
> Sealed with magic's kiss!

Grill pork on an oiled rack set 5 to 6 inches over glowing coals for 2 minutes on each side. Move pork off to side of grill, turning once, until just cooked through, about 3 minutes more on each side. Transfer to a platter and let stand, loosely covered, 5 minutes. Serve pork with mango on top or on the side as garnish.

Adaptive Suggestion: Substitute chicken for pork to encourage a healthy relationship.

Makes 4 servings

PORK PERSPECTIVES

- Pliny and Plutarch speak of more than fifty ways to season pork.
- Paleolithic people killed and ate wild pigs.
- Chinese citizens ate nearly every part of the pig but for the skin at least 5,000 years ago.
- By 7000 B.C.E. pigs were domesticated.
- In Rome pig was a food of the elite.
- Hebrew custom considers the pig unclean and therefore unfit for consumption.
- New Guinea myth says the pig was created as a sacrificial food.
- In Greek tradition a pig represented the fertile earth.
- Pork was so popular in Rome that some had to be imported from Gaul.
- Germanic warriors who fell in battle were posthumously awarded a pig (note that this may tie into the Celtic myth that claims feasts in the otherworld consist of boar or pig that never runs out.
- Fifteenth-century Latvian recipes specify the use of pork ribs.
- Early Americans dug a pit, filled it with wood, and burned it until only hot coals were left. Then they would put a forked stick on each side and place a spiced whole pig or rack of ribs on a long pole, turning it slowly over the heat, using some type of mop, a large basting brush, to keep the meat from burning.

Solar Goose

The goose was sacred to many gods and goddesses, including Osiris, Isis, and the sun god Ra. The bird gained its reputation by laying the cosmic egg that gave birth to the entire universe. Because of this associ- ation the bird was featured at solar feasts, making it an ideal food for Summer and Winter Solstice to honor the fires above, those on our grill, and those in our soul. In the New World, turkey has replaced goose at the table, and it can be utilized similarly.

BASIC BRINE

For a 5–6 pound goose

Enough water to completely cover bird with space to spare
1 cup salt and ½ cup sugar per gallon of water

1 bay leaf
½ lemon, sliced
½ orange, sliced

Bring the goose and the brine to boil in a pan large enough so that the goose doesn't touch the sides. Turn off the heat, cool, and refrigerate for 24 hours. Remove the goose and pat it dry in preparation for stuffing and spicing.

PREPARATIONS

Since you have twenty-four hours, try to time this so that you can pre- pare and stuff the bird either at dawn or noon, both of which are very positive times symbolically for the sun (the first for hope, the second for fullness of power). You already used two sunny fruits in the brine, but you may want to consider side dishes that also have solar value. For example, make a green salad garnished with red and yellow pepper around a center of cashews (a solar nut), and offer some sun- flower seeds as a light snack or favor. Additionally, decorate your table with a bright yellow candle that can be lit at the start of the meal to celebrate the sun. You may want to add a prayer, chant, or song at this juncture, depending on what solar occasion you're celebrating.

STUFFING

1 chopped red onion	Chopped fresh sage and lemon
1 chopped red-and-yellow	balm
apple	Herb butter (your choice)
1 chopped citron	Poultry seasoning to taste
Diced garlic to taste (2 cloves	
is nice)	

Combine first five ingredients. Note that the bird need not be stuffed full. The main reason for these ingredients are both their symbolic attributes and the overall aromatic appeal they give to the goose. I also like to stick a few pats of herbed butter under the goose's skin so it stays moist while grilling, and sprinkle the skin with my favorite poultry seasoning.

You need to create an indirect heat so that the goose is on the cooler side and can cook slowly. Using toothpicks, secure a tent of tinfoil over the breast so it doesn't burn or stick to the skin. You'll also need a meat thermometer that you can place in a thick portion. When the grill reaches a medium heat, close the bird inside and let it cook until the meat thermometer reaches 165 degrees F. Then remove the foil, turn off the grill, and leave the bird in a bright window for 20 minutes' resting time. This way it can absorb more solar energy.

SERVING SUGGESTION

If you'd like a sunny sauce to go with your goose, try this golden blend. Melt 1 tablespoon butter in a saucepan. Add 1 tablespoon olive oil, 2 tablespoons Dijon mustard, 2 tablespoons lemon juice, 2 tablespoons orange juice, 1 tablespoon grated lemon peel, and 2 cups chicken broth. Bring this to a low rolling boil and let it reduce by ⅓. Serve it like a gravy.

Alternative Cooking Method: If you would prefer, the goose can be cooked equally well in a 300-degree-F. oven. The interior temperature of the bird should reach 165 degrees F., and you should cover and baste the goose regularly, as you would a turkey.

Makes 5–6 servings

Bountiful Baby-Back Ribs

I owe a debt of gratitude to the person who first decided to roast these delectable items over a fresh fire. They're among our favorites for inspiring both providence and bounty, being that the swine are associated with the fertile nature of the Great Mother, and Earth itself, in Celtic, Oceanic, Tibetan Buddhist, Hinduism, and Sumero-Semetic settings. To this foundation we add a sweet-savory rub so that life itself is sweet and zesty!

RIB RUB

1 tablespoon garlic powder
1 tablespoon onion powder
½ tablespoon fresh ground
   black pepper
1 teaspoon ground cardamom
1 teaspoon each orange and
   lemon powder (or rind)

1 teaspoon paprika
1 teaspoon powdered ginger
½ teaspoon kosher salt
½ teaspoon cayenne pepper
½ teaspoon chili powder
¼ cup brown sugar

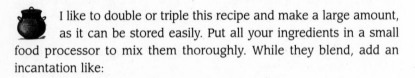 I like to double or triple this recipe and make a large amount, as it can be stored easily. Put all your ingredients in a small food processor to mix them thoroughly. While they blend, add an incantation like:

> *Meat when rubbed with herbs and zest*
> *Brings to us, providence!*
> *When heated 'pon my sacred grill*
> *Life becomes bountiful!*

PREPARATIONS

Bounty and providence are strongly associated with the earth element, so you may want to honor those energies in your sacred space with a small living plant, or four green candles placed near the northern area of the room (north is the region of Earth in most Wiccan traditions). If you choose the plant, place a coin in the soil before you start cooking (so prosperity grows). If you choose the candles, light them before you start cooking the ribs.

RIBS

1 rack baby-back ribs	Plastic food wrap
3 tablespoons apple cider	Aluminum foil
1 teaspoon orange extract	

 Most good butchers remove the sheath from the back of baby ribs before selling them, but check to make sure this has been done. If it hasn't, loosen one edge of the thin fat layer and grab hold of it with a paper towel. Pull slowly and evenly back (the towel keeps your hands from slipping and makes this step *much* easier).

Next, take a handful of the rub mixture and massage it into the surface of the ribs. Coat them on both sides evenly (don't skimp). Repeat your previous incantation four times while you rub.

Lay the ribs on a large sheet of plastic wrap (enough to cover them completely and securely. Drizzle the mixture of cider and extract over top, then wrap up the bundle. Around this, place another layer of aluminum foil. Put this in the oven at 200–225 degrees F. for about 2 hours (until the meat starts retracting from the bones). Remove from the oven.

At this point the ribs are ready for the grill, but if you want them to be even more flavorful you can drop them in some marinade. I use a blend of orange juice, a hint of soy, and a fruity wine. Whether you marinate or not, these will take but a few minutes to finish over a medium grill heat. Place them on the grill after it's heated and brush with your favorite barbecue sauce.

Last but not least, move your candles or plant to the center of the serving table to act as a focus for manifesting your energies.

Makes 2 servings

Blissful Beef Kabobs

*In ancient times beef was often eaten by those who presided over impor-
tant religious rituals in which a bull or cow was given as an offering.
Thus it has connections with the spiritual quest, as does the cinnamon in
the marinade below. Additionally, there were a variety of cow goddesses
who had great power in ancient myths because they nourished the world.
With these historical facts in mind, this beef can be prepared to nourish
your inner kitchen witch so you can follow your bliss!*

MARINADE

1 (12-ounce) bottle of dark
    beer
⅓ cup (packed) dark brown
    sugar
3 tablespoons lime or lemon
    juice
2 tablespoons minced red onion
3 garlic cloves, chopped
2 tablespoons Worcestershire
    sauce

2 tablespoons whole-grain
    mustard
2 tablespoons olive oil
1 teaspoon meat tenderizer
    (may only be necessary on
    less expensive cuts)
½ tablespoon minced peeled
    fresh ginger
½ tablespoon cinnamon

Lay your marinade ingredients before you. Close your eyes and
take three deep cleansing breaths. Meditate for a few minutes
on your spiritual path—what has brought you to this place and where
you wish to go in the future. As you do, put your hands above the
ingredients palms down, and visualize sparkling white light pouring
into them (Note: If you think of your path as having a specific color—
use that hue in the imagery.) Continue until your palms feel warm and
the ingredients have been saturated with those vibrations. Combine
ingredients.

KABOBS

The ingredients here are measured out so that three people get five pieces each of all items—five being the number of spiritual pursuits. The peace slices also support this goal as the fruit of Paradise.

36 ounces top loin, cubed (you can use other less costly cuts)

15 small mushrooms

15 slices sweet pepper

15 cherry tomatoes

15 slices onion

15 slices fresh peach

 Set aside a small portion of marinade to use for brushing at the grill. Place all the ingredients in the remaining marinade. Cover this and keep it in the refrigerator for about 24 hours, stirring regularly so the meat is evenly soaked. If you're using wooden skewers soak them in herb water or wine for 1 hour before threading them. Place the kabob components on the skewers in a manner that's visually pleasing, thinking of the Path of Beauty as you do. Bring the grill up to a high heat to sear the meat on all sides, then lower the temperature to a medium heat and cook until the veggies are tender (longer if you like well-done meat).

SERVING SUGGESTIONS

Make sure each person receives five of each item when you serve out the meal. Consider adding a simple white candle to the dining table to honor Spirit. Also, if you'd like a nice sauce accompaniment try the wine reduction sauce in the next chapter.

Makes 5 servings as a main course

Classic Comfort Chicken Grille

There is something welcome and familiar about a classic barbecued chicken. The aromas at cookouts can be enticing to the point of distraction, and joining in the fellowship always seems to leave a warm smile on people's faces. Add to that the mythology and lore associated with this bird, which connects it to solar energy (blessings) and health, and you have a perfect dish to inspire soothing social energy.

CHICKEN FOR FOUR

4 pounds chicken pieces
(bone in)
4 quarts water

½ cup kosher salt
½ lemon, sliced

 Place the chicken pieces in the water with salt and lemon, bringing all to a boil for 15 minutes. Cool and transfer meat to marinade.

MARINADE

A dependable and tasty marinade for chicken is simple Italian dressing or your favorite vinaigrette. Sprinkle this lightly over the meat and let it sit for at least 1 hour, basting regularly. Each time you baste the chicken, consider adding an incantation like:

Comfort of friends and family
Comfort of the heart
Comfort at my hearth and home
Comfort never part

Grilling Sauce

If you're pressed for time, it's perfectly acceptable to use your favorite over-the-counter barbecue sauce instead of this recipe.

1 cup light brown sugar, packed	1 tablespoon seasoned salt
1 cup honey	1 tablespoon soy sauce
¼ cup steak sauce	½ tsp minced garlic
⅔ cup ketchup	¼ tsp salt
2 tablespoons cider vinegar	⅛ tsp ground black pepper
2 tablespoons Worcestershire sauce	⅛ tsp dried oregano
1 tablespoon meat tenderizer	⅛ tsp ground ginger

 Place all the ingredients in a small saucepan over low flame and stir until the honey and all spices are well blended. Note that it's easier to apply this sauce warm while grilling the chicken.

Grilling Directions

Turn the grill up to a high heat. Sear chicken on both sides, then adjust the grill to a medium-low heat. Coat one side of the chicken with the sauce and close the grill for about 5 minutes. The sauce should appear sticky and somewhat "cooked" to the meat's surface before you turn it. Repeat this process four times while repeating the incantation you used to energize the marinade. Serve.

Makes 4 servings (about 3 cups of sauce)

Serving Suggestions

What's a classic grille without some type of salad as a side dish? Recipes for some of these dishes are located in chapter 10.

Just for the Halibut

Fish represents the power of water, and specifically generative energy (or regeneration). Fish served with bread and wine often make up the offeratory meal for goddesses of love and fertility. Combined with the nuts in the accompanying sauce you can use this fish for any area of your life that you wish to be more fertile (imagination, the garden, whatever!).

HALIBUT

4 pieces halibut fillet
1 cup white wine
2 tablespoons lemon juice

1 teaspoon garlic juice
1 teaspoon onion powder
   (optional)

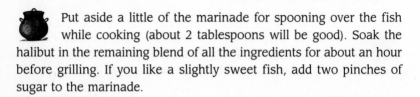 Put aside a little of the marinade for spooning over the fish while cooking (about 2 tablespoons will be good). Soak the halibut in the remaining blend of all the ingredients for about an hour before grilling. If you like a slightly sweet fish, add two pinches of sugar to the marinade.

PECAN SAUCE

1 tablespoon olive oil
1 cup (6 ounces) chopped
   shallots
½ cup (2 ounces) pecans,
   chopped

½ tablespoon butter
½ teaspoon basil (for love if
   you're hoping to conceive)
½ teaspoon finely grated fresh
   lemon zest

PREPARATIONS

Yellow is a creative, productive hue, so consider adding highlights of it to your workspace. While the fish marinates, create your pecan sauce over a low flame. Stir the mixture clockwise to draw positive energy (the heat here also supports fertility). Focus on the area of your life to which you're going to apply the finished energy, just as you'll apply the sauce to the fish!

Place the marinated fish skin side up on a medium-heat grill that's sprayed with non-stick cooking oil. Let the fillets cook for about 3 minutes so that they're just starting to turn translucent. Flip them and spoon the reserved marinade onto the fish. Close the grill for an additional 3 to 5 minutes. The fillets will flake easily with a fork when cooked through. Serve with the pecan sauce either on top or on the side for dipping.

SERVING SUGGESTION

The pecan sauce tastes very nice with asparagus (which is a symbol of male virility), or with rice (a component that inspires luck).

Makes 4 servings

Mystical Mushrooms

Throughout Europe a ring of mushrooms was the sign of fairy goings-on. Due to the hallucinogenic nature of some mushrooms, eating them was associated with psychism in regions as far apart as Siberia and North America. This dish builds on that ancient mystical foundation by including celery seed, thyme, and anise—all of which support psychic awareness.

MUSHROOMS

1 tablespoon peanut oil
2 cups chopped green onions
2 tablespoons minced garlic
1 tablespoon minced peeled
    fresh ginger
½ teaspoon celery seed

½ teaspoon thyme
1 cup chicken broth
½ cup hoisin sauce
4 whole star anise
4 large shiitake mushroom
    caps, stemmed

Preparations

Take a little anise seed oil and dab it on your third eye (the area on your forehead between your eyes), saying *"Open my eyes within and without. Let vision be clear, remove all doubt!"* To keep the energy of your incantation going, dab a little of the oil on a candle and burn it while you cook.

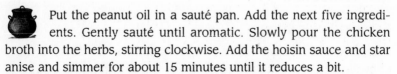 Put the peanut oil in a sauté pan. Add the next five ingredients. Gently sauté until aromatic. Slowly pour the chicken broth into the herbs, stirring clockwise. Add the hoisin sauce and star anise and simmer for about 15 minutes until it reduces a bit.

While you're doing this lay the mushroom caps in a flat pan. Pour the sauce while it's still warm (not hot) over the mushrooms. Let these soak in the sauce at room temperature for 30 minutes then take them to the grill, which you'll want on a medium-low temperature (the mushrooms cook fairly quickly). Because you haven't left the marinade overnight you can use this right from the same pan for basting. It usually takes about two turns of the mushrooms 3 minutes per side—to cook (longer if the caps are thick). Serve with one of the star anise pieces on top of each for a decorative spiritual flair.

Serving Suggestion

If you want to serve this as an appetizer for more than four people, slice up the mushrooms and put them over a bed of lettuce with the following as a dressing: 4 tablespoons lime juice, 2 tablespoons peanut oil, 1 tablespoon cider vinegar, 1 tablespoon honey, 1 pinch salt.

Makes 4 servings as a main course

Opportunity Sesame Shrimp

In Hindu custom people anoint themselves with sesame oil to bring luck and keep away evil influences. The purported power of sesame was seen in the Arabian knights when the way to hidden treasure was made clear by saying, "open sesame!" Here we're utilizing that energy combined with the prolific nature of shrimp to inspire all manner of openings, especially passionate ones.

SHRIMP

1½ pounds jumbo shrimp, peeled and deveined

3 tablespoons sesame oil

3 tablespoons soy sauce

3 tablespoons bourbon whiskey

2 teaspoons minced fresh ginger

Pinch of dried crushed red pepper

½ teaspoon Chinese five-spice powder

2 garlic cloves, crushed

1½ tablespoons honey (orange blossom is nice)

Fresh chopped chives

PREPARATIONS

If weather permits, open windows and doors during the preparation process for this dish. So doing opens the way for prospects to find you! If you wish, leave one door or window closed until just before serving then recite the incantation given later in this recipe when you open it.

 Rinse the shrimp under cold running water and blot dry with paper towels. Put aside while you create the marinade sauce.

In a large container, combine all but the chives. Put the shrimp in and cover them. Place the shrimp in the fridge for an hour. Try to stir or shake every fifteen minutes for the best results.

Using a slotted spoon, remove the shrimp from the marinade, and pour it into a saucepan. While you're warming your grill to medium heat, bring the marinade to a boil until it forms a glaze-like texture (about 3 minutes after the boiling begins). Remove from the heat and set aside.

Place the shrimp on the grill, turning every two minutes until nicely browned (you can brush them with a bit of glaze to keep them moist). When they're bright red, they're ready to serve. Transfer to a platter and sprinkle with the chives (keep a pinch in hand and mix it with sesame seeds). Now go to your door or window, open it and say:

> *Open sesame*
> *Sesame open the way*
> *Bring good prospects this very day!*

SERVING SUGGESTION

Have a warm baguette on hand. Prepare this butter and have it handy for dipping (both the shrimp and the bread!): Combine 2 tablespoons margarine or butter melted with ½ teaspoon grated lemon peel, 1 tablespoon lemon juice, ½ teaspoon Worcestershire sauce, and ¼ teaspoon minced garlic.

Makes 6 servings

Kinship Potatoes

I'm often amazed at how many people neglect to use the grill for side dishes and vegetables. If you have a good heat going, there's no reason not to make your entire menu in one spot. Potatoes, being a root vegetable, offer strong foundations to this dish, and the dill provides the aroma of kinship and strong family ties.

POTATOES

Five medium-size white potatoes (red if you want a little more love)
4 tablespoons Italian-style salad dressing

2 teaspoons dill weed
Salt and pepper to taste

Preparations

Kinship is all about togetherness, so get people in your household to help with this. Perhaps one person could wash the potatoes, another dice them, another toss with the herbs, another still bless them, and finally wrap them in aluminum foil. Hold hands around the bundle and say something like:

> Kinship, trust, and unity
> Cooked within each bite
> When heated through and tasty
> Let the magic take to flight!

 I usually make this as a side dish, so it's the first thing to go on the grill. Toss the diced or sliced potatoes with the other ingredients and wrap them securely in one layer of foil. Put them on an upper shelf if possible for 10–15 minutes per side (the more potatoes, the more time required), then bring out your main dish. Continue turning the potatoes until the main dish is cooked. The chef may wish to recite the same incantation again upon each turn to reinforce the magic while the fire warms your hearts to perfection.

Serving Suggestion

For a simple and symbolic serving surface, place a heaping spoonful or so of these potatoes on a large lettuce leaf, which will bring peace into your magical equation.

Makes 5 servings

MOONLIGHT MARINADES AND SUNSHINE SAUCES

What is sauce for the goose may be sauce for the gander but is not necessarily sauce for the chicken, the duck, the turkey, or the guinea hen.

—ALICE B. TOKLAS

The term *sauce* comes from a French word meaning "a relish" (basically any liquid or semi-liquid substance that makes food taste, smell, or look better). While sauces vary dramatically from era to era and culture to culture, there seem to be five on which all chefs still depend. The two oldest, and most flexible to creating the base for other saucy mixes, are béchamel sauce and mayonnaise. The other three are velouté, brûne (brown), and blonde (a golden yellow). This chapter explores a variety of traditional and inventive sauces that you can use in combination with many of the other recipes collected herein. No matter your choice, a sauce will magically "top" off your creation, something like the highpoint of a chant where energy builds to perfection.

Plum Dandy Sauce (for Health)

Thomas Culpeper, an eighteenth-century English herbalist, recommended plums both for well-being and for their pleasurable taste. The word plum *means "desirable," which gives this fruit an extra dimension of being able to improve the health of our passions! In either case, this sauce matches nicely with chicken (another health-oriented food metaphysically), but it also creates a unique flavor sensation when served on salmon (for profuse wellness). This sauce is also complementary with beef and ham.*

SAUCE

4 ripe red plums, cut into 1-inch chunks
1 tablespoon finely grated peeled fresh gingerroot
1 garlic clove, diced
2 tablespoons brown sugar, firmly packed
2 tablespoons water
1 tablespoon soy sauce
¼ teaspoon Chinese five-spice blend
1 tablespoon sake
2 scallions or green onions, chopped
Hot sauce to taste (optional)

SPELL PREPARATIONS

Because you're generating positive energy, I suggest preparing this dish on a waxing or full moon. Wear a color that you associate with health and recovery. If you're making this spell recipe with the intention of directing it toward a relationship, I suggest using dark red plums, the color of love and desire.

In a saucepan simmer all ingredients except hot sauce and scallions, covered. Stir occasionally for about twenty minutes until the plums start to fall apart. Uncover, add the vinegar and simmer until sauce is consistency of ketchup. Stir regularly to keep it from sticking and heat for about 10 more minutes. Stir in scallions. Add hot sauce if desired.

Makes 1 cup

Peanut Recompense Sauce

A Chinese legend tells of a family trying to protect their crop of peanuts from crows. The son of this family was tending his fields when an old, hungry man appeared. The son showed him kindness, and in return was given a magical jewel that had to be placed underground with his bare hands. This, of course left him bloody and tired, but the next day all the peanuts followed the jewel underground. He no longer had to fend off the birds. This legend is shared with children to teach them the value of hard work and generosity as yielding their own rewards. Accordingly, apply this sauce when you need your sincere efforts to be appreciated and manifest in positive results (in other words, you're not working for peanuts!).

SAUCE

⅓ cup smooth peanut butter
¼ cup chicken broth
2 tablespoons unsweetened
    coconut milk
1 teaspoon lemon or lime juice

1 teaspoon soy sauce
1 teaspoon fish sauce (only if
    using on fish)
½–1 tsp. hot sauce

PREPARATIONS

Orange is the color associated with the harvest. Since you want your hard work to reap a fine harvest of magic, carve an orange candle with a symbol of the area of your life in which you desire those rewards. Light it just prior to making your sauce, saying:

The gold of rich rewards be mine
May fortune on my life now shine
As in this sauce my magic blends
So manifestation can begin!

NUTTY FACTS

Peanuts are actually legumes. They probably originated in South America. History tells us the Maya and Incans both cultivated peanuts, sometimes using them as a food for the dead. This connection came about because they grow underground, thus associating them with the underworld.

Although the peanut itself has a long history, having been found in Peruvian mummy tombs, peanut butter is a relatively young food. In 1890, an enterprising physician, Dr. John Kellogg (of corn flakes fame), created peanut butter as a healthy animal protein substitute that was easy to digest for patients with no teeth. The manufacturing process was mechanized by George A. Bayle Jr., and a patent for a peanut butter machine was issued to Abrose W. Straub in 1903. In 1904, peanut butter was thrust into the limelight at the St. Louis Universal Exposition by concessionaire C. H. Sumner, where it was promoted as a health food. When innovative agricultural scientist Dr. George Washington Carver developed an improved version of the butter, it attracted even more enthusiasts. In 1922, peanut butter went commercial when J. L. Rosefield of Rosefield Packing Company of Alameda, California, perfected a process to keep the oil from separating in the peanut butter and to prevent it from spoiling. He marketed his commercial peanut butter, under the name "Skippy," as "churned" peanut butter, a smoother, creamier version of the coarse-textured original.

Puree the ingredients in a blender or food processor 1 day ahead of time and refrigerate. Bring to room temperature before using. You can brush this on fish while grilling or use it as a serving sauce.

ALTERNATIVES

For a sweeter sauce add a dollop of honey (for sweet success), and for a more Oriental-style sauce add sesame seeds (that open the way).

Makes 1 cup

Nature Goddess Sauce

The rich green color of this sauce gives it strong connections with any nature goddess whom you'd like to honor (or Earth itself, especially in spring). It's also the color of new endeavors and slow but steady growth.

SAUCE

½ cup white salad dressing (generic is fine)

½ cup sour cream

¼ cup chopped green onion

¼ cup chopped scallion

2 tablespoons fresh chopped parsley

2 tablespoons chopped tarragon

1 tablespoon anchovy paste (optional)

1 tablespoon lemon juice

¼ teaspoon salt and pepper

PREPARATIONS

To honor nature, utilize this as part of your next outdoor gathering. Before making it, take a walk outside and sit beneath a lush tree. Take in the color, aroma, and energies you feel. Breathe deeply of the earth's richness, then carry that feeling with you while you prepare your sauce and other dishes.

Puree the ingredients together until very smooth. Serve the sauce with crackers, chips, shrimp cocktail, bread sticks, or warm pita.

ALTERNATIVE

If you'd like a warm dip, add ½ cup of your favorite cheese to this sauce and simmer it over a double boiler until it's smooth. Cheese adds the energy of love to the dish.

Makes 1 cup plus

Suppression Sauce

The form of steak sauce used during the Victorian era was heavy on the vinegar, as vinegar helped to preserve the meat, at a time when refrigeration was scarce. A vinegar sauce also neatly covered the flavor of meat slightly past its prime. With this in mind, use this sauce when you wish to keep something personal or private until you can handle it yourself.

SAUCE

2 tablespoons olive oil
1 red onion, finely chopped
1 stalk of celery, finely chopped
Pinch of sugar
1 teaspoon celery seed (or ½ tsp celery salt)

1 tablespoon Dijon mustard
1 cup ketchup
¼ cup beef broth
3 tablespoons wine vinegar
2 tablespoons Worcestershire sauce
2 tablespoons honey

PREPARATIONS

On a scrap piece of paper draw an eye. This represents those people trying to peek into your personal business. Now, take a dark cloth and wrap it completely around that image like a blindfold, saying something like:

No evil shall you see
None to hear, none to speak
You may look, but not find what you seek
Until I fix them, these problems shall hide
From your gossip, from your snooping
And stay out of your mind.

 Put the oil, onions, and celery in a frying pan to gently sauté until golden brown. Stir in the remaining ingredients, bringing them to a low-rolling boil. Maintain the heat at medium-low for another 20 minutes. This sauce will last for 3 to 4 weeks in the refrigerator.

ALTERNATIVE

Switch out the beef stock for apple cider when making this for pork and add a pinch of ginger to the blend. For a hotter sauce, add a few drops of chili sauce or Tabasco (to taste). The hotness is even more protective.

Makes about 3 cups

Grilling Up Cordial Conversations

The amiable nature of anise combines in this recipe with mustard, which is known for its healing properties, and honey—a flavoring known to bless the consumer with the gift of gab. Utilize this sauce when your words have been harsh and you need to find the right way to fix the situation during or after dinner.

SAUCE

2 tablespoons vegetable oil

1 medium onion, finely chopped

1 celery rib, finely chopped

2 teaspoons anise seeds, lightly crushed with a rolling pin

1 teaspoon celery seeds

1 tablespoon dry mustard

1 cup ketchup

1 cup bottled chili sauce

¼ cup apple cider or apple juice

3 tablespoons cider vinegar

2 tablespoons Worcestershire sauce

2 tablespoons honey

PREPARATIONS

Warm up a little extra apple cider for yourself, and add to it a sprinkle of anise and honey. Stir it counterclockwise, saying:

> *Angry words shall be no more*
> *Ire and judgment, my mouth abhor*
> *When next ——————— and I meet*
> *Only healing words will I speak*
> *And let this sauce like balm be applied*
> *So our relationship is rectified!*

Sip on the cider-tea while you make the sauce.

In a medium saucepan, heat the oil and cook the onion and celery over medium heat until softened, about 5 minutes. Add the anise seeds and cook, stirring, for a minute longer, then also mingle in the celery seeds with the mustard. Stir until the mustard dissolves. Add the remaining ingredients. Increase the heat a bit so that the whole blend comes to a boil, then turn the heat down and simmer over low-medium heat for about 15 minutes. Keep stirring, this will thicken as it cooks.

Note that this sauce is best left to sit in the refrigerator overnight before grilling. It will then keep safely in your refrigerator for about 3–4 weeks.

Makes enough sauce for about 5 pounds of barbecue

Lemon Love Sauce

The Jews in Roman times and the Japanese decorated bridal chambers with lemons to represent everlasting love. A French custom from the time of the Crusades was for a knight to show his fidelity by making for his lady a cloven lemon. This was not an inexpensive gift—lemons came from the Holy Land, and cloves were worth their weight in gold.

SAUCE

½ cup dry white wine
1 cup chicken broth
3 tablespoons lemon juice
2 teaspoons grated lemon zest
1 teaspoon diced onion
1 teaspoon diced garlic (shallots may be substituted for garlic or onion)

1 teaspoon fresh minced thyme
1 teaspoon each salt and pepper
¾ teaspoon ground allspice
2 teaspoons corn starch
Water
Parsley for garnish

PREPARATIONS

Since you're making this for the one(s) you love, think in terms of creating the right atmosphere in which to serve your dish. Have finger bowls with rose water, a candle for each person, and wear something you know he or she likes. Additionally, sprinkle some fresh rose petals decoratively on the table, adding an empowering phrase like:

> *Let love be warm, let love be real*
> *Love within this sauce I seal!*

Pour the white wine in the saucepan, adding the broth, lemon juice, and zest. Bring this to a boil and let it reduce by half a cup. Add the remaining ingredients except the cornstarch and water, whisking them into the blend. Let this simmer for about 5 minutes. Meanwhile mix the cornstarch with just cold enough water to thin, and stir it into the hot base to thicken it. Pour this over your main dish (chicken is one choice) so that the sauce forms a heart. Finish with a sprig of bright green parsley so love flourishes.

Makes about 2 cups

Jumpin' Ginger

Ginger is strongly associated with magic. The ancients felt that only shamans and mages could tap and control its powers, especially to drive away malicious spirits that cause disease. Soy is thought to provide endurance. These attributions combined with health-giving orange make a zesty sauce that activates and amplifies whatever energies you put into the rest of your meal.

SAUCE

2 teaspoons sesame oil
1 ½ teaspoon fresh gingerroot, peeled and chopped
½ cup soy sauce

2 green onions, sliced thin
2 tablespoons rice vinegar
Splash of hot sauce

PREPARATIONS

Mix a bit of ginger powder with water and wash your hands in it. Focus on allowing them to absorb the herb's energy so that you can carry that vibration with you while you cook. While your hands are still wet, raise them slowly in the air, saying:

> *Higher still and higher*
> *Rise—the magick power*
> *When simmered by the fire*
> *The energy grows higher*

Continue repeating this like a chant until your voice naturally reaches a crescendo, then go directly to making your sauce.

GLORIOUS GINGER

Ginger has been a part of human history for at least 3,000 years. In Sanskrit, it was called *srngaveram*, meaning "horn root," because of its branching appearance. For a while in Roman times the use of ginger declined greatly. Later on, Marco Polo's trip to the Orient brought the herb to Europe's attention and made it a popular and costly spice. Queen Elizabeth I of England is credited with the invention of the now famous holiday gingerbread-man cookies. Today you can find ginger pickled, preserved, crystallized, fresh, and ground.

Place the sesame oil in a small frying pan and gently sauté the gingerroot therein. Cool, and then mix with the remaining ingredients. Let this sit covered in the refrigerator for 24 hours before using. Goes well with anything on which you would use normal soy sauce (in particular pot stickers).

Makes ³⁄₄ cup

Vigor Sauce

Native Americans consider beans a gift from the Great Spirit and the earth goddess who sustains us. In this setting beans represented life and continuance. The phrase "full of beans" can be heard in a new way: actually meaning full of energy or life.

Sauce

2 tablespoons olive oil
1 cup chopped green and/or red bell pepper
½ cup chopped onion
2 garlic cloves, minced
1 (16-ounce) can of black beans, drained

1 cup chicken broth
1 tablespoon Worcestershire sauce
Dash of red pepper

Preparations

In thinking of vitality, make sure you've had a good night's rest before starting this recipe. Also get up on the right side of your bed to encourage health, and bless your vitamins saying:

> *When taken within, this spell begins*
> *Health come to stay*
> *By night and by day.*

You may also want to consider burning a vitality-aligned incense like pine or orange while you cook.

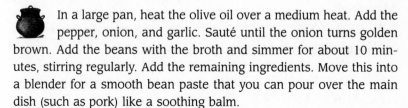 In a large pan, heat the olive oil over a medium heat. Add the pepper, onion, and garlic. Sauté until the onion turns golden brown. Add the beans with the broth and simmer for about 10 minutes, stirring regularly. Add the remaining ingredients. Move this into a blender for a smooth bean paste that you can pour over the main dish (such as pork) like a soothing balm.

Makes about 6 cups

Marinades

Linguists speculate that the word *marinade* comes from a Latin term *aqua marina* which was actually a way of pickling fish. This transformed into the Italian *marinara* over time, but no one seems absolutely sure when! No matter its origins, however, it's quite certain that our ancestors knew the value of flavoring and tenderizing meat. Documentation shows that people in pre–Columbian Mexico were wrapping meat in papaya leaves before cooking for that purpose. Interestingly enough, papain—a marvelous meat tenderizer made from papaya—is still used commercially today.

From a spiritual perspective, a marinade saturates your ingredients with its energies and your intention. Together with sauces, these two provide an inventive kitchen witch with yet even more able companions for his or her culinary kit.

Safety Marinade

In some spiritual traditions, especially those of Voudon, rum is sacred to certain deities. It may also be sprinkled around a space to chase away any mischievous entities that might be lingering nearby. Combined with garlic and the zesty nature of Worcestershire, the following makes an excellent protective blend.

MARINADE

¼ cup dark rum

2 garlic cloves, crushed (use a garlic press or just smash 'em with the side of a big knife on a cutting board)

1 cup of brown sugar, packed

¼ cup soy sauce

½ cup chili sauce

¼ cup Worcestershire sauce

Dash of pepper

PREPARATIONS

Safety and protection are at least 50 percent proactive in nature. So, before you begin, take a brief accounting of your work space, considering various safety issues that might affect you or someone else in your home. For example, knives loaded into the dishwasher point up make for a hazard, so turn them, to likewise turn the potentially harmful energy away from you. Other traditional ways of "turning" energies that seem counterproductive include turning an item of clothing inside out and turning chairs around. As you do, consider adding an incantation like:

Neither destroyed nor created; negativity abated
By a turn of the hand, a turn of time, a turn of fate,
A magical rhyme

In a saucepan over low heat, put half the rum and all of the remaining ingredients. Let this blend simmer until the sugar is dissolved and the aroma of the herbs begins to take on a strong tealike quality. Let this cool, then add the remaining rum. Pour over your chosen ingredients (this is particularly nice on beef and chicken) and refrigerate for about 24 hours, turning to coat your main component evenly at least two or three times during that period.

Serving Note: If you wish to reduce this by one-third to one-half by slow simmering, it becomes a rather nice sauce (note, however, that you should *not* use the remaining marinade for the sauce—but instead create a new batch for that purpose).

Makes 1½ cups

Fit 'n' Trim Mediterranean Marinade

The traditional diets of the Mediterranean region were mainly based on the foods from a rich diversity of plant sources and included fruits, vegetables, whole grains, beans, nut seeds, and of course olive oil. Modern research has begun to show how this diet is quite healthful, so use this marinade to saturate your main dish with restorative qualities. Good on poultry, meat, or seafood (and may also be used as a baste).

Marinade

¼ cup lemon juice
¼ teaspoon hot pepper flakes
¼ teaspoon cracked black
    pepper
½ teaspoon coarse salt
4 strips of lemon zest
3 garlic cloves, crushed
¼ cup fresh parsley, coarsely
    chopped

4 tablespoons each fresh basil,
    cilantro, dill, oregano,
    coarsely chopped
½ cup extra-virgin olive oil (a
    flavored blend may also
    be used)

Preparations

It's time to pump up and work out! If you want to be healthy, act healthy. Don your favorite sweats and take a brisk walk or do another exercise that you find invigorating. As you do, consider adding some affirmations to the process such as, "I am healthy" or "I am fit and strong." When you're done, go to the kitchen and whip this marinade into shape!

Combine the lemon juice, pepper flakes, cracked pepper, and salt in a ceramic bowl. Whisk until the salt dissolves. Add the remaining herbs and slowly whisk in the olive oil. Use this marinade as soon as possible. The fresher the herbs, the more flavor.

Makes about 1 cup

Anger Abating Sauce and Marinade

Beer has been made for thousands of years. The art of brewing fermented grains into beverages goes back as far as the Pleistocene epoch, and Egyptians made beer from barley. One Egyptian myth says that Ra quelled Sekmet's anger with beer. I based this recipe on that myth. Apply the first marinade-sauce recipe to replace negativity with healing, and the second marinade to help restore emotional or situational balance.

Sauce 1

1 (12-ounce) bottle lager beer
¾ cup fresh lime or lemon
    juice
6 garlic cloves, minced
1 teaspoon powdered chicken
    bouillon

1 teaspoon Worcestershire
    sauce
1 teaspoon soy sauce
1 teaspoon hot pepper sauce
1 teaspoon ground black
    pepper

Preparations

The beer in this recipe cools the other ingredients, just as you wish it to cool heated tempers. So focus on that component first by placing it in the freezer briefly before using. The short chilling effect supports your goal. Then pour it into a bowl where the other ingredients wait, saying:

Ire and negativity—quell
By the stirring of this spell

 This is a simple case of putting everything together and stirring well. The combination can be used either as a marinade or as a basting sauce. Excellent on pork in particular.

Makes 2 cups

Sauce 2

¼ cup rice wine (mirin) or
    sweet sherry
¼ cup cider vinegar
⅓ cup sugar
2 tablespoons fresh
    gingerroot, chopped

⅔ cup light-colored beer (an
    Asian beer is a good
    choice)

Preparations

Before you begin, sit down and draw two yin-yang symbols on two pieces of paper (equal sized). Across the middle of the symbol write the world *balance*. Place this little charm in each of your shoes so you walk in balance while making the marinade.

In a saucepan combine all the ingredients. Simmer until the mixture reduces by one-third cup. Add this to your chosen base component 24 hours before cooking and let it soak in the refrigerator, turning it regularly to maintain that delicate balance. Each time you turn the base, you may want to add a brief prayer or incantation like:

As without so within, let symmetry begin.
As below so above, replace anger with love.

Makes 1 1/2 cups

MUSTARD MUSE

Ancient Hebrews and many people from the Far East cultivated mustard seed to create anointing oils. At this juncture in history the plant was much larger than what we see now, sometimes growing to fifteen feet (complete with nesting birds!). Hindu myth says that mustard seed could enable one to fly through the air and locate treasure. Here it's also associated with fertility. Greeks so revered mustard that they felt it was a gift from Asclepius, the god of medicine. This association with health didn't stop there, however. Native Americans and Europeans alike used mustard pastes or plasters to alleviate various ailments, from colds to infections.

Zealous Marinade

The mustard's fiery nature gave it a reputation both for healing and as an aphrodisiac. This recipe builds on that dual rep and is meant to improve your interest and zeal when a relationship gets a tad dull.

MARINADE

2 tablespoons Dijon mustard
1 tablespoon red-wine vinegar
¼ cup olive oil

1 tablespoon dried summer
  savory, crumbled
1 tablespoon water

PREPARATIONS

It's very important that you take the time to rid yourself of any lingering negativity toward your mate before preparing this marinade. Sit for a few moments and hold on to a piece of paper. Also have some matches and a fireproof dish nearby. Let all the things that brought you to this apathetic point in your relationship pour into the paper. When you feel completely empty, burn it with a prayer for renewal. Turn your back once it's gone out, and leave the past behind. Cook expectantly.

 Whisk together all the ingredients and dredge your chosen base component (such as ribs) in the marinade for at least 15 minutes before cooking.

Makes about ½ cup

Banishing Brandy Marinade

Historically, people discovered that it was possible to separate water from wine to create a liquid close to pure alcohol. The Germans called this product "burnt," which became the basis for the term brandy. *We're using the symbolism of that preliminary separation in this recipe to help sort the "good" energy from the "bad" and retaining only the positive in and around your sacred space.*

MARINADE

2 cups dry white wine
¼ cup brandy
1 carrot, grated
1 onion, grated

2 bay leaves
2 to 3 sprigs thyme
2 to 3 sprigs marjoram
  or parsley

PREPARATIONS

As you gather your ingredients for this, try to move in a counter-clockwise manner. You're also going to want to stir counterclockwise to "turn away" any energies that aren't life affirming and helpful. Focus on your goal while you're working.

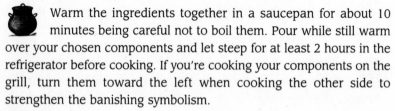 Warm the ingredients together in a saucepan for about 10 minutes being careful not to boil them. Pour while still warm over your chosen components and let steep for at least 2 hours in the refrigerator before cooking. If you're cooking your components on the grill, turn them toward the left when cooking the other side to strengthen the banishing symbolism.

Makes 2½ cups

Mojo Marinade

The word mojo *is African in origin, coming from the Fula language term* moco'o, *meaning shaman. A similar word,* moco, *in the Atlantic Island region of South Carolina means "magic" or a charm. Overall the meaning is very similar to the Native American concept of "medicine", which is all about finding your power, tapping it, and applying it for personal or global wholeness. There's a whole lot of mojo in the herbs and spices of this recipe, so why not whip them up to full power for manifesting your personal gifts in the most positive way possible?*

MARINADE

½ cup olive oil	4 teaspoons salt
¼ cup diced garlic	Pepper to taste
¼ cup chopped red onion	1 teaspoon cumin
2 cups orange juice	1 teaspoon ginger
¼ cup lemon juice	1 teaspoon Cajun spice mix
¼ cup lime juice	(your favorite brand)

PREPARATIONS

Your personal center of power is located near the navel. This is why many teachers of sacred sound instruct that one learn how to bring up chants, songs, and mantras from that region and release the energy outward. Before you start to make this mixture, try taking a deep breath, to fill that region of your body completely. Release that breath with a personal power word, chant, or phrase that makes you feel strong, secure, and centered. I often use the "om" for this activity because it reaffirms the self (the "I am"). Repeat this at all four corners of your preparation area and in the center to literally claim your space and power.

Place the oil in a frying pan and warm it. While you do, blend the garlic, onion, orange, lemon, and lime juice together. Carefully pour those into the warm oil (NOT HOT—it will flame!). Continue warming until the garlic and onion are golden brown. Add the remaining ingredients and cool. Transfer this to your blender and mix well before pouring over the main component.

Makes 2–3 cups of marinade

Good as Gold Marinade

A Haitian story tells us of a young girl who had a very evil stepmother who nearly starved her. One day the girl grew tired of the abuse and ran as far as she could. When she grew weary, she stopped and prayed for relief. As she did, an orange seed fell upon her, and she planted it. The resulting tree produced the sweetest, juiciest oranges imaginable. When the girl returned home to show them to the stepmother, the woman of course wanted to see the tree. So the girl showed her. She sang to the tree and it grew bigger and bigger. She sang again and it grew smaller— at which point the stepmother could not resist climbing into the tree to gather a fruit. When she did, the girl sang and sang until the tree branch in which the stepmother sat broke and brought her down to her death. Thus she gained her freedom and had a viable crop so she'd be good as gold the rest of her life.

Marinade

1 yellow bell pepper	1 tablespoon orange zest
1 cup orange juice (fresh squeezed is best)	1 tablespoon orange flower water
⅓ cup vegetable oil	1 tablespoon wine vinegar
1 clove elephant ear garlic	½ teaspoon salt
1 tablespoon soy sauce	

Preparations

Gold is the keynote for this recipe. When you prepare it, wear something bright yellow or gold in color and have a yellow-gold candle burning as brightly as a blessed sun in your work space. Additionally, if you have any yellow tableware, using it will definitely support the goal, as will serving other edibles that have solar associations (like sunflower seeds).

 Cut the yellow pepper into small chunks and place it along with the other ingredients into a blender. Mix at medium speed until smooth. Coat the primary ingredient overnight in the refrigerator with the marinade, and cook it the next day.

Makes 1½ cups

MOLASSES SPECIFICS

- If you oil your measuring device, molasses will slip off of it more easily; heating your measuring utensil also helps.
- Dark (or black) molasses should not be substituted for light in a recipe as it will overpower the other flavors of the recipe.
- Golden molasses is somewhat buttery and can be used to top bread, ice cream, and pancakes as well as a component for glaze.
- Dark molasses has a caramel flavor and lends a color to dishes.
- Dark molasses causes dishes to brown more quickly.

Destination—Determination!

Treacle *was the original name for molasses. Oddly enough the word was first assigned in old French to poison antidotes, but slowly transformed to meaning a sweetener by the 1700s. The word* molasses *comes from a Portuguese word* melaco *meaning "honey." Because of its sticky, thick nature, this recipe uses molasses as a sweet way of inspiring tenacity so that you can stick to your guns!*

MARINADE

1 ½ cups dark molasses
¾ cup sherry
6 tablespoons lemon juice
1 ½ cups tomato sauce
1 garlic clove, minced
1 chili pepper, seeded and minced

Pinch of cayenne pepper
1 teaspoon minced candied ginger
1 teaspoon orange zest
¼ teaspoon fresh thyme
¼ teaspoon nutmeg

Preparations

Determination seems to come from one part willpower and one part consistent reminder! The will is something you muster, but to help with the memory portion, write on a piece of paper the area of your life where you want this marinade's energy to settle deeply. Dab that paper with rosemary (for the conscious mind) and put it up on your refrigerator or somewhere else that you will see it often. Each time your eyes catch the paper, consider reciting an empowering incantation like:

> *To this task my mind is glued*
> *My magic grants me fortitude!*

Put the ingredients in your food processor or blender and mix thoroughly, remembering that this process also whips up energy. Refrigerate overnight before using on things like chicken, quail, duck, goose, or hen.

Makes 4 cups

CASSEROLES
AND COVEN-CRAFT

For ordinary people, food is heaven.

—CHINESE PROVERB

The word *casserole* has an interesting history, originating in ancient Greece with a term for cup (*kuathos*). In Latin this became *cattia*, meaning both a ladle and a pan. In Old French it transformed again to *casse*, and finally *casserole*. But the newer word has not always meant food served in a common dish. In the eighteenth century a casserole was a dish of rice molded into a pot and filled with a savory blend of chicken or sweetbreads. Sometimes this included a border of mashed potatoes. It wasn't until the late 1800s that the word was used to describe a blend of meats and vegetables with stock cooked slowly in the oven.

Besides what the frugal witch already knows (namely that casseroles save money), they offer another benefit. Slow cooking blends flavors into harmony. You also don't have to fuss over a casserole. Once assembled it pretty well takes care of itself and

> ### Casserole History
>
> In China people use sandpots to prepare something similar to a casserole. Meat or fish gets placed along with water or a savory sauce into a rough pot. The pots themselves come in a variety of shapes. In any case, however, these go into charcoal burners that act like a chafing dish!

you can do other things! Thus I offer casseroles in this book as the perfect accompaniment to coven meetings in that you can either assemble one for your family while you head out, or take one with you for an after-Circle treat!

Safety Shellfish Casserole

Wealthy people in Rome imported oysters from Britain, while they were the food of lower classes in China. Despite this disparity, oysters have strong connections with protection of those things we hold dear (just like a pearl within the shell). Thus, make this dish when you feel your coven needs extra warding.

Casserole

2 quarts oysters
¼ pound (1 stick) butter
3 whole scallions, chopped
1 green or red bell pepper, seeded and chopped
½ pound mushrooms, sliced
¼ cup flour
½ cup heavy cream
¼ cup grated imported Parmesan cheese
Freshly grated nutmeg
½ teaspoon paprika
Salt
Freshly ground black pepper
½ cup bread crumbs

Oyster Facts

The European oyster is rounded in appearance and offers delicious flavor. Its cousin, the Portuguese oyster, is larger, not quite as tender, and provides a robust flavor for those who enjoy shellfish. American oysters are similar, those grown in cool northern waters being preferred for their pleasing shell shape (it makes for a handsome half-shell serving appearance). Asian oysters grow the largest, with a capacity to reach ten inches in length. These must be cooked or sun dried before consumption.

Preparations

Create a sacred space in your kitchen before you cook, being sure to tell the elemental powers your goal in having them present. Stir the ingredients counterclockwise to support the goal of turning any negative energies away from you. This is also the perfect time to invoke your pantry protector if you've chosen one in prayer, asking him or her to bless your food and your group.

Preheat the broiler. Grease a 9-by-13-inch ovenproof serving dish. Drain the oysters thoroughly and set aside. Melt 2 tablespoons of the butter in a heavy casserole. Add the scallions and pepper to this butter and sauté until the onion is golden brown. Add the mushrooms and oysters and continue sautéing for 5 more minutes.

In a separate pan, melt 2 tablespoons of the remaining butter. Stir in the flour. When smooth, add the cream, and stir over a medium heat until it begins to boil and thicken. Add the cheese slowly so it integrates. Stir this into the oyster mixture in the casserole pan and season with nutmeg, paprika, salt, and pepper. You can make the casserole a day ahead, refrigerating overnight (to cool negativity and increase the flavor). Return it to a simmer on top of the stove the next day before proceeding.

Pour the mixture into the prepared dish and top with the bread crumbs and dot with the remaining butter (if you want you can add a bit of powdered cheese to this blend for richer flavor). Place under the broiler until browned and bubbling—about 10 minutes, depending on the depth of the casserole.

Makes about 4 servings

Any Meal Casserole

The Any Meal casserole is prized for its flexibility and versatility, and that's exactly what we're using it for magically too. This dish works as breakfast, lunch, snack, or dinner, so that no matter the time of the coven meeting, you're always prepared!

CASSEROLE

1 pound maple- or hard-wood-cured bacon

½ cup chopped shallots

2 garlic cloves, minced

½ green pepper, chopped

½ cup oil-packed sun-dried tomatoes, drained and chopped

2 tablespoons chopped fresh parsley

5 large eggs

3 large egg yolks

1 cup half-and-half

1 cup whipping cream

1 cup grated mozzarella cheese

1 cup grated provolone (or other cheese of your choice)

½ teaspoon salt

PREPARATIONS

The recipe requires that you precook the bacon, so while you're doing that focus on your goals of being both versatile and prepared. Add an incantation like this one each time you turn the bacon (which is also flexible):

> *By fire and earth, water and air*
> *I charge this dish to help us be prepared*

Proactive thoughts and words and deeds
By my will, this spell is freed!

Preheat oven to 375 degrees F. Grease a 13-by-9-by-2-inch glass baking dish with butter or olive oil. Precook the bacon until it's done all the way through but not crisp. Drain, leaving just a bit of the fat in the pan. Set aside the bacon, then add shallots and garlic to the bacon fat. Sauté 5 minutes. Add sun-dried tomatoes and parsley; stir until mixed. Spread this mixture in the dish, layering the bacon and tomatoes evenly.

In a large bowl, whisk eggs, egg yolks, half-and-half, whipping cream, 1½ cups of the combined cheeses, and salt. When this is mixed completely pour the egg mixture over the bacon and tomatoes. Sprinkle the remaining cheese on top. Bake until the casserole is golden brown (about a half hour). Let it sit at room temperature to finish out for another 5–10 minutes before serving.

SERVING IDEA

Play around with additions to this dish that better reflect the time of day in which you're serving it. For example, if it's lunchtime use yellow pepper to honor the sun.

Makes 5–6 servings

South of the Border Solution

This casserole has tons of fiery energy provided by the spices and the generative nature of the beans. Use it to put a fire under a situation, especially one that you'd like to be resolved with all due expediency.

Bean Quandary

In the sixth century B.C., Pythagoras began a religious movement that included dietary laws, at least one of which was a ban on bean eating. It seems that Pythagoras believed that beans could cause not only arousal, but that they were strongly connected to the world of the dead. One story claims he died while fleeing an enemy in the war between Acragas and Syracuse because he refused to cross a bean field, fearing spirits of the dead would possess him.

Casserole

1½ cups crushed tortilla chips

1 pound shredded cooked chicken or turkey meat (no skin)

8 ounces garbanzo beans, drained

8 ounces chickpeas, drained

8 ounces white kidney beans, drained

8 ounces black beans, drained

1 (15-ounce) can sweet corn, drained

1 (8-ounce) can chunky-style tomato sauce

1 cup prepared medium-hot salsa

1 cup chopped red onion

2 tablespoons freshly chopped chili pepper, seeded

1 teaspoon cumin

1 green bell pepper, cut into ¼-inch dice

¼ cup chopped fresh cilantro leaves

1 tablespoon minced garlic

Salt and freshly ground black pepper, to taste

6 ounces grated Monterey Jack cheese

6 ounces grated sharp Cheddar cheese

Preparations

The use of canned items in this dish allows you to put it together very quickly, and thereby supports the symbolism of fast resolutions. As you open each can, focus on opening the way for the energy of that food to enter the blend. Visualize sparkling light pouring out of the can and into your mixing dish.

 Preheat oven to 350 degrees F. Grease a 13-by-9-inch baking dish, then scatter the crushed tortilla chips evenly on the bottom. Combine the remaining ingredients except the cheeses. Place half of this mixture evenly in the baking dish with a layer of cheese over the top. Cover with the remaining half of the chicken mixture; then sprinkle the rest of the cheeses over the top. Bake for 30 minutes.

Serving Suggestion

Have sour cream, diced tomatoes, and pineapple chunks with which people can garnish the casserole. Fresh cilantro is also a nice addition.

Makes about 8 servings

Comfort Casserole

In the southern United States, this dish comes under the classification of warm, welcoming comfort food. There's no reason not to stick with that association so that every bite transmits calming, soothing, and reassuring energies to everyone enjoying it.

Casserole

5 pounds chayotes

1 medium red onion, chopped

1 medium yellow onion, chopped

1 each red and yellow sweet peppers, chopped

1 stick butter

2 cloves elephant ear garlic, minced

2 pounds large shrimp, shelled and de-veined

¼ teaspoon cayenne

Salt and pepper to taste

¾ cup salted crackers, finely ground

2 tablespoons fine dry Italian-style bread crumbs

Chay-What?

A chayote, a member of the gourd family, is a pear-shaped fruit cultivated as a vegetable that can be found at many international markets. It has a lovely nutty taste and was favored by the Aztec and Maya alike. In China its name means "Buddha's hands" because it looks a bit like two hands clasped in prayer (thus another implication of comfort and solace!). Botanically chayote is related to squash and cucumber.

Preparations

When making comfort foods one should be . . . well . . . comfortable! Don a piece of clothing that really puts you at ease and in the right frame of mind so you can extend your personal comfort into the food you're preparing.

 Cover the chayotes with water in a large pot. Simmer until tender (about 1 hour). Drain, halve, peel, pit, and chop them. Set aside.

Preheat oven to 400 degrees F. Sauté the onions and peppers with 6 tablespoons of the butter. When the onions have turned golden brown, add the garlic and chayotes, stirring regularly until most of the liquid has disappeared. Add the shrimp, cayenne, salt, pepper, and crackers. Transfer this blend into a shallow 3-quart baking dish and sprinkle with bread crumbs. Dot the top with the remaining butter and bake for about 15 minutes until the crumbs turn golden brown.

Makes 8–10 servings

BROCCOLI BASICS

Romans were growing and eating broccoli by the first century C.E. The type they cultivated, called calabrese, is the most common variety eaten in the United States today. One favorite Roman recipe called for boiled broccoli mixed with cumin, coriander, chopped onion, olive oil, and sun-made wine.

Fair Weather Broccoli

Roman farmers called broccoli "the five green fingers of Jupiter." In Roman mythology Jupiter is the god who controls the skies, so if your coven wants a rain-free gathering, he's the being to petition for assistance. However, as the "maker of agreements": an offering or other suitable gift might be wise—specifically baked goods, as he is also the patron of bakers!

CASSEROLE

3 medium-size heads of broccoli	1 tablespoon cornstarch diluted in ½ cup cold milk
3 eggs, beaten	1 medium onion, chopped
1 cup ricotta cheese	Salt and freshly ground black pepper, to taste
1 cup grated extrasharp Cheddar cheese	1 cup buttered bread crumbs
½ cup asiago cheese	

PREPARATIONS

I am somewhat hesitant to tinker with the weather because of the broad-ranging effects on the planet. However, there are times when we need a little cooperation from Mother Earth for important rites (like a handfasting). In these instances, I suggest taking some home-baked item outside. Break it up in a circle around the area where the ritual is planned. As you walk ask for a specific amount of time during which the unwanted weather will simply "hold off." When you're done with the offering go about cooking, but be aware that you will typically get *exactly* the amount of time for which you ask—no more, no less!

 Preheat oven to 350 degrees F. Boil the broccoli heads in water for 10 minutes then drain. Chop the broccoli with the stems and set aside.

In a deep bowl, beat the eggs, adding the ricotta, cheeses, and the cornstarch–milk mixture. Mix thoroughly then sprinkle in the chopped onion, salt, and pepper. Add the drained broccoli, mixing again. Pour this into a buttered or greased ovenproof dish and bake topped with bread crumbs for 30 minutes. Let stand at room temperature for 5 minutes before serving.

Makes about 8 servings

Sweet Life Dessert Casserole

While most of us think of a casserole as a main or side dish, a little clever adaptation allows it to become dessert too. This is a bit like a blintz, but with a twist that makes it fast and easy. Lore tells us that blintzes helped secure sweet freedom for a Russian Jew appointed to Stalin's kitchen. It was only one of two recipes he knew, and Stalin loved them. Eventually he escaped, telling his story of victory and safety thanks to this sweet dish.

CASSEROLE

Batter

4 large eggs
1 ¼ cups milk
2 tablespoons sour cream
¼ cup butter, melted

¾ teaspoon orange extract
1 ⅓ cups all-purpose flour
1 to 2 tablespoons sugar
1 ¼ teaspoons baking powder

Filling

2 (8-ounce) packages farmer
cheese
1 (16-ounce) container ricotta
cheese

2 large eggs
3 tablespoons sugar
2 tablespoons orange juice

To Serve

Vanilla yogurt
Sliced fresh strawberries and mandarin oranges

Preparations

Ponder what sweet wishes you have for your group. Make a list of the top three. When you crack the eggs for this dish, reserve two egg-shell halves. Place your list of wishes inside and gently secure them together with a natural cloth and a touch of glue. Place this in the ground so that all good things will grow from your efforts (and the eggshell will enrich your soil even as you wish to enrich the coven)!

 Preheat the oven to 350 degrees F. Butter or grease a 9-by-13-inch baking dish and have it ready.

In a blender combine all batter ingredients. Process until very smooth. Measure 1½ cups of this, and pour it in the bottom of the baking dish. Put this in the oven for 10 minutes until it sets up.

While the batter sets, combine all the filling ingredients in a large non-aluminum bowl, and mix. Spread this evenly over the top of the baked portion. Stir the rest of the batter once and gently pour this over the cheese filling, making sure it's all covered. Bake an additional 35 to 40 minutes, until the top is also set.

Let the casserole rest for about 10 minutes before cutting it into squares. Serve with the toppings or another sweet blend of your own. If you wish, drizzle with honey or flavored sweet cream.

Makes 6–8 servings

Self-Control Cabbage

Humankind has consumed cabbage for more than 4,000 years, and the Egyptians even worshipped it as a deity. Egyptian, Greek, and Roman mythology all link cabbage with the ability to temper the effects of wine, allowing the eaters to remain focused and clear headed no matter the situation. With this in mind, prepare this casserole for those times when your group has difficult decisions to make, or situations for which to find logical solutions.

CASSEROLE

1 small red cabbage, cored and shredded

1 small white cabbage, cored and shredded

8 cloves

2 pounds boneless pork chops

2 tablespoons olive oil

1 large onion, chopped

1 large ripe tomato, diced

1 green apple, cored and diced

1 cup diced celery

2 bay leaves

1 tablespoon red-wine or cider vinegar

1 teaspoon sugar

Salt and pepper, to taste

4 red potatoes, quartered

PREPARATIONS

The conscious, logical mind is ruled by the sun and the element of air. So, try to prepare this dish in a sunny region, preferably with a window open so a fresh wind of reason can inspire the magic.

Blanch the cabbage in boiling water and set it aside. Insert 2 of the cloves into each pork chop then brown them in olive oil (about 5 minutes a side). Remove the chops, and brown the onion in the same pan. Once the onion is cooked, return the chops to the pan adding the remaining ingredients. Cover partially and let simmer for 15 minutes. Uncover the pot and keeping the heat at medium-low continue cooking for about an hour more so the meat and potatoes are tender. Do not let this boil or it becomes mushy.

ALTERNATIVES

This recipe works well using brisket, too, if you first boil the brisket until it's tender. Cut it into large slices, and substitute 1 heaping tablespoon of honey and a diced orange for the cloves and tomato.
Makes 6–8 servings

Barley Betterment

Many myths about barley connect this grain with the cycle of death and rebirth—endings and new beginnings. Typically the barley is entrusted to the underworld (the dark earth) where, in time, its seeds spring up anew. This recipe combines this renewing effect with the health-giving qualities of chicken broth for those times when your group is having trouble finding closure with people or situations.

CASSEROLE

½ pound mushrooms
4–5 tablespoons butter
1 medium onion, chopped very fine
1 bundle green onions, chopped

1 cup pearl barley
Salt and pepper to taste
1 teaspoon soy sauce
2–3 cups beef or chicken broth

PREPARATIONS

As I read about the history of barley, the phrase "where one door closes, another opens" came to mind. Using that idea, go to the door farthest from your kitchen and close it firmly. As you do, mentally accept whatever ending or closure you feel your group needs to move on. Then, move to the door closest to the kitchen and open it saying:

> *Open the path . . . open the way*
> *Where there's an end, there's a beginning*
> *Let it become clear today!*

You can utilize this incantation or something like it while you're creating the dish to support your goal.

Preheat oven to 350 degrees F. Slice the mushrooms and set aside. Heat the butter in a skillet and add the chopped onions. Cook for 3 or 4 minutes then add the mushrooms. Cook another 4 minutes, stirring occasionally. Add the barley, mixing it well with the other ingredients, and browning it lightly. Season the barley blend with salt, pepper, and soy to suit your personal tastes. Pour this into a greased casserole dish. Cover the whole blend with chicken broth so that there's about ½ inch extra over the top. Securely cover the casserole and bake for 25 minutes. If you find the barley isn't quite done, add more broth. Watch to see when the liquid becomes absorbed and test again for tenderness. Taste the barley for doneness. Add more broth, if necessary, and continue cooking until the liquid is absorbed and the barley tender. Serve as an accompaniment to duck, game, goose, squab, or other kinds of poultry—wherever you would use wild rice.

VARIATIONS

For stronger health-oriented energy add chopped chicken or turkey to this dish along with some garlic. Without the mushrooms this makes an excellent convalescent meal.

Makes 4–6 ½-cup servings

Cornerstone Casserole

For the longest time writers didn't distinguish between parsnips and carrots, and until the advent of various other starch and sugar groups they were used for baking and thickening. As a root vegetable, along with the earthy nature of potatoes, they combine in this dish to provide foundations and grounding when you feel that things have gotten a bit too etheric, or when you're laying cornerstones for new projects.

CASSEROLE

12 parsnips (medium size are
best for flavor)
1 red onion
2 medium russet potatoes
3½ tablespoons unsalted
butter

2 teaspoons salt
1 teaspoon freshly grated
nutmeg
Pepper to taste
⅔ cup mascarpone or whole-
milk ricotta cheese

PREPARATIONS

Save the peelings from the potatoes and parsnips in this recipe. Put them in a planter with good soil and the seed from some type of flowering plant that can thrive indoors. Name the seed after your goal. From this day forward tend it with care, continuing to focus on the task of creating firm foundations. By the time it begins to sprout, your foundations should be taking shape nicely!

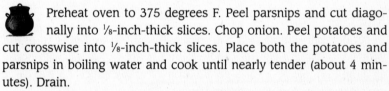 Preheat oven to 375 degrees F. Peel parsnips and cut diagonally into ⅛-inch-thick slices. Chop onion. Peel potatoes and cut crosswise into ⅛-inch-thick slices. Place both the potatoes and parsnips in boiling water and cook until nearly tender (about 4 minutes). Drain.

In a large skillet cook the onion in 3 tablespoons of the butter over moderately low heat, stirring, until softened. Add salt, nutmeg, and pepper to taste and cook mixture over moderate heat, stirring occasionally. Gently toss the potatoes and parsnips with this blend. Grease a 3-quart oven dish. Arrange half of the potatoes and parsnips in the dish with a layer of cheese over the top. Repeat with the second half, dotting the top with the remaining ½ tablespoon of the butter. Cover with foil and bake until heated through and bubbling (about 1 hour). Cool at room temperature for about 10 minutes before serving.

Makes about 4 servings

Kinship Casserole

Tomatoes were once called love apples. They combine in this dish with herbs like basil and binders like cheese, both of which have the ability to generate warm, affectionate fellowship.

CASSEROLE

2 tablespoons butter

2 tablespoons virgin olive oil

8 ounces ground sweet Italian sausage (without casing)

1 cup diced eggplant

1 cup diced zucchini

1 cup diced red bell pepper

¼ cup chopped red onion (red is the color of love)

2 garlic cloves, minced

2 cups plum tomatoes, chopped

2 tablespoons chopped fresh parsley

2 tablespoons chopped fresh basil leaves

Black pepper to taste

4 ounces grated mozzarella cheese (or use a blend of Italian cheeses)

PREPARATIONS

Decorate your eating area with highlights of red and pink to mirror your goal. Carve a central candle with a heart and dab it with corresponding oil like rose for a gentle aromatherapy effect. As you carve consider adding an incantation like:

> *Good friends, good fellowship, good food, good feelings*
> *In the candle's light, let our hearts be warmed*
> *Around the table let our minds know harmony*
> *With each other, let our spirits be blessed.*
> *So be it.*

Preheat oven to 350 degrees F. Melt the butter in a pan, add olive oil, then add the sausage meat to cook completely. Remove the cooked meat with a slotted spoon, leaving the drippings for sautéing the eggplant, zucchini, pepper, onion, and garlic. Cook until the onion is tender and golden brown. Put the sausage back in the pan, and add the tomatoes, parsley, basil, and pepper. Simmer for 15 minutes over low heat. Transfer the entire blend to a 9-inch-square baking dish and sprinkle the top with cheese. Bake for about 20 minutes, until the cheese melts.

Makes about 6 servings

Pentagram Casserole

Among both the Egyptians and Druids, the onion was honored as an emblem of the universe, each layer representing part of heaven or the underworld. Egyptians went so far as to swear oaths with their right hand on an onion to show sincerity. And, like garlic, the strong odor of this plant was respected as a powerful ward against evil (just as we sometimes use a pentagram as a protective symbol). This dish incorporates five different onions, one for each point of the pentagram, to encourage supportive and protective energy for whatever magic your group has in mind.

CASSEROLE

2 medium bunches scallions, cut crosswise into 1-inch pieces
2 medium white onions, sliced
2 medium red onions, sliced
1 large Spanish onion, sliced
1 large cooking onion, sliced
2 garlic cloves, minced
3 tablespoons butter
¼ cup heavy cream
½ cup freshly grated Parmesan cheese
½ cup freshly grated Romano cheese
1 tablespoon olive oil
2 cups fresh bread crumbs

PREPARATIONS

To honor the symbolism of the pentagram, have five candles ready (one each red, yellow, blue, green, and white). Set the yellow one at northeast, the red one southeast, the blue one southwest, the green one northwest, and the white one due north on a flat surface in your kitchen. Light each one, starting in the east, saying:

The power of air,
The power of fire
Raise the magic ever higher
The power of water
The power of earth
Fill this dish, my magic—birth!

Leave the candles burning while you cook.

Grease a 1½-quart shallow baking dish. In a large frying pan cook the onions and garlic in butter over moderate heat until softened and nicely browned (about 20 minutes). Stir in cream and cheeses (retaining ¼ cup total of the two), then transfer to baking dish.

Warm the olive oil in the same skillet and add the bread crumbs. Mix these with the remaining cheese and sprinkle evenly over the top of the casserole. The flavor of this casserole improves if left for one night in the refrigerator. Take out and bring to room temperature before baking uncovered at 350 degrees F. for about 20 minutes, until the top turns golden brown.

Makes 4–6 servings

Here's the Beef

Beef has often been the food of the elite, and it has long been among the favored offerings to various deities. But considering the frugal nature of this casserole, this dish isn't suited to "wealth" but geared toward those times when you just need a little more providence to make ends meet.

CASSEROLE

2 medium onions, sliced	1 cup beef gravy
1 garlic clove, diced	2 tablespoons Worcestershire
¼ cup chopped celery	sauce
3 tablespoons butter	2 cups cooked rice
2 cups diced beef	Fresh dill

PREPARATIONS

Green and gold are the colors that support financial providence. High-light your kitchen or eating area with those, and consider wearing some clothing in those hues too (so you "don" providence). While you're cooking this dish try adding a little chant like

> *In this dish, my needs be met*
> *In this meal, my magic set!*

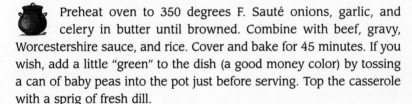 Preheat oven to 350 degrees F. Sauté onions, garlic, and celery in butter until browned. Combine with beef, gravy, Worcestershire sauce, and rice. Cover and bake for 45 minutes. If you wish, add a little "green" to the dish (a good money color) by tossing a can of baby peas into the pot just before serving. Top the casserole with a sprig of fresh dill.

Makes about 4 servings

Spinach Strength

The contemporary cartoon character Popeye the Sailor got extraordinary strength from eating spinach. Not surprisingly the vitamins in spinach are good for developing overall physical vigor, so we can utilize both the cultural inference and known physical qualities of this vegetable to inspire fortitude when we need it most.

SPINACH

Spinach originally came from Persia, where it was known as "aspanakh." By the 1300s, it had spread to Europe and Britain, where it was popular in religious communities, particularly during Lent. It was being cultivated in North America by the early part of the nineteenth century. The "spinach capital of the world," Lenexa, Kansas, holds an annual spinach festival to celebrate this vegetable's importance in local history.

CASSEROLE

1 (12-ounce) package frozen spinach, thawed

½ pound extra-wide egg noodles, freshly cooked

1 pound savory chicken, diced small

1 cup sour cream

3 tablespoons pesto sauce

1 bunch green onions, diced

1 garlic clove, crushed

1 cup grated Cheddar or Swiss cheese

PREPARATIONS

Inner fortitude is a function of will. Take time before preparing this dish to sit quietly and meditate. Visualize a color of light that to you represents strength pouring down from above. Let that light fill you from your toes upward until you feel as if you can contain no more. While you prepare this dish, release some of that strength into each ingredient by seeing the same light pour from your hands and saying:

> *From the strength within let the magic begin*
> *Pour into this dish, by my will and my wish*
> *Each bite provides, fortitude abide!*

 Preheat oven to 350 degrees F. Grease an 8-by-8-by-2-inch glass baking dish. Blend everything but the cheese in a bowl and transfer the blended ingredients into the baking dish. Sprinkle the grated cheese over the top. Bake until set, about 35 minutes.

Makes 4–6 servings

Insightful Yams

Throughout Oceana yams are regarded as sacred vegetables, having either been given by the gods or stolen from them. Yams are also nearly as important as bread in terms of being a "staff of life." Ancient people here carried out elaborate rituals to ensure fertile fields and a good yam harvest. Some believe that yams have generative abilities. This dish uses them in combination with carrots to improve psychic productivity and fruitfulness.

CASSEROLE

8 large carrots, peeled and grated
1 large potato, peeled and grated
1 large yam, peeled and grated
⅔ cup golden raisins
½ cup butter
½ cup golden brown sugar, packed
4 large eggs
1¼ teaspoons salt
1 teaspoon baking powder
¾ teaspoon ground cinnamon

PREPARATIONS

Take a handful of carrot peelings and dip them in warm water. Let them steep for a minute, holding the cup in your hands, and repeat this incantation five times:

> *Open my vision*
> *Let me clearly see*
> *Of what was and what will be*

Dab the carrot juice on your third eye before making this dish.

Preheat oven to 350 degrees F. Grease a 13-by-9-by-2-inch glass baking dish. Combine the carrots, potato, yam, and raisins in large bowl. Melt the butter in a medium-size saucepan over low heat. Add sugar and whisk until sugar dissolves and mixture is smooth. Remove from heat; cool completely. Whisk eggs, salt, baking powder and cinnamon into butter mixture, blending completely. Pour this over the vegetables; mix well. Season with salt and pepper. Transfer to prepared dish. Bake until vegetables are tender, about 90 minutes.

Makes 4–6 servings

Priest/ess Pie

A priest/ess is a shepherd to his or her coven. This person guides and provides spiritual sustenance. Thus this dish is an adaptation of traditional shepherd's pie, complete with leeks to sustain the soul!

CASSEROLE

10 ounce pearl onions

4 medium leeks, white part only, cut into ½-inch-thick slices

2 pounds boneless meat (your choice), cut into 1-inch cubes (or use hard tofu or mushrooms for a vegetarian version)

2 teaspoons salt

½ teaspoon black pepper

5 tablespoons all-purpose flour

3½ tablespoons butter, softened

2 tablespoons chopped garlic

½ cup dry white wine

1½ tablespoons tomato paste

1 cup broth (match to your meat or vegetables)

1 cup water

2 teaspoons chopped fresh thyme

5 carrots, cut diagonally into ⅓-inch-thick slices

2 medium turnips, peeled and cut into ½-inch pieces

2 stalks celery, large cuts

2 parsnips, large cuts

Casserole Topping

2 cups instant mashed potatoes	1 cup milk
1 cup warmed heavy cream	1 teaspoon garlic powder
	½ cup cheese (your choice)

Preparations

Being a good leader requires both the conscious mind and strong instincts. So bless your components in both sunlight and moonbeams before using them, saying:

> *Powers of All hear my plea*
> *Help me in my quest to lead*
> *Grant strength and perspective*
> *Wisdom and balance*
> *In every bite, let this energy dance!*

 Blanch onions in a 3-quart pot of boiling salted water. After 1 minute transfer them to a bowl of cold water. Drain the onions, and rinse off leek slices. Preheat oven to 350 degrees F. Sprinkle your chosen meat with the salt, pepper, and flour, coating evenly. Meanwhile melt the butter and brown the meat for about 5–7 minutes. Set aside but retain the bits in the pan. To this add the garlic, wine, and tomato paste. Let this reduce by half (5 minutes). Slowly stir in the broth, water, thyme, onion, leeks, carrots, turnip, celery, and parsnip, returning the meat to the dish as well. Bring this to a simmer, then pour into an ovenproof dish. Cover with foil and bake for 1½–2 hours until the meat is tender. Top the pie with the garlic and cheese mashed potatoes (follow the directions on the box, substituting cream and milk for the water called for). Put this under the broiler for a few minutes to achieve a golden brown hue and melt the cheese.

Makes about 6 servings

MEAT AND MEDITATIONS

He who has wine and meat will have many friends.

—CHINESE PROVERB

Meat is an important part of the American diet, often central to at least one meal a day. From a health standpoint, it provides iron, vitamin A, and vitamin B along with necessary amino acids. Nonetheless all kinds of taboos are associated with meat, more indeed than with any other food. Examples include the Muslim prohibition against eating pork and blood, the Hindu prohibition against eating beef, and the English distaste for even considering eating horsemeat.

The word *meat* has a very general meaning that has pretty well stayed the same since medieval times—namely "animal flesh." For our purposes here, I'll be giving an overview of beef, pork, lamb, ham, bacon, and sausage. I have left out veal for ethical reasons. Those readers who are vegetarian can likely find ways to adapt these recipes to your diet, but you'll probably be happier with the strict vegetable fares offered in other chapters.

BEEF BEETS?

Beef was not an important part of the American diet before the Civil War. Cattle were not indigenous to the Americas, and cows didn't exist in the New World until the Spanish introduced them via Mexico in 1540. In the eighteenth century, the Spanish and French colonists began to raise cattle in North America.

Beef

Roast beef, medium, is not only a food. It is a philosophy. Seated at life's dining table, with a menu of morals before you, your eye wanders a bit over the entrées, the hors d'oeuvres, and the things à la, though you know that the roast beef, medium, is safe, sane and sure.

—EDNA FERBER

Beef is the meat of domesticated cattle, specifically *Bos Taurus*. The name may resonate with kitchen witches who have a particular interest in astrology, a science in which the sign Taurus represents the earth and the creative force of the universe. Additionally, the eye of the bull in the constellation Taurus shines so brightly that it came to represent illumination, and the light that is an expression of creation. Egyptians called this constellation "the interpreter of the Divine voice," lending it further symbolic value for improved communications, especially in spiritual matters.

More mundanely, beef eating has often been restricted to the wealthy. It therefore carries vibrations that can support the goal of prosperity. Magical practitioners additionally note that eating meat

139

after a spell or ritual helps ground and center personal energies, giving foundation to your aspirations.

Discourse Roast

Horseradish is not really a radish at all, but a member of the crucifer family—namely kin to cabbage, turnip, and mustard. Magically speaking it's an excellent purifier, and when blended with the beef it aids in clearing up miscommunication.

1 tablespoon red-wine vinegar	Salt and pepper to taste
1 tablespoon cider vinegar	2 scallions, minced
2 tablespoons coarse-grained mustard	¼ cup minced watercress
1 tablespoon oil	½ cup mayonnaise (or generic salad dressing)
1 tablespoon bottled horseradish, drained	1½ pounds roast beef, thinly sliced

PREPARATIONS

Communication comes under the element of air. To honor that element in your sacred pantry, light a white or yellow candle, open a window, and consider burning some air-oriented incense like mint, which also clarifies and encourages positive discourse. When you light the incense you can add an incantation like:

> *Welcome powers of the wind,*
> *With your help this spell begins*
> *Grant to me words spoken with gentle care*
> *With my thanks, Powers of the air.*

Whisk together the vinegar, mustard, horseradish, and salt and pepper in a small bowl. Add the oil, continuing to whisk until emulsified. Add the scallions, watercress, and mayonnaise, mixing thoroughly. Arrange the beef on a platter and serve it with the mustard sauce drizzled over the top (if you wish, you can create a pattern with the sauce that supports your goal).

Makes 6 4-ounce servings

Affluent Almond Meatballs

Almonds originated in the Middle East. In spring, the almond trees were the first to flower and so long as they survived the frost, the trees would soon grant a wealth of gifts (their nuts) to humans. Additionally almond trees provided fuel, oil, and a lovely aromatic flower that was sacred to several deities. Since the almond heralds the rebirth of Earth's abundance, for the following dish we're going to nestle a bit of this symbolic prosperity in the center of each meatball.

1 pound ground chuck
1 medium onion, chopped fine
2 small garlic cloves, minced
1 teaspoon salt
1 teaspoon freshly ground
    black pepper
1 cup fresh bread crumbs
2 large egg yolks
Whole almonds
2 tablespoons olive oil

½ pound mushrooms, sliced thin
    (about 2 cups)
½ cup medium-dry sherry
2 cups low-salt chicken broth
2 teaspoons Worcestershire
    sauce
2 tablespoons butter, softened
2 tablespoons flour
2–3 tablespoons minced fresh dill
Sour cream for topping (optional)

Preparations

Take 4 of the whole almonds, a green or gold colored swatch of cloth (4 by 4 inches), and 4 small sprigs of the fresh dill. Tie the almonds and dill into the cloth (sachet style), saying:

> *A pinch of dill and focused will*
> *Prosperity obtain, adversity wane*
> *Four almonds gather abundance from Earth*
> *And grant this spell a successful birth!*

Carry this charm with you. When you need a little extra money quickly you can open the sachet and release one of the bits of dill to the wind. Never use the last one though; always refill the charm.

Stir together the ground meat, half of the onion, garlic, salt, pepper, bread crumbs, and egg yolks. Form into meatballs about an inch in diameter with one almond neatly secured in each. In a frying pan, brown the meatballs gently in the olive oil. Remove from pan to a paper towel to drain off grease.

Meanwhile in the same skillet add the rest of the onion and cook until soft. To this add the mushroom, sherry, broth and Worcestershire. Bring this to a boil and reduce it by about a third. Blend the butter and flour together, then whisk this into the liquid a little at a time. Continue to boil for about 2 minutes, then reduce heat. Put the meatballs back in to warm for about 8 minutes. Stir in half the dill; use the rest as a garnish to go on top of the sour cream.

Makes 3–4 servings

Backbone Beef

Most people are familiar with the phrase "grow a backbone." This recipe calls for marrowbones, which symbolically provides the resultant dish with a great deal of fortitude and stability.

MADEIRA

This is a fortified wine typically aged in wood. It has various colors from pale to a tawny brown, and has four styles. The pale gold Madeira is very dry. Verdelho is sweeter and more potent. Boal is sweeter still and offers a full body flavor. Finally Malmsey is very sweet, dark, and incredibly rich. The two heavier wines are typically served as dessert wines.

3 pounds beef marrowbones, both ends of marrow exposed

2 cups red cooking wine

⅓ cup finely chopped red onion

½ cup chopped mushrooms

1 small carrot, finely chopped

2 large sprigs fresh thyme

1 bay leaf (not California)

1 garlic clove, crushed

2 cups beef stock

2 teaspoons cornstarch mixed with just enough water to liquify

1 tablespoon Madeira

¼ teaspoon salt

3 pounds beef tenderloin

¼ teaspoon salt

¼ teaspoon black pepper

1 tablespoon vegetable oil

1 tablespoon butter

1 tablespoon Worcestershire sauce

1 cup beef broth

1 cup water

½ teaspoon salt

Preparations

Fortitude is a function of the will (think of a stubborn child and you get the idea). The real question is to what aspect of your life do you wish to apply this energy? If you need emotional strength, for example, you'll probably want to temper the water element in your environment and increase earth energies to provide more grounded viewpoints. You can accomplish this using the appropriate colors and aromas in various ways, as well as by having a special potted plant named after your goal. Keep that plant where you can see it. When you water the plant—you're "grounding" excess emotional energy!

Soak the marrowbones in warm water for 10 minutes. Press the marrow out of each, then cut it in ⅛-inch thick sections. If you wish you can store the bones in the freezer for later use in making soup stock. Cover the marrow in cold water and chill for 24 hours, making sure to change the water twice, at 12-hour intervals.

Meanwhile boil the next seven ingredients in a saucepan until the liquid is reduced by half. Add beef stock and return to a low-rolling boil. Add the cornstarch and Madeira, whisking thoroughly. Simmer until thick (about 3 minutes) then add salt. Set this mixture aside.

Preheat the oven to 350 degrees F. Sprinkle the beef with salt and pepper. Heat the oil, butter, and Worcestershire sauce in the roasting pan to brown the beef on all sides and seal in the juices. Roast for 45 minutes, let cool slightly, then transfer to a cutting board and slice the beef into ½-inch thick pieces.

While the roast is cooking, bring broth, water, and salt to simmer. Add the marrow to poach for 10 minutes. Pour the sauce over the meat, using the marrow rounds as a decoration around the serving platter.

Makes 8–10 servings

Pork

*Two ordinary foods, combined together, ignite a
pleasure far beyond the capacity of either of its parts
alone. Like rhubarb and strawberries, apple pie and
cheese, roast pork and sage, the two tastes and textures
meld together into the sort of subtle transcendental
oneness that we once fantasized would be our
experience when we finally found the ideal mate.*

—JOHN THORNE

PORK PROHIBITION?

Ancient people avoided pork for differing reasons. In Greek tradition, pig was connected to vegetation deities like Adonis and Demeter and believers avoided eating it out of respect for these gods. In Egypt, pigs were associated with Seth, a rather dark entity, and therefore many Egyptians refused to eat pork. Certain African tribes regarded pork as an unclean food. Even so, humankind began domesticating wild pigs by around 7000 B.C.E.

Depending on what culture you study, pork has a variety of symbolic values. The Celts strongly associated it with renewal, resurrection, and fertility. In the oceanic cultures, it represented prosperity, providence, and affluence, much as did beef. One Oceanic myth has it that before pigs came into the world, people had to eat each other. So the goddess gave birth to a pig and turned herself into a mother sow, enabling more and more pigs to be born and supply humankind with food.

Wealthy Roast

Prepare this roast and watch financial improvements come your way! Celtic people believe that the food of paradise is pork, which is available throughout eternity (so this dish safeguards prosperity too). To these symbolic qualities we add honey for success, and ginger to drive the magic toward manifestation.

1 teaspoon each butter and olive oil
1 teaspoon powdered ginger
½ cup soy sauce
1 cup orange juice
⅓ cup orange rum
½ cup apple juice
¼ cup honey
½ cup minced chives or green onions
2 tablespoons minced garlic
1 (2-pound) pork roast

Preparations

This is really a simple dish to prepare so you can easily mingle magic with the process (as shown in the directions). However, to give it a bit more power, consider burning prosperity-generating incense while you work: choices include bayberry, honeysuckle, and mint.

Preheat oven to 325 degrees F. Put the butter and olive oil in your roasting pan and brown all sides of the roast on the stovetop to keep the juices inside. Next, in a mixing bowl blend all the remaining ingredients except the pork. Pour this over the roast, saying:

> *Honey, make my life sweet*
> *Ginger, my fortunes soon to greet*
> *Fruit and honey, bring sweetness and joy*
> *By this spell, prosperity deploy!*

Roast for an hour, basting regularly (if you have a food injector, use that to flavor the interior of the meat as it cooks). Each time you baste, add a second incantation, like:

> *Bless this roast by the sacred fire*
> *as it cooks, abundance grows higher!*

When the roast is done, let it set at room temperature while you cook down the juices for gravy. For two cups of hot (nearly boiling) au jus, add 2 tablespoons of cornstarch mingled with just enough cold water to liquefy. Stir until thickened.

Makes 6–8 servings

Connection Chops

First discovered more than 4,000 years ago, peppercorns were cultivated as early as 1000 B.C.E. This spice was so costly that some shady suppliers mixed in mustard husks, juniper berries, and even floor sweepings and ground charcoal to stretch their supply and profits. To the underlying energy of importance and worth of pepper, we're adding a sweet potato–apple topping to renew a healthy physical relationship between two people based on equality and mutuality.

Chops

4 pounds pork chops
4 cups water
⅓ cup kosher salt
⅓ cup brown sugar
1 tablespoon dark soy sauce
2 teaspoons toasted
    peppercorns

2 garlic cloves, crushed
4 ¼-inch-thick slices fresh
    ginger
2 star anise
2 bay leaves
2 tablespoons oil

Topping

6 tablespoons butter
2 tablespoons finely chopped
    fresh ginger
4 medium sweet potatoes,
    peeled and thinly sliced
1 teaspoon five-spice powder

2 green apples, peeled and
    diced
2 tablespoons brown sugar
½ cup apple juice
Salt and freshly ground black
    pepper to taste

Preparations

Since the purpose of this dish is twofold (namely improving your enjoyment of each other and equality in the relationship) each person should make an effort to do something special for the other. Wear each other's favorite cologne or perfume, put on sensual clothing, and play romantic music to set just the right mood. Remember this is about making magic together!

Twenty-four hours before your dinner, combine all the ingredients (except the oil) in a large dish that can easily hold the pork to marinate. Refrigerate overnight, turning regularly. The next day, drain the chops and fry them in the oil until cooked thoroughly. Each time you turn the chops, think of warming up your partner even as the pork is warming slowly and evenly.

While the pork cooks, make the sweet potato–apple blend. Begin by putting the butter in the bottom of a frying pan with the ginger. Let this sauté for about 4 minutes. Add the sweet potatoes with five-spice powder and cook for about 15 minutes turning regularly. Add the apples. When the potatoes and apples are crisp-tender, pour in the brown sugar and apple juice. Salt and pepper to taste. Let this simmer until nearly all the liquid is gone, and top each pork chop with a healthy serving.

ADAPTATIONS

Some people like to mash this blend, or serve it with a drizzle of sweet cream.

Makes 8–10 servings

Cycle Circles

Pork already has strong associations with the wheel of life. In this case, we'll be fashioning ground pork into neat circles, which strengthen the connections with the cycles in our lives. These are served with a spicy dip for energy. What cycle you want to encourage or break is up to you!

MEATBALLS

¾ pound lean ground pork

1½ tablespoons paprika

1 tablespoon salt

1 tablespoon garlic powder

½ tablespoon black pepper

½ tablespoon onion powder

¼ tablespoon cayenne pepper

½ tablespoon dried oregano

½ tablespoon dry parsley

½ tablespoon dried thyme

½ cup chopped onions

¼ cup chopped bell peppers

2 teaspoons chopped garlic

3 tablespoons unsalted butter

3 tablespoons plus ¾ cup flour

1½ cups water

½ teaspoon salt

Pinch cayenne

1 cup cooked medium-grain rice

¼ cup chopped green onions

2 cups dried fine bread crumbs (Italian style)

1 large egg

2 tablespoons milk

6 cups vegetable oil, for frying

Sauce

<table>
<tr><td>1 cup mayonnaise</td><td>2 teaspoons minced fresh parsley</td></tr>
<tr><td>2 tablespoons minced green onions</td><td></td></tr>
<tr><td>1 tablespoon minced shallots</td><td>1 teaspoon minced garlic</td></tr>
<tr><td>1 tablespoon Creole mustard, or other spicy, whole-grain mustard</td><td>1 teaspoon fresh lemon juice</td></tr>
<tr><td></td><td>1 teaspoon hot red pepper sauce</td></tr>
<tr><td></td><td>Pinch salt</td></tr>
</table>

Preparations

Much here depends on whether you're trying to inspire a specific cycle or break one. For motivating a positive cycle, make sure you turn the meatballs sunwise while frying and perhaps add an incantation, like:

> *Turned toward the sun, this spell's begun*
> *Bring a new cycle my way, let it begin today!*

For changing a negative cycle the alternative incantation might be something like this while you turn the meatballs from right to left (moving them counterclockwise).

> *Turned away—negativity at bay*
> *Old cycles broken—by my will I have spoken!*
> *In this meat, my spell's complete*

Brown the pork with all the herbs that follow on the list (up to the butter). Cook for about 5 minutes, then drain off the fat. Return the meat to the pan, adding onions, bell pepper, and garlic and continue to cook for another 3 minutes.

Meanwhile, in a medium pot, melt the butter over medium heat. Add 3 tablespoons of the flour and, stirring constantly for 5 minutes, make a dark brown, even roux. Add the pork to this blend and cook for a minute longer before adding water, salt, and cayenne. Bring to a boil, and lower the heat to a simmer. Simmer until thick, adding the rice, green onions, and ½ cup of the bread crumbs just prior to removing it from the heat. Let the mixture cool so you can handle it easily.

Whisk the egg in one shallow bowl, put the ¾ cup flour in another, and the remaining seasoned bread crumbs in a third for dredging. Shape the meatballs to a size you like, dipping them in flour then the egg wash, the final coat being the bread crumbs. Fry the meat balls lightly in the oil until golden brown. Drain and serve with the sauce for dipping, which is made simply by combining all the ingredients and mixing them thoroughly.

Makes about 6 servings

Lamb

The only gift is a portion of thyself . . . the poet brings his poem; the shepherd his lamb . . .

—RALPH WALDO EMERSON

In many settings lamb symbolizes innocence, purity, and the ability to give freely to others without expectation. Additionally, according to the Hebrew stories of lamb's blood, it also carries protective energy and the ability to forestall ill fates.

As with beef, the name for domestic sheep—*Ovis aries*—is worth considering symbolically too. Astrologically Aries is the first constellation to welcome the sun, an icon of hope and blessings. Those born under this sign are said to be as bright, courageous, liberating, energized, and charismatic as that spring sun. Thus

---

LAMB

Egyptians, Greeks, Hebrews, and Africans alike offered sheep to their deities. While modern Jews don't sacrifice lambs as the ancients did, the lamb bone that appears on the seder plate at every Passover feast serves as a remembrance of the lamb their forebears sacrificed before leaving Egypt.

---

your lamb dishes can be saturated with any (or all) of these attributes depending on your needs and goals.

Aspiration Lamb

Nettle is a remarkably adaptable and long-lasting plant. Besides being edible, it can be used for making sturdy cloth, thread, rope, and twine. Unlike, say, cotton, nettle can be harvested twice a year for several years before being replanted. With such durability in mind, prepare this dish when you need the courage and tenacity to pursue your dreams (no need to count sheep!).

2 ounces fresh mushrooms, rinsed and quartered	2 ounces ground lamb
Butter	1 ounce hazelnuts, roasted and roughly chopped
1 garlic clove, minced	1 tablespoon chopped parsley
Salt and pepper to taste	1 teaspoon chopped thyme
Thyme sprig	1 teaspoon chopped savory
2 ounces wild nettles, blanched, squeezed dry, and chopped	1 ounce bread crumbs
	1 egg, beaten
1 shallot, minced	1 rack of lamb

Preparations

Consider to what area of your life this particular goal applies. For example, if you're dreaming of a career change, that's an earth-oriented goal and can be supported by using greens and browns in the sacred space as well as using an aromatic like patchouli, which provides a rich foundation in which your dreams will grow to fruition.

Sauté the mushrooms in a pat of butter (about 1 tablespoon) until they begin to release their moisture. Add half the garlic, salt, pepper, and thyme. Chop fine and chill.

Meanwhile sauté the nettles with the remaining garlic, salt, pepper, and thyme, using another pat of butter. This also needs to cool then be mixed into the mushroom blend. In another bowl, mix the shallots, ground lamb, hazelnuts, herbs, and bread crumbs Moisten with the egg, adding just a little at a time, until the consistency is spreadable. Mix this into the previous mushroom spread and chill.

Season the rack of lamb with salt and pepper, then sear it on all sides in butter. Let this cool. Fork the meat at regular intervals on the surface then rub the entire rack with the lamb-nettle-mushroom mixture evenly. Wrap the leg with plastic wrap so it's completely sealed inside, then wrap it again with foil. Heat the oven to 375 degrees F., cooking 45 minutes per pound (for medium). Turn it every 20 minutes while cooking.

Make sure you unwrap the lamb in a dish that can catch the juices so you can use them in serving.

Additions

Try adding some crushed pineapple to the meat juices when you serve the lamb. The pineapple will help open people's minds and hearts to welcome your ideas.

Makes about 8 servings

Greek God/dess Lamb

Olives and feta blend together in this dish to create a meal that's fit for celebrating a special occasion with the domestic god or goddess in your life. Olives offer peace and bless your union, while cheese bears the energy of love. For those of you who honor a Greek god or goddess— olives are sacred to Apollo, Artemis, Athena, Poseidon, Hercules, and the Moriae. Other regional deities to whom lamb was sacred include Hera, Zeus, Dionysus, and Pan.

4 pound boneless leg of lamb

salt and pepper to season

3 tablespoons olive oil

½ cup cured black olives, chopped

¼ pound feta cheese, crumbled

¼ pound goat cheese

6 garlic cloves, sliced thin lengthwise

1 onion, sliced thin

½ cup sun-dried tomatoes, chopped and lightly coated in olive oil

1 teaspoon crumbled dried rosemary

1 cup red cooking wine

1 ½ cups beef broth

½ cup water

1 tablespoon cornstarch dissolved in 2 tablespoons cold water

PREPARATIONS

Take out all your recipe-spell components and focus on your goal. Hold your hands palm down over all of them, then recite a blessing something like this:

> *Rosemary—so we remember all good things*
> *Cheese—true love toward each other brings*
> *Olives—grant blessings and ongoing peace*
> *Lamb—pure intention that will never cease!*

Lay the lamb out, bone side up, and season lightly with salt and pepper. Rub with 2 tablespoons of the oil. Mix the olives and cheese and tomatoes together and spread it over the lamb, leaving about an inch all around the edge. Evenly distribute the garlic and onion slices over the top of the cheese-olive spread. Now roll up the lamb (starting on the short side) and tie it with kitchen string.

Put the roll in a roasting pan and cover the exterior with the remaining oil, rosemary, salt and pepper to taste (if you wish a bit of mint is also nice). Roast at 325 degrees F. for 20 minutes per pound to finish medium-rare. The roast should stand for 15 minutes before serving.

While the roast rests, add the wine to the pan drippings. Heat to boiling and reduce by half. Put in a bit of rosemary, broth, and water. Let this boil to reduce by half again. Mix the cornstarch with just a little water and blend it into the drippings to make a thick gravy.

SERVING IDEA

Slice the lamb and arrange it in a circle in the center of your platter. Lay out cooked whole carrots from that center point so the whole dish looks like a spring sun rising!

Makes 10–12 servings

Power Patties

The solar energy of lamb combines with pomegranate sauce in this dish to pack quite a magical energy wallop. Mesopotamians connected pomegranates with a solar god who annually died and was reborn as a pomegranate tree. Numerous other cultures believed that pomegranate supplied both physical and proverbial fertility; it may well give this dish the profuse boost you seek.

1 ½ pounds ground lean lamb
½ cup fresh bread crumbs
½ cup chopped fresh cilantro
½ cup minced red onion (red is a good power color)
¼ cup chopped fresh mint
1 large egg
1 large shallot, minced
1 tablespoon lemon juice
2 teaspoons ground cumin
1 ½ teaspoons salt
1 teaspoon freshly ground black pepper
½ teaspoon cayenne pepper
¼ teaspoon ground allspice
2 tablespoons olive oil

Sauce

1 cup finely chopped red onion

3 garlic cloves, chopped

2 cups diced tomatoes

2 tablespoons fresh lemon juice

2 tablespoons tomato juice (spiced is fine)

¼ teaspoon ground allspice

1 tablespoon pomegranate molasses (available at Middle Eastern markets) or pomegranate juice mixed with molasses

6 large pitas

Plain yogurt (not skimmed)

½ cup chopped green onions

Preparations

It's good to start raising energy before you prepare this dish, then let the cooking process bring everything to an apex. There are several ways of raising energy, but I like to dance sunward around my kitchen while chanting something like:

> *Higher, higher feel the power*
> *Growing moment by moment*
> *And hour by hour!*

This helps charge your sacred space with harmonic energies.

Combine all the ingredients listed with and including the lamb, except oil, in a large non-aluminum bowl. Let this sit overnight in the refrigerator. The next day, shape the lamb into patties (about ¼ cup of the blend for each). Put the 2 tablespoons of olive oil in a large frying pan and sauté the patties until golden brown (4 to 5 minutes per side). Using a slotted spoon set aside the patties and retain the drippings. For the sauce, put the onion and garlic in the pan, and sauté for 5 minutes. Stir in tomatoes, lemon juice, tomato juice, and allspice. Let this come to a low rolling boil then stir in the pomegranate molasses. Return the patties to the skillet, reduce heat to low, cover, and simmer for 20 minutes.

While the patties cook, warm the pitas. Lay these on a platter with the lamb patties on top. Let the sauce thicken, and then pour it over the top (if you wish, draw an invoking pentagram with the sauce as you pour). Dollop with yogurt and sprinkle with green onions.

Makes 5–6 servings

Ham

It was a comfort in those succeeding days to sit up and contemplate the majestic panorama of mountains and valleys spread out below us and eat ham and hard boiled eggs while our spiritual natures reveled alternately in rainbows, thunderstorms, and peerless sunsets. Nothing helps scenery like ham and eggs.

—MARK TWAIN

The curing of hog meat most likely first became popular in central Italy in the early Roman period. It's interesting that the Roman word for salt-cured hog leg was *Perxctus*. This is what we now know as prosciutto! Later in history Columbus introduced hogs to

HAM IN HISTORY

Ham typically means the hind leg of an animal, specifically from boar, lamb, goat, or venison. Classical writings tell us that Romans had heard about the hams made by Gauls using curing, brining, and/or smoking. Cato also writes about ham being made in Northern Italy by layering legs of pork in salt, followed by a drying and smoking process. By medieval times hams were quite common in Europe, with most cottage dwellers keeping a pig specifically for making ham that could provide food for the winter.

Cuba, Hernando de Soto brought them to Florida in the late 1400s, and colonial settlers had hogs to hunt and eat in the 1600s.

Sweet Life Ham

In Polish tradition ham represented joy and abundance. Combine this with the Anglo-Saxon meaning of the word ham *(namely a homestead), and we have the perfect sweet dish to bring happiness into our homes!*

½ cup honey butter (softened)
¼ cup real maple syrup
2 tablespoons sweet hot
    mustard

1 teaspoon orange extract
1 teaspoon ginger powder
Pinch of vanilla powder
1 spiral-cut ham

PREPARATIONS

Look through your music collection and find those tunes that really set your feet to tapping and lift your spirits. Play that music while you sage your home to rid it of any lingering negative energy that could put a damper on the evening's meal. Decorate the table with bright, happy accents to support the overall goal.

This dish goes together very quickly. Just mix the honey butter with the syrup and spices and spread mixture between each slice of the spiral-cut ham. Reserve a little to put on top. Place the ham in a baking dish and cover the bottom with about ¼-inch of water to keep it from burning. Cover and cook according to the directions with the ham. Check the pot periodically; baste the ham and add more water if necessary.

Makes 2–4 servings per pound

Passion Ham

The lore of celery seems to be twofold. Romans ate the stalks to increase passion, while celery seed was said to improve psychic awareness. Why not have the best of both worlds in this dish by using your sensitivity to make intimate moments more enjoyable?

10 celery ribs
½ pound thinly sliced smoked ham
¼ cup minced fresh parsley
¼ cup mayonnaise
2 tablespoons Dijon mustard

2 tablespoons chopped pickles (optional)
½ teaspoon Worcestershire sauce
½ teaspoon cider vinegar

Preparations

Get everything ready ahead of time for a steamy evening with your significant other. Lay out something really sexy, and dab the space with passionate aromatics like ginger or lavender (to attract a man) or vetivert or violet (to attract a woman). As you move around the space, add an incantation like:

> *Good food, good feelings, let interest grow higher*
> *Passion and playfulness, lit by magic's fire!*

Cut the celery into 32 (1¼-inch) pieces. Keep the trimmings in your freezer to use in vegetable stock (if desired). Next, take half of the ham and pulse it in a blender or food processor until finely chopped. The other half should be minced by hand. Stir these together with the remaining ingredients, liberally filling each of the celery stalks with the blend. This makes a great appetizer (to whet both your appetite for food and each other). It's also a good late-night snack in case everything goes really well!

Makes 5 servings (2 stalks each)

BACON AND SAUSAGE

Bacon is made from a salted side of pork. Originally bacon (*bacoun* in Middle English) referred to any type of fresh or cured pork, but that usage died out by the seventeenth century. The term itself comes from the Germanic *bakkon* and Teutonic *backe*, referring to the back of the animal.

And what of sausage? Unlike our modern notions of sausage being made from meat stuffed in a casing, the ancients didn't limit the filling to meat. They used fish, fowl, cheese, and leeks too. And that tubular shape wasn't always favored either. Some sausages were round, square, flat, or spherical!

Bacon and Sausage

Those that respect the law and love sausage should watch neither being made.

—MARK TWAIN

Ever wonder how the phrase "bring home the bacon" started? Well, a small English town in the twelfth century was given a unique challenge by the local clergy. If a man could stand before God and the congregation and claim he had not argued with his wife in a year, he would be given a side of bacon. Thus anyone seeing such a man returning home with the bacon knew he'd shown great patience and forbearance. With this in mind, the presence of bacon in our magical meals can imply providence, self-control, moderation, and endurance.

Sausage also has symbolic value, often that of frugality and necessity. In ancient Greece the art of sausage making meant using all that was left from prime meat. Additionally the word *sausage* itself comes from the Latin *salsus*, meaning salted (or preserved). This provides the additional quality of safeguarding and conserving your energy once it is manifest.

Lucky Bacon

The Chinese call kumquats gam gat sue, and they're considered fortune foods. The word gam rhymes with the Chinese word for gold, and the word gat rhymes with the Chinese word for luck. Additionally, the shape of these little oranges represents unity and perfection. Combined with bacon, this dish would be ideal for bringing financial or business luck.

2 pounds Canadian bacon
   (maple or smoked is fine)
1 cup orange marmalade
1 tablespoon lemon juice, or
   to taste

2 tablespoons dry mustard
Fresh kumquats for garnish

PREPARATIONS

Make yourself a luck-drawing charm for the kitchen. Save a nice-looking spice bottle and fill it with a magnet (to draw luck your way), allspice berries, nutmegs, and star anise (all of which improve fortune). Keep this over your stove where the gentle heat will keep it active. (Open the bottle when you want luck to arrive quickly.)

Preheat oven to 350 degrees F. Put the bacon in a shallow baking pan and pour the marmalade mingled with the lemon juice and mustard over the top. Bake for a half hour, basting every 2 minutes. Serve with the fresh kumquats on the top.

Makes 6–8 servings

Sausage Stipulation

When there's a necessity facing you and you can't seem to figure out how to take care of it, try this dish. The sausage provides a foundation of reasonable perspectives, while the beer—as a "safe" beverage when water wasn't always drinkable—helps you find the most secure options.

3 pounds uncooked bratwurst	1 cup water
1 onion, thinly sliced	1 tablespoon vegetable oil
6 garlic cloves	Mustard
3 cups dark beer, as needed	

Preparations

You can use a little charm like this while you're cooking or eating to support the energy:

> *Sausage served upon my plate,*
> *help me to stipulate!*
> *A difficult need we face head-on*
> *Let reason find a way—be gone*

 Prick each sausage with a pin to release some of the fat when cooking. Arrange the onion slices on the bottom of a sauté pan large enough to hold all the sausages (oil the pan). Place the sausages on top and add beer, garlic and water to cover (3 parts beer to 1 part water). Gradually bring the liquid to a simmer. Cook 10 minutes. Remove the brats from the liquid and let it simmer down to half the volume. Add some of your favorite mustard to this to thicken—serving it on the side for dipping.

Makes 8–10 servings

PRAYERFUL POULTRY

The key to everything is patience. You get the
chicken by hatching the egg—not by smashing it.

—ARNOLD GLASOW

Poultry has a very colorful history. First domesticated in Asia, people there would have been upset if someone ate chicken, because it has an aspect of the divine! As you might expect, the symbolic value of poultry also varies depending on the era and setting. Some Chinese attribute to the cock the knowledge of good and evil and also believe it to be a messenger between Earth and heaven. Persians thought the cock was a symbol of light and awareness, and Egyptians associated chickens with fertility. Other values given the cock specifically (in heraldry, among other places) were those of vigilance, alertness, and safety.

Goose and turkey were similar. These two birds were linked with the seasonal round and solar deities, which is one reason that they still appear on holiday tables. Additionally Egyptians felt that a goose laid the golden celestial egg from which all things originated (fertility). Both chickens and geese in China represent yang (male) energies.

Chicken

I start with a chicken. A good chicken. A cheap chicken wouldn't make a rich soup.

—Elsie Zussman

Wild chickens originated in Thailand and in southeast Asia, which is also where they were first domesticated. As early as 3000 B.C.E. this animal was being used in China, arriving in Africa 500 years later. The appeal of the chicken was its economy and ease of care, and its relatively small size—which made it simple to consume the whole bird in one meal (so nobody had to worry about the meat spoiling before the advent of refrigeration).

Overall, besides the Western connection with health, the chicken symbolized illumination and new beginnings since roosters announce the dawn. In Buddhism the first enlightened animal was a Tibetan chick, and in China the chicken represents happy, unified families. This is why it's among the most popular foods at Chinese New Year.

Conclusion Chicken

The combination of chicken and mustard helps guide fact finding so that you'll gain the information and insight necessary to make a good decision on whatever crossroads you face. The maple syrup ensures that your choice will makes you truly happy.

1 good-size boneless chicken
    breast
¼ cup cider vinegar
¼ cup sesame oil
2 tablespoons soy sauce
1 teaspoon salt
1 teaspoon powdered ginger

2 tablespoons brown sugar
2 slices orange
¼ cup orange liqueur (or
    cooking wine)
⅛ cup spicy mustard
¼ cup maple syrup
Pat of butter

PREPARATIONS

Fact finding requires both logic and instincts working simultaneously, so look to in-between times (like noon or dawn) for gathering your recipe ingredients. Doing so encourages balanced perspectives.

Pierce the chicken with a fork to break through any illusions that may exist about your options. Marinate it in a blend of the vinegar, oil, soy, salt, sugar, ginger, and the juice of the two orange slices. Leave the meat to soak for 6 hours in the refrigerator, turning it regularly saying something like:

> *Reveal wherein the best future lies*
> *Help me in my Path to decide*

Meanwhile, create the glaze by mixing the liqueur or wine, mustard, syrup, and butter together in a saucepan. Set this aside. Brush the glaze on the chicken as you grill or bake it, turning every 7 or 8 minutes. You can also reduce the remnants down to make a nice energizing sauce!

Makes 1 serving

Vision Chicken

Most myths about the lime tree refer to a linden (which is of the same family). In Germanic and Swedish stories, the linden is a magical tree that attracts fairy folk, and it's under the bows of these long-lived trees that ancient stories are often shared. This special energy mingles with the illuminating nature of chicken and with the psychic energy of apricots to produce a dish that opens our inner vision to the unseen realms, and allows us to share those images in stories and songs.

8 pound chicken wings	1 cup soy sauce
1 cup fresh lime juice	$\frac{2}{3}$ cup sugar
1 cup apricot preserves	4 large garlic cloves

PREPARATIONS

This dish benefits from making it during in-between times (like dusk, dawn, midnight) as that's when fairy activity is said to be strongest. Other times include Samhain and Lammas, which are fairy holidays. If this timing proves problematic, bring items into your kitchen that will appease your fairy guests when they arrive, such as sweet breads and small cups of mead.

Preheat oven to 425 degrees F. Halve wings at joint. Divide wings between two large roasting pans, arranging in single layers. Puree remaining ingredients in a blender and pour mixture over wings, dividing evenly between pans. Bake wings in upper and lower thirds of oven 50 minutes. Turn wings over and switch position of pans in oven, then bake 45 minutes to 1 hour more, or until liquid is thick and sticky.

Alternatively, you can deep-fry the wings until they're halfway done, then transfer them to the roasting pans and baste with the puree with every turn until the wings are cooked and the sauce sticky. At this juncture I like to sprinkle on sesame seeds (another excellent "eye opener").

Makes 8 one-pound servings

Warm Affection Lemon Chicken

Yin (lemon) and yang (chicken) team up in this dish, generating positive energy for warm affections, be it toward friends or mates. The chicken also produces an overall sense of harmony and unity for those partaking of the meal.

2 lemons, sliced into 12 thin slices each (a multiple of 4 for foundations)

Olive oil (if you can find a citrus-flavored blend—all the better)

Salt

4 skinless, boneless chicken breasts

Salt and pepper

Garlic powder

All-purpose flour

5 tablespoons olive oil

½ cup sliced green Italian- or Greek-style olives

1½ cups chicken stock

¼ cup butter

PREPARATIONS

Pink is the color for gentle feelings (it's not overly pushy). So bring a pink candle into your working space. Light it saying something like:

In this food affection bind
In the light of this candle affection shines
And as we eat, my guests please bless
With love, and hope . . . hear my behest

Note that this is designed somewhat as a prayer, so if you wish you can direct it to your pantry protector or protectress!

Preheat oven to 325 degrees F. Line a baking sheet with parchment paper, and arrange the lemon slices on the paper. Brush them with olive oil and sprinkle on a little salt. Bake until the slices are lightly browned at the edges.

Sprinkle the chicken with salt, pepper, and garlic. Dredge chicken in flour to coat both sides; shake off excess. Heat the olive oil in a frying pan over high heat. Cook the chicken in the oil, turning every 3 minutes until golden brown. Stir in the olives and stock. Let this come to a boil, and allow the liquid to reduce until it becomes very thick (about 5 minutes). Add the butter and lemon slices.

FLAVORING OPTION

To bring more love and devotion into this dish, you can add 2 teaspoons of orange extract to the sauce and a cup of mandarin oranges (drained) with the butter and lemon.

Makes 4 servings

Security and Strength Stuffed Chicken

The green color of the spinach in this recipe gives it growth-oriented energy. Cheese was the food of Grecian athletes, providing them with endurance and strength. This combination of spinach blended with chicken motivates vigor and tenacity, with strong roots to hold sure to your ideals.

2 tablespoons extra-virgin olive oil

1 small onion, diced

1 large garlic clove, minced

¼ cup chicken stock or water

1½ pounds spinach, washed

2 ripe plum tomatoes, diced

2 ounces goat cheese, room temperature

2 ounces cream cheese, room temperature

Coarse salt

Freshly ground black pepper

4 large boneless, skinless chicken breasts (sliced with a pocket)

Coarse salt

Freshly ground black pepper

PREPARATIONS

A suitable deity to call upon for assistance with this dish is Apollo, whose son (it's said) gifted humankind with cheese. Bay leaves are sacred to Apollo, so take a large one and use a toothpick to inscribe on the leaf one word that best describes your goal. Burn the leaf in a fireproof dish (like an incense burner). The smoke will transport your prayer to the heavens and the four winds while you work.

Preheat oven to 325 degrees F. Warm the oil in a sauté pan, adding the onion and garlic to cook lightly. Add the stock and spinach, letting it cook down until the spinach is done. Transfer this mix to a bowl and add the tomatoes, cheeses, salt and pepper.

Season each chicken breast lightly with salt and pepper and create a pocket. Stuff the pocket with a healthy portion of the spinach mix. Wrap these in plastic wrap to keep the filling from falling out. Wrap again with foil, and place the packets in the oven for about 15–20 minutes. Remove from the oven and leave at room temperature for 5 more minutes. *Carefully* remove the plastic, using a sharp knife or scissors. Cut the chicken in ½-inch-thick slices to serve.

Note: If you have access to a Greek seasoning blend, use this on the chicken breasts instead of the salt and pepper.

Makes 4 servings

Goose

A goose is a goose still, dress it as you will.

—HENRY DAVID THOREAU

Geese were not always considered dumb (as the phrase "silly goose" suggests). Ovid called them wiser than dogs and deemed them household protectors. Greeks and Romans kept them as household guardians to warn of attack. The goose was sacred to Hera, a goddess of love and watchfulness. Other deities who held the goose as sacred include Mars, Hermes, Apollo, Eros, Ejpona,

Goose

The term *gooseflesh* arose in the Middle Ages, when geese were plucked for their feathers several times a year. The naked goose's skin formed little bumps where the feathers had been removed, especially when it was cold. Human skin takes on a similar appearance when cold, and thus is called "gooseflesh" or "having goosebumps"!

Brahma, Isis, and Ra. Other cultures connected them with the energies of awareness, the air element, the sun, inspiration, swiftness, happiness, and providence.

Hospitality Goose

Throughout South America and the Caribbean, pineapples symbolized friendship and welcome. People put fresh pineapples outside their huts to invite guests, akin to putting out a welcome mat! These customs translated over into early American homes where pineapples were carved into various pieces of furniture. Pineapple makes an ideal complement to goose, whose energies are largely associated with family and love.

4 ounces dried figs, stems discarded
4 ounces dried apricots
8 ounces dried pineapple
4 ounces dried pear
4 ounces dried mango (or papaya)
2 tablespoons brandy
1 tablespoon whole allspice
1 tablespoon mixed peppercorns (black, white, green, and pink—all four elements!)
½ stick butter, melted
1 (12-pound) goose
⅓ cup finely chopped shallots
⅔ cup brandy
1 cup chicken stock
1 cup pineapple juice
2 tablespoons orange preserves

169

PREPARATIONS

The pineapple is the key energy component in this dish. Find the largest piece of your dried pineapple and cut an image of a house from it, while envisioning your home and saying:

> *My heart and hearth are open*
> *Heed these words as they're spoken*
> *This is a house of hospitality*
> *And through this food, this spell is freed!*

By the way, this is a particularly welcoming dish to serve people the first time they visit your sacred space or home.

Simmer all the dried fruits in water for about 20 minutes. Drain and set aside, tossing with the brandy. Crush the allspice and the peppercorns, then stir them into the butter. Remove any excess fat or quills from the goose. Gently lift the skin from the breast portion and push part of the butter-spice mixture underneath. Use the remaining to evenly cover the goose's skin. Stuff the interior of the goose with as much of the fruit mixture as possible, reserving at least 1 cup for the pan sauce.

Roast in a pan at 325 degrees F. for 4 hours, skimming excess fat and basting the goose every half hour. Let rest for 30 minutes covered with foil while you make the fruited gravy.

Take the drippings from the goose (skimmed of fat), adding shallots and stirring until golden brown. Add the brandy, stock, juice, reserved fruit, and preserves. Simmer, stirring regularly, until sauce thickens.

Note: You can use a thickener like cornstarch if you'd like it thicker. Carve goose and serve with the fruit stuffing on the side.

Makes 8–10 servings

Golden Goose

Children know the story of the goose that laid the golden eggs. Adults wish that life would be so easy. However, we'll use the symbolism in this recipe, bringing golden apples into the equation for a healthy providence that blends with the goose's domestic quality.

1 (13-pound) goose, giblets and neck discarded
Salt and pepper
3 garlic cloves, thinly sliced
8 Golden Delicious apples, peeled, cut into 8 wedges each (earth number)

¼ cup fresh lemon juice
6 tablespoons sugar
¼ cup apple brandy
1½ teaspoons ground cinnamon

PREPARATIONS

Gold is the name of the game today! Use whatever gold accents you have for your table and working space. Additionally, leave the apples in sunlight to charge for 4 hours. Bless them, saying

> *I don't have the eggs but I've got the goose*
> *In these apples my magic—loose!*
> *Needs abate, wants cease*
> *Providence come—the spell's released!*

Preheat oven to 350 degrees F. Rinse the goose completely, then let dry. Season with salt and pepper inside and out. Cut small slits all over goose, placing the garlic slices securely into the slits (symbolically this helps protect those financial improvements when they arrive). Place goose on rack, breast side down, in a large roasting pan. Roast for 2 hours, basting regularly. Remove and discard all but about 6 tablespoons of the excess fat. Turn the goose over, and continue to roast and baste it for 90 minutes more.

While the goose cooks prepare the apples by tossing them in a bowl with the lemon juice, about 6 tablespoons of the goose fat,

sugar, apple brandy, and cinnamon. Bake in a lightly greased pan during the last hour that the goose roasts. Slice the goose and assemble the apples on each plate so they form the shape of a golden egg!
Makes 9–10 servings

Duck

When I see a bird that walks like a duck and swims like a duck and quacks like a duck, I call that bird a duck.

—RICHARD CARDINAL CUSHING

Pliny thought that ducks were wind and weather prophets. Among the Hebrews the duck represented long life (or immortality); in Egypt the duck was sacred to Isis; and in Greek tales Poseidon had dominion over this bird. The Chinese and Japanese look to the duck for felicity, fidelity, and cooperation in relationships. American Indians see the duck mediating between the sky and water, and this bird is often present in creation myths.

JUST DUCKY

According to dream keys, a duck showing up in your dreams means that you or someone you know is very adaptable and fully competent in dealing with emotional issues. Ducks are also considered good dream omens of positive change and overcoming adversity.

Crispy Conciliation

To the aspects of cooperation afforded by duck, we add pears for a long-lasting solution to the problems being addressed. According to Gaelic stories, pears were the fruit of paradise that offered immortality. This dish is doubly effective when the mediation is happening between women since the pear is an icon of the feminine.

1 ½ pounds boneless duck breast

Salt to taste

Olive oil

1 firm-ripe Bosc pear

2 tablespoons apple or pear brandy

1 vegetable bouillon cube

¾ cup apple or pear juice

½ teaspoon cornstarch

1 tablespoon green peppercorns, lightly crushed

1 teaspoon fresh thyme leaves

PREPARATIONS

Mediation and reconciliation require a healthy dose of both logic and intuition—so consider charging the pear in both sunlight and moonlight to achieve that balance. Also each person partaking in this dish should bring along a symbol of his or her anger that can be easily destroyed. Destroy the symbol after dinner, leaving that negativity behind you, then returning to the table to talk things through.

Trim any excess fat from the duck. Pat with salt. In a medium-hot pan add olive oil and fry the duck for 25 minutes until the skin is very crispy and brown. Carefully remove excess fat as the duck cooks (you can think about removing excess negative feelings as you do!). Put the duck breasts on a serving platter and cover them with foil to keep warm.

While the duck fries, peel and dice the pear. Pour off all but about a tablespoon of fat from the skillet and sauté the pear until lightly browned. Add the brandy, peppercorns, and bouillon cube. Mingle the juice with the cornstarch, stirring this slowly into your sauce. Add thyme, stirring until thickened. Pour this over the breasts in the pattern of a peace sign to support your goals.

Makes 6–8 servings

Relationship Remedy

The earliest recorded mention of what we know as rhubarb dates back to 2700 B.C. in China, where the plant was cultivated for medicinal purposes. Coupled with duck and ginger, in this recipe, rhubarb helps give all willing parties the energy to begin healing a damaged relationship.

18 (¼-inch-thick) slices
  sourdough baguette
1½ tablespoons melted butter
6 ounces rhubarb stalks,
  trimmed and diced
1½ teaspoons peeled and
  grated fresh ginger

⅓ cup water
3 tablespoons brown sugar
¼ cup mayonnaise
¾ pound smoked duck breast,
  skin and fat removed
Cilantro for garnish

PREPARATIONS

Take an image of the person with whom you're trying to make amends (one that you don't mind getting messy for this spell). Apply any type of medicinal cream to the edge of the picture, saying:

> *Where things once did not go well*
> *Return your heart to peace and health*
> *And where our relationship bent or broke*
> *Remedial powers I now evoke!*

Keep this image in a safe and special place throughout the meal (say, on your altar).

Brush the bread slices with butter and toast them in the oven for 5 or 6 minutes. Meanwhile simmer the rhubarb, ginger, water, and sugar to tenderize the rhubarb (about 3 minutes). Set the pan in ice water to cool. Drain the rhubarb, reserving 2 teaspoons of the liquid. Mix the reserved liquid with mayonnaise. Carve a slice of duck for each piece of bread. Spread the mayonnaise on each piece of toast, top it with duck, and garnish with a dollop of the rhubarb and cilantro.

Makes 9 2-slice servings

Turkey

*Radical historians now tell the story of Thanksgiving
from the point of view of the turkey.*

—MASON COOLEY

While you might not think so, a wildlife biologist will tell you that turkeys in the wild could teach humans a thing or two. They know how to fade into an environment and when to spread their tail

TALKING TURKEY

Urban mythology claims that the phrase "talk turkey" was first used on a hunting trip. Two men agreed to split whatever they caught. When one of the two divided the game they had shot, he took the two turkeys and left the two buzzards for his companion, who said "Stop talking birds, let's talk turkey."

By the way, the North American turkey was purportedly named by explorers in the late 1500s who mistakenly thought it was a European turkey cock.

feathers in showy pride. They know how to forage and when to flock or stay close to the roost. Perhaps this is why Benjamin Franklin wanted the turkey to be America's national symbol.

Turkey Equilibrium

This dish blends simple "turkey wisdom" with plums. In China and Japan, plums are the fruit of life, and they signify never-ending energy. Eat this dish to internalize a whole new sense of balance between spirituality and mundanity, work and play, sounds and silences.

½ cup plum jam
2 teaspoons Chinese five-spice powder
2 tablespoons water
1½ teaspoons salt
1 (12-pound) turkey

Salt and pepper to taste
5 to 7 cups of your favorite dressing (one made with currants is a nice choice)
½ stick butter, melted

GRAVY

Pan juices from roast turkey
About 3½ cups turkey stock
½ cup dry red wine

¼ cup plum jam
2 tablespoons cornstarch
Water

PREPARATIONS

On a piece of paper, make a yin-yang symbol, and color it with a hue that represents the area of your life where you want to bring balance. Bless this token, saying:

> *As above so below*
> *As within so without*
> *Bring my life into symmetry*
> *By my will, this spell is freed!*

Leave this where you can see it while you cook, then carry it with you as a charm afterward to help the manifestation process.

Simmer the jam, powder, water, and salt until well mixed. This will be the glaze. Set aside. Season the turkey with a little salt and pepper, and stuff it with whatever you've chosen (try to find a blend that supports your goal). Distribute half the butter under the turkey skin. Use the remaining butter to brush the turkey for the first 90 minutes (at 350 degrees F.). Continue roasting, basting occasionally with the plum glaze, until the stuffing reaches an internal temperature of 170 degrees F. (about another 90 minutes). If the glaze becomes too brown, cover the turkey with foil. Let the turkey stand for 20 minutes while you make the gravy.

Transfer pan juices to a large measuring implement, skimming the fat. Add enough turkey stock and wine to pan juices to total 4½ cups. Put this in a pan over a medium heat. Reduce to two cups of liquid, then add the jam. Thicken by mixing the cornstarch with a touch of water, and slowly mixing this into the plum gravy. When you serve make sure to apply the gravy evenly to complete the symbolism of balance.

Makes 8–10 servings

Sharing and Caring Turkey

Cabbage is one of the oldest known vegetables. One fable from Europe talks about a person wanting cabbage so badly that he stole some from his neighbor and was banished to the moon, giving rise to our stories of a "man in the moon." The magical association of cabbage with lunar energies has been notable ever since. This intuitive energy mingles nicely with the Native American symbolism for turkey as the give-away bird— the ability to offer kindness and share what we have in times of need.

TURKEY

1½ pounds boneless turkey breast tenderloins

1 large red onion, sliced

3 tablespoons olive oil

1 tablespoon balsamic vinegar

4 bay leaves, halved

1 teaspoon salt

½ teaspoon black pepper

½ teaspoon ground allspice

CABBAGE

¼ cup olive oil

6 cups finely shredded red cabbage

½ cup red onion, thinly sliced

3 tablespoons balsamic vinegar

3 tablespoons golden brown sugar

½ teaspoon ground allspice

Salt and pepper to taste

PREPARATIONS

The phrase "practice random acts of kindness" has a lot to do with this dish. Many times we simply need to be more aware of our ongoing opportunities to offer a hand of help and hope. To encourage this in yourself, take an entire week before making this dish and try to watch for just such moments. When you see one, jump into the fray and "give away" good energy. By the end of the week you should have a lot of positive energy stored up to channel into this dish (which, in turn, will keep that awareness flowing in your life).

Put the turkey with all the following ingredients in a large bag to marinate overnight in the refrigerator. Shake it several times for even flavoring. The next day, just prior to cooking the turkey, heat the olive oil in a frying pan, adding the cabbage and onion. Cook until the cabbage is soft. Transfer the mixture into a bowl, and add the vinegar, sugar, allspice, and salt and pepper. Chill the mixture while you cook the turkey. Roast the bird in a 350-degree F. oven until its internal temperature reaches 165 degrees F. When done, turn twice, 4 minutes per side, brushing it each time with the marinade. Put the glazed turkey on a platter, and serve it with the cabbage spreading all around it (like a bright sun spreading cheer everywhere it touches).

Makes 6–8 servings

Earthy Turkey

Various Native American myths tell a similar story—of a deity who came to Earth and wherever he or she walked, squash, beans, and corn sprouted on the land, and became staples for early tribes. This gives these particular edibles a strong connection with Earth energies, especially when combined with the wild turkey, who is part of the Mother's network of life. Adding to this symbolism, the pie circle symbolizes the planet and makes a womb within which your energy bakes to perfection.

FILLING

1 ½ cups peeled and seeded butternut squash, cubed
3 cups salted water
1 cup frozen baby lima beans, thawed
1 cup frozen baby corn, thawed
3 tablespoons unsalted butter
3 tablespoons all-purpose flour

1 cup turkey broth or chicken broth
2 tablespoons minced fresh sage
Salt to taste
5 ounces frozen pearl onions, thawed
3 cups cubed cooked turkey

CRUST

1 ¼ cups all-purpose flour
1 ½ teaspoons double-acting baking powder
½ teaspoon salt
2 tablespoons butter, cut into bits

1 ½ cups extrasharp Cheddar cheese, grated
4 slices of bacon, cooked until crisp, crumbled
½ cup milk

PREPARATIONS

This is an ideal dish to make for Earth Day, or any day focused on healing our planet. Plan the entire day's activities so that everything you do blesses and rejuvenates the planet's energy grid. Also think of this pot pie as a miniature "earth" (a focus for your spell), and empower the components by saying:

> Earth's abundance within this dish
>> Powers hear my prayer and wish
> Heal our world, make it whole
>> As above, so below
> As without, so within
>> Let your healing powers begin!

Put the squash and water in a saucepan and bring it to a low-rolling boil for about 8 minutes until it just starts getting tender. Using a slotted spoon, remove the squash from water, and put the lima beans and corn in the saucepan. Cook for about 4 minutes, until tender. Add these to the squash, retaining 1 cup of the water, and discarding the rest.

Preheat oven to 425 degrees F. Melt the butter over medium heat. Slowly add flour, whisking so it becomes thick. Add the broth, a little at a time, stirring constantly. Once this is well blended, add the sage and salt. Simmer for 10 minutes. Put the drained squash, beans, corn, and onions into the sauce and add the turkey. Set the mixture aside to put it into the crust when done. Note that if you're pressed for time you can skip making the piecrust here, and just use a prepared crust from the supermarket.

To assemble homemade crust, mix together the flour, baking powder, salt, and butter until crumbly. Stir in the cheese and bacon, slowly adding enough milk so the dough holds together. Roll it out on a floured surface and put it in your pie dish. Or, if you feel creative, put the turkey mix in a baking dish and drop small balls of the crust on top (like earth dumplings). Bake until the crust turns golden brown.

Makes 6–8 servings

Game Hen

*The cocks may crow but it's the hen that lays
the egg.*

—MARGARET THATCHER

While the rooster struts his stuff, the hen became the symbol of maternal instinct, family defender, and productivity. An image of a hen and her chicks in ecclesiastical sculpture represents God's providence. And in ancient times, an image of a hen kissing a rooster was the symbol of a legitimate marriage.

Eros Hen

If the hen rules the roost in your home, then this dish will also allow her to whip up a night of playful pleasure and romance. In Greek and Roman mythology, the raspberries in this recipe are associated with passionate love and are sacred to Venus and Eros.

1 (¾-pound) Cornish game
    hen, halved
Salt and pepper to taste
1 teaspoon dried thyme
2 tablespoons olive oil
2 small onions, chopped
2 garlic cloves, chopped

2 cups chicken broth
⅔ cup dry red wine
⅔ cup frozen raspberries
2 teaspoons (or more) sugar
¼ teaspoon ground allspice
Cornstarch, if needed

PREPARATIONS

This isn't the time to be shy—do something daring. Greet your significant other in something sexy and wear an alluring perfume or cologne. Set up the area where you wish to play so that it's welcoming. Bless this space with a prayer to Eros and Venus that the night be filled with love, joy, and physical bliss.

Preheat oven to 350 degrees F. Season the hen halves with salt, pepper, and thyme. Put these in a large frying pan over medium heat with the oil and brown on both sides for about 7 minutes each. Transfer the halves to a baking dish, and bake for 60 minutes.

Meanwhile, pour all but 2 tablespoons of oil out of the frying pan. In the remaining oil, sauté the onions and garlic for 5 minutes. Add the broth, wine, raspberries, sugar, and allspice. Boil this down so it reduces and thickens, stirring regularly. If you find the sauce isn't thick enough, add a little cornstarch. Pour this playfully over the surface of the hen when serving. (And perhaps keep a little set aside as edible body paint!)

Makes 2 servings

Fertility Dumplings

The hen is highly symbolic of fertility. Making these dumplings egg-shaped only emphasizes that value both visually and spiritually. The key is to focus on the part of your life to which you want to bring fertility as you shape these dumplings (so eating them will be like hatching the energy!).

Salt and pepper to taste
5- to 7-pound hen
3 cups chopped onions
1 ½ cups chopped carrots
1 ½ cups chopped celery
6 garlic cloves, peeled
3 bay leaves
4 sprigs of fresh thyme
2 cups flour
1 ¼ tablespoons baking powder
1 teaspoon salt
4 tablespoons solid vegetable shortening
½ cup milk
½ cup heavy cream
½ cup chopped green onions
2 tablespoons minced parsley

Preparations

On a piece of paper write the area of your life where you wish to direct this energy. Put the paper in a cup, under a bowl, or in something else that's "womb"-shaped, and leave it in a sunny window while you work saying:

> *Let the magic flow, and energy grow*
> *By my will, make ——————— fruitful*

Fill in the blank with the area of your life that's written on the piece of paper. Repeat this phrase throughout your cooking process. When you're done, remove the paper and burn it to send your wishes to the winds, and "heat up" the magic.

 Sprinkle salt and pepper inside and out all over the hen. Put it in a large stockpot with the onions, carrots, celery, garlic, bay leaves, and thyme. Add additional salt and pepper to taste. Cover with a gallon of water. Bring to a boil, then turn the heat down and simmer until the meat begins to come off the bones. During the boiling process remove excess fat that rises to the surface. Cool the stock, then strain it. Reserve the strained stock, hen, and one cup of the mixed, cooked vegetables and herbs.

Put the stock back in the pot and simmer. Meanwhile, remove the meat from the hen, discarding skin and bones. Tear the meat into small pieces and put them into the stock. Separately combine the flour, baking powder, oil, milk and salt along with one cup of the vegetables, mashed up completely. Stir. Dust the dough with a little flour so that it takes on a consistency that's easy to handle. Using a tablespoon, shape your dumpling eggs and drop them into the stock. Cook for about 15 minutes then add the cream, green onions, and parsley to the stock. Cook for an additional 15 minutes before serving.

Makes 5–6 servings

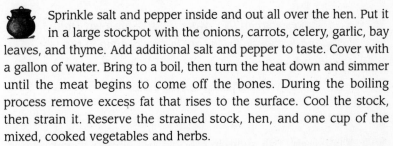

9

SOLITARY PATH SEAFOOD

Shakespearean fish swam the sea, far away from
land; romantic fish swam in nets coming to the
hand.

—WILLIAM BUTLER YEATS

While some fish swim in schools, not all neo-Pagans choose to participate in groups. Sometimes constrained by circumstances or location, other times simply more comfortable on their own, these people have to find a way to keep reaching for and defining the sacred without any guru or guide but their own inner voice. Fish is an ideal helpmate in this pursuit. Throughout the world fish was often regarded as a sacred food, as a good catch literally could mean the difference between life or death for entire villages. For our purposes here, the sustenance we seek is also food for the soul—something to inspire, motivate, and keep us walking the Path of Beauty with confidence.

Fish

*The laying of fish on the embers, the taste of the
fish, the feel of the texture of bread, the round and
the half-loaf, the grain of a petal . . . the rainbow
and the rain.*

—HILDA DOOLITTLE

As one might expect, a variety of deities have been associated with fish. Seafood was sacred and utilized in the rites for Atargatis, Ishtar, Isis, and Aphrodite. Often sacred fish were kept in special ponds at the temple so that none but the priests or priestesses could harvest them for rituals.

Hinduism tells us that Vishnu incarnated once as a fish to save humankind from the flood. Philistines worshipped Dagon, a sea god that was part man and part fish. Aphrodite took the form of a fish when fleeing Typhon, and Oannes (lord of the deep in Sumerian beliefs) wore a fishskin robe.

Babble Fish

This dish accents creative communications, especially with know-it-alls, wiseacres, gossips, conversation hogs, and people who are quick to jump into discussions just to hear themselves talk! The yellow parsnips, carrots, and pepper reflect the air element, which empowers our words.

2 medium carrots
2 medium parsnips
1 yellow pepper (large)
2 tablespoons butter
2 cups sliced cabbage
1 tablespoon white vinegar

¾ cup soy sauce
4 (4–5 ounce) fish fillets (your choice)
¾ pound sweet potato, peeled and cooked tender

Preparations

Grab a breath mint before working this spell. Since you're working on the best possible communications, doing so will emphasize your goal. Additionally, mint supports effective interactions.

Cut carrots, parsnips, and yellow pepper into thin strips. As you do, focus on anything that stands between you and speaking your mind. In a large frying pan (indoors or on the side burner of your grill), place the butter, carrots, parsnips and pepper, to fry. As the carrots and parsnips become tender, add the cabbage to the fray, along with the vinegar and soy sauce. Coat vegetables evenly (you want the magic to flow evenly into all the components) while saying:

> *Parsnips help my words to flower*
> *Carrots and cabbage add magical power*
> *And with my will, this sauce saturates*
> *Improve my words, and my fate!*

When the vegetables are close to being fully cooked, place the fish on a low-heat grill. Carve a symbol that represents your goal into the fillet using a knife (like the rune of communication). Brown the fish about 5 minutes on each side (adjusting for thickness). The potatoes and the root vegetables create the firm foundations for your spell. The profuseness of fish ensures that you'll never be at a loss for words! Eat slowly, letting the energy of each bite linger on your tongue.

Makes 4 servings

Consciousness Trout

In Yeats's poem (opposite) he speaks of "fire in the head," an old Irish term for inspiration and heightened awareness. Hazels are a magical tree found near wells of wisdom. The trout used here replaces the Salmon of Wisdom in other stories as the key to unlocking the subconscious and superconscious mind.

TROUT:
"THE SONG OF WANDERING AENGUS"

I went out to the hazelwood,
Because a fire was in my head,
Cut and peeled a hazel wand,
And hooked a berry to a thread;
And when white moths were on the wing,
And moth-like stars were flickering out,
I dropped the berry in a stream
And caught a little silver trout.

When I had laid it on the floor
And gone to blow the fire aflame,
Something rustled on the floor,
And someone called me by my name:
It had become a glimmering girl
With apple blossoms in her hair
Who called me by my name and ran
And vanished in the brightening air.

—WILLIAM BUTLER YEATS

FISH

2 cups pecans
1 cup all-purpose flour
2 (12- to 14-ounce) trout,
   filleted

Salt and pepper to taste
3 large egg whites, beaten
   to blend

SAUCE

1 ½ cups fresh orange juice
1 cup dry white wine
⅓ cup chopped onions
¼ cup chopped garlic
¼ cup wine or cider vinegar
1 ½ tablespoons fresh lemon
    juice

1 large fresh thyme sprig
2 fresh rosemary sprigs
¼ cup whipping cream
6 ounces (1 ½ sticks) butter,
    cut into 12 pieces
Salt and pepper to taste

GARNISH

4 tablespoons virgin olive oil
1 carrot, peeled, cut into
    matchstick-size strips
    (also good for "vision")
1 yellow bell pepper, thinly
    sliced (yellow is the color
    of psychism)

6 cups cabbage, thinly sliced
¼ stick unsalted butter
Chopped fresh chives or green
    onion

PREPARATIONS

The third eye (the area on your forehead between your eyes) is the chakra associated with spiritual awakening and awareness. Before making this dish, take a few minutes to meditate. Visualize a blue-white light swirling clockwise in the area of your third eye, opening like an iris. When it's about half open in your mind's eye, put your meal together, allowing the improved insights to guide your own bits of flair.

Place the pecans and 1 tablespoon of the flour into a food processor or blender and grind until very fine. Pour this onto a plate. Put the rest of the flour on a second plate. Season the fish with salt and pepper, followed by dipping it into the flour (shake off excess). Brush this with egg whites and then coat with pecans. Place the coated fish on a wax-paper-lined baking sheet. Chill.

For the sauce, combine first seven ingredients in a medium saucepan. Bring to a boil over medium heat and continue to boil for

10 minutes. Add rosemary and continue cooking until the liquid is reduced to ½ cup total. Strain the liquid into a clean saucepan, add the cream, and bring to a boil again. Immediately reduce the heat to low, whisk in the butter, and add salt and pepper.

Next, heat the olive oil in a dutch oven and toss in the carrots and peppers. Turn the heat to high, add the cabbage and stir until all the vegetables are wilted. Season and set aside while you fry the trout. Melt 1 stick of butter in a frying pan and fry the fillets until golden brown (about 2 minutes per side). Continue turning until fish is opaque (about 8 minutes total). Serve with warm sauce and vegetables for garnish. Sprinkle chives and green onions over the top of everything.

Makes 4 servings (one fillet each)

Salmon Savvy

In the days before Saint Patrick and Christianity, the five provinces of Ireland enjoyed peace and regular exchanges of scholarship and learning. The Druids and poets led the way. Among these leaders was Finneigeas, a man who grew up on the river Boyne watching for the Salmon of Knowledge, a fish that would grant the person who gathered it the most wisdom in Ireland. Thankfully we can simply go to the supermarket to gather our salmon, and then bless it with magic to gain wisdom and knowledge.

½ cup sweet rice wine (mirin)
2 tablespoons soy sauce
¼ cup rice vinegar

1 tablespoon finely grated peeled fresh ginger
4 (6-ounce) pieces salmon fillet

Sauce

2 tablespoons soy sauce
¼ cup honey
1 tablespoon fresh lime juice

2 teaspoons wasabi powder
1 tablespoon water
Lime wedges for garnish

PREPARATIONS

Take the salmon fillets and put your hands palm down over them to bless them saying something like:

> By the heart and oven's glow
> Let me learn what I need to know
> A wise eye, true words, and keen mind
> In this dish let magic shine

You can repeat this incantation anytime during the preparation process as you feel inspired.

Stir together mirin, soy sauce, vinegar, and ginger. Put these in a dish with the fish, skin-side up. Marinate at room temperature for 15 minutes. Preheat your broiler while making the sauce.

Put the soy sauce, honey, and lime in a saucepan over a medium flame. Bring to a boil, stirring regularly, until thickened (4 to 5 minutes). In another small bowl mix the wasabi and water.

Oil the broiler pan, placing it about 5 inches from the heat. Broil the fish skin-side down until translucent, about 5 to 6 minutes. Serve the fillets with the sauce on the side for dipping. Garnish with lime wedges.

Makes 4 servings

Good Luck Haddock

The Scottish regard haddock as very fortunate fish. They think that this was the fish chosen by deity to feed many people in the story of the loaves and fishes. Specifically the black spots around the gills are where they believe Christ held the fish as he gave them to the people. To this foundation we add oranges and cheese that more specifically can encourage luck with love.

Fish Tails

In Gaul water spirits were known as *peisgi*, which is potentially derived from the Latin *piscos*, or fish. So it's not surprising to discover that many of the myths of water spirits include discussions of a variety of fish forms, with an equal variety of powers—including that of becoming invisible. Because of these stories and ideas many Highland wells that held fish were regarded as so sacred that no one was to try to catch the creatures. In fact, to this day two wells still exist in Nant Peris where the local people replace any fish that dies with a new one, to always keep the well filled. The deceased fish, by the way, are buried with proper ceremonial form.

An Irish myth, as mentioned elsewhere in this chapter, speaks of the Salmon of Knowledge, which gain their powers by eating hazelnuts as they fall from trees into the water. The sea god Manannan appears to the hero Cormac and tells him the fish he's seen in his vision live in a promised land where the water heals the mortally wounded. Should any human eat of those fish, it would make him the wisest of all.

Interestingly enough we see this symbol emerge in Christianity in talking about the disciples being fishers of men. Fish were used to feed the masses, and it was the fish that became an icon of the resurrection. This of course is how the pre-Christian holy wells found their way into church myths—by having the persona of Christ transform instead of a fish spirit. Additionally—to pull the iconology all together—there was a much earlier association between salmon and rebirth, thanks to soul transference.

3 large oranges

3 tablespoons olive oil

3 cups thinly sliced red onions

3 garlic cloves, thinly sliced

1 (14½-ounce) can diced
tomatoes in juice

1 cup dry white wine

⅓ cup sliced pitted black
olives

6 (5-ounce) haddock fillets

3 ounces drained feta or goat
cheese, thinly sliced

3 tablespoons chopped fresh
chives

PREPARATIONS

Wear an outfit that includes something in your lucky color. Gather together your ingredients and energize them with an incantation, like:

> *In oranges fine, providence shines*
> *In fish and chives, fortune's alive*
> *By my will and this rhyme, good luck is mine!*

 Peel the oranges, focusing on peeling away anything that stands between you and good fortune. Also get as much pith off as you can. Segment.

In a large skillet heat the oil to medium. Add the onions and garlic and sauté until browned. Add the tomatoes and wine, and bring the mixture to a boil. Reduce to a low heat and simmer for 5 minutes. Stir in the orange segments and the olives, laying the fish over the top. Cover and continue to simmer for about 15 minutes until the fish is translucent. Serve the vegetables and fish garnished with the sliced cheese and chives.

Makes 6 servings

Stability Halibut

In the Pacific Northwest, the halibut is regarded as the symbol for a spirit who has undergone unusually great changes, and as a result has become very strong and stable. Such spirits, and the people who possess them, are also fervent protectors of life and its sacredness. The dark green beans in this dish allow that energy to grow, and the lemon juice provides clarity so we can apply that energy in the best possible places.

1 pound green or wax beans	½ cup (1 stick) unsalted butter
4 (7-ounce) halibut fillets	5 scallions, white part only,
Kosher salt and freshly ground	finely sliced
white pepper to taste	1 tablespoon capers, drained
2 tablespoons oil	and rinsed
¼ cup dry white wine	1 large, ripe tomato, peeled,
2 tablespoons fresh lemon	seeded, and diced
juice	

Note: If you'd like to use your verbal or written communication abilities to safeguard something you hold sacred, use yellow beans in this dish. If you're interested in generating community-oriented energy, use fresh snow peas in the pod instead of beans.

Place a pot of salted water over high heat and bring to a boil. Put in the beans you've chosen to "heat up" the energy. Cook until tender, drain, and set aside, keeping them warm.

Next, season the halibut on both sides with salt and pepper. Prepare a large sauté pan with oil over medium-high heat. Season the halibut on both sides with salt and pepper. Cook the fish until gently browned, and for an additional 4 minutes on each side after that. Remove from heat and keep warm while preparing the sauce. Pour off the remaining oil in the frying pan, then put the wine and lemon juice into it. Scrape up any little bits of fish and seasoning left in the pan and stir into the liquids. Reduce the sauce by half, then turn down the heat to whisk in the butter. While it cooks try adding a little verbal component:

> *Stability grow where it belongs*
> *Deep inside, I'm constant and strong*
> *And as this dish cooks to perfection*
> *Let magic be on the menu's selection*

Add the scallions, capers, and tomato. Season with salt and pepper, pour over the fish. Serve immediately with the beans.

Makes 4 servings

Holy Mackerel

Mackerel was a sacred and ancient Christian totem, probably evolving from its earlier symbolic representation of fertility and continuity. A "mackerel sea" denotes the presence of stormy ripples caused by large schools of this fish in the water, and a mackerel sea is considered a positive omen for a good catch. Mackerel are superb swimmers, symbolically giving this dish the ability to help you navigate your spiritual path with power and confidence.

6 large whole mackerel (ask to have it gutted and the backbone removed)

¼ cup olive oil

4 white onions (white is for Spirit), grated fine

1 cup pine nuts

⅓ cup ground walnuts

2 cups black currants

2 teaspoons fresh ground black pepper

½ teaspoon cinnamon

½ teaspoon allspice

½ teaspoon cumin

1 bunch parsley

1 bunch dill

Kosher or fresh ground salt

½ cup flour

4 eggs, blended together in a flat bowl

3 cups bread crumbs

1¼ cups olive oil

PREPARATIONS

If possible have a bowl of seawater at hand. If not salt a little water from your tap. This is about to become representative of living waters. Breathe upon the surface of the water (to give it life, and ripple the surface as the mackerel do when they swim). Whisper your prayer to the water for guidance and surety. Dab some of the water on your heart chakra, and pour the rest onto the earth to carry those prayers on the water droplets throughout the world.

Carefully squeeze the fish to remove the skin from the meat without tearing it, since the skin will be stuffed in this recipe. Doing this will also give you the chance to remove any small bones missed earlier. Chop the mackerel meat and set it aside.

Put the olive oil in a large frying pan, add the onions and sauté until golden brown. Add pine nuts, walnuts, currants, and all the spices. Cook for 5 minutes, stirring regularly. Chop the parsley and dill (reserving a few sprigs of each for decorative garnish), and stir the chopped herbs into the onion mixture. Stuff this filling into the fish skins. Salt and flour the stuffed skins and roll them in egg, then in bread crumbs. Turn these back into the frying pan (adding more olive oil as needed) and fry on both sides. Arrange on a platter, and garnish with the reserved green sprigs to encourage spiritual growth.

Makes 6 servings (one fish each)

Bass of Honor

At Chinese New Year a bass might be served whole, signifying prosperity, and it would be placed on the table pointing to the guest of honor.

1½ cups finely chopped green tomatoes

1½ cups finely chopped red watermelon

⅔ cup minced red onion

1 (3-inch) fresh red or green chili pepper minced (including seeds)

¼ cup chopped fresh cilantro

1 teaspoon fresh lime juice

¾ teaspoon salt

6 (6-ounce) center-cut pieces striped bass fillet with skin

1½ tablespoons olive oil

Salt to taste

PREPARATIONS

To what area of your life do you want to bring honor? Bring an emblem of that into your sacred space (for example, if you're a painter bring your favorite brush so it will be saturated with the energies you're about to create). Leave it in a spot where you can see it easily to direct the power into that item.

 Heat the broiler on high for 10 minutes and then turn it down to a moderately high heat. Mix together tomatoes, watermelon, onion, chili, cilantro, lime juice, and salt. Use as salsa.

Pat the fish dry, then brush it with the oil and season it with salt. Broil the fish, starting with skin sides down, on a lightly oiled rack. Turn once until just cooked through (about 8 minutes). Serve topped with the salsa and perhaps a side of rice.

Makes 6 servings

Victorious Sole

One Welsh legend tells us that the leek is linked to Saint David because he ordered his soldiers to wear this vegetable on their helmets for victory, after they had fought a victorious battle against the Saxons in a field full of leeks.

½ pound sea scallops
1 large leek (white part only)
2 tablespoons drained and
    minced bottled pimiento
1 large egg white, beaten
    lightly

1 teaspoon salt
½ teaspoon white pepper
¼ teaspoon garlic
4 (½-pound) sole fillets

Preparations

Since we think of blue ribbons in connection with success and victory, bring a blue candle into your sacred space and carve it with one word representing the area of your life where you wish to bring victory. Focus on that and chant something like this while you carve:

> *By my will and magic's decree*
> *This meal will bring me victory!*

Light the candle and then go about making the dish.

Place all the ingredients except the fillets in a food processor or blender. Puree completely, and let this mixture sit overnight in the refrigerator, covered, to improve flavor. If you do not have enough time, chill it for a minimum of 1 hour.

Place the sole fillets between two sheets of waxed paper and flatten them (using a meat pounder or rolling pin) until they're about ⅛-inch thick. Cut each fillet into three pieces. Spread a heaping tablespoonful of the scallop mixture evenly on each piece. Roll these up and wrap them in plastic food wrap.

Pat the rolls in a steamer and allow them to cook in full steam for about 4 to 5 minutes. Chill for 2 hours. Peel off the plastic, then cut each roll crosswise into 1-inch pieces. Arrange in an eye-pleasing way on a platter. Makes a nice appetizer or side dish.

Makes about 4 pieces

Friendship Cod (for Male Companionship)

Cod was the most popular fish in Portugal for a long time where over 1,000 recipes existed for any day of the week—anytime of the year. History tells us that the fishermen of this region went to the northern waters for cod, which became such a dependable food source that they called the fish "the true friend." The asparagus in this recipe gives it a strong masculine overtone. So, make this dish to find a dependable, long-term male friend, or when wishing to improve your relationship with an existing male friend.

2 pounds baby asparagus, trimmed	6 (6-ounce) cod fillets
6 tablespoons unsalted butter	2 teaspoons fennel seeds, chopped

PREPARATIONS

If doing this for an existing friend it's more fun and functional to prepare the meal together. Take a moment's pause before cooking to share with each other all the things that have made you better friends

Adore Asparagus?

Asparagus probably originated in Greece or Turkey. Egyptians regarded it as food for the gods, while the Arabs and Romans believed this vegetable had powerful aphrodisiac qualities. Apicius, first-century Roman epicure, gave directions for releasing those qualities through cooking. His instructions were to fry asparagus in lard and add egg yolk/hot pepper.

Galen, a second-century Greek physician, claimed asparagus had medicinal properties, some of which modern medicine has corroborated. Pliny the Elder (Rome—first century), called asparagus "prodigia ventras," meaning good for digestion. It was a highly prized vegetable in Rome, Greece, and Egypt, looked upon as a delicacy, fit for the gods.

over time, and those things you hope will continue to grow in the future.

If making this to find a friend, try not to put any faces or names to your desire, simply focus on the goal of friendship while you cook, and allow that energy to be internalized when you consume the dish. (In this way you will carry the energy with you into social situations where you might meet the person you seek!)

Cut asparagus tips into 2-inch-long pieces, and peel the remaining stalks. Cut those into 1-inch strips, cooking them in a pan of salted water until tender. Transfer the cooked stalks into a blender, adding 2 tablespoons of the butter and just enough of the cooking water to make a smooth sauce. Transfer the sauce into a medium saucepan and simmer.

Boil the tips in salted water for 4 minutes, just until crisp-tender. Drain and set aside. Melt the remaining butter in a large frying pan and sauté the fish until golden brown on both sides (about 8 to 10 minutes total). Pour sauce on each plate, top with the fish, then garnish with the asparagus tips and a sprinkling of fennel.

Makes 6 servings

Friendship Mussels (for Female Companionship)

Mussels are strongly symbolic of the feminine, and they are also representative of the mouth (for communication). In the language of dreams, mussels are said to imply increasing social contact that will lead to happiness.

½ cup heavy cream

1 tablespoon buttermilk

2 large egg yolks

1½ tablespoons butter

2 large shallots, finely chopped

1 tablespoonful garlic (optional)

3 tablespoons brandy

3 tablespoons fresh lemon juice

1 generous pinch of saffron threads

40 mussels, scrubbed and debearded

Salt and pepper to taste

1 cup dry white wine

Fresh chives

PREPARATIONS

See the preparations for the Friendship Cod, immediately preceding this recipe.

 Combine the heavy cream with the buttermilk and let stand at room temperature until slightly thickened. Beat this mixture with the egg yolks, blending thoroughly.

In a skillet, melt the butter and sauté the shallots and garlic until tender. Remove from the heat and add the brandy. Carefully ignite, and then let the fire burn itself out. Whisk in the lemon juice and saffron. Set this aside.

Life Gives You Lemons

- Lemons came to Europe from India some 8,000 years ago, brought back by Crusaders, and Columbus transported them to the New World.
- The best lemons are those with a thick peel and heaviness in relation to their size.
- An average lemon provides about 3 tablespoons of juice and 1 tablespoon of peel.
- To release the juice from a lemon more readily, let it warm up first. Then roll it on a counter to loosen the rind.
- If you don't have zest for a recipe, you can substitute two tablespoons of juice for one teaspoon fresh rind, or one teaspoon dried rind.
- Have a nasty, stubborn odor? Try rubbing the area with freshly cut lemon.
- A bit of lemon juice sprinkled on freshly cut potatoes or apples keeps them from turning brown.

Cook the mussels in a large pot of boiling water until they open (symbolically this opens the way for friendship and good feelings). Do not eat any that don't open (they're probably bad). Take the top shell off the mussels and put the bottom shell with the meat in a large bowl. Cover while making your sauce.

Strain about three cups of cooking liquid from the mussels and pour it into the pan with the shallots, wine, and garlic. Bring to a boil over a medium heat until it reduces by one-third. Beat the cream mixture into this liquid very slowly. Cook to a personally pleasing thickness, season with salt and pepper, then serve poured over the mussels topped with chives.

Makes about 4 servings

Shellfish

*Tis the voice of the lobster; I heard him declare, you
have baked me too brown, I must sugar my hair.*

—Lewis Carroll

Shellfish plays a role in a wide variety of mythologies. Looking at the crab as an example, Sumerians associated both it and lobster with Nina, the goddess of the waters. Incas considered crab an aspect of the Great Mother, and it's also a totem for Melanesian clans. The Greeks tell us lobster was sacred to Perseus.

Overall shellfish have protective symbolism (most often because of their outer shell), and they may also represent fertility and passion.

"Hang in There" Crab Cakes

The crab is a symbol of great strength and power in gripping and holding. It can be found on the coats of arms of several noble families, implying both power and unity. In this recipe, we apply the symbolic value for those times when you need to hold on tight to get through a difficult situation.

½ cup minced blackened red
  bell pepper
1 teaspoon vegetable oil
⅓ cup salad dressing
  (mayonnaise)
1 large egg
1½ tablespoons coarse mustard
2 teaspoons lemon juice
¾ teaspoon dried tarragon,
  crumbled

½ teaspoon minced garlic
Splash Worcestershire sauce
  (optional)
Salt and pepper to taste
1½ cups Italian-style bread
  crumbs
1 pound flaked crabmeat
Butter and olive oil for frying

Don't Be Such a Crab

In global Shamanic traditions, crabs are important because they move on both land and water, and thus, like the frog, sometimes ended up being used in medicine rites. Most often the crab is considered female, however, where the frog is considered male. Among the Maori people crabs are connected with solar eclipses.

And what of those born under the sign of the Crab (June 21–July 23)? Cancers are not very direct (notice how crabs scuttle sideways). They prefer to go around the wall instead of over it. Crabs are also homebodies, and if they can't be at home, they take things along that will always make them feel comfortable, much as a crab carries its shell.

PREPARATIONS

Keep one crab claw with which to create a tenacity charm. You'll want to clean this out completely with salted water to get rid of any fishy smell. Place an image of the area of your life where you want to apply this energy into the crab's claw (so it holds on!). If you can't find a token, write it on paper instead. As you place either into the claw add an incantation, like:

> Hold on tight
> Stay true and sure
> In this claw, magic secure!

Hang the charm somewhere in your kitchen while you cook, and consider carrying it into the situation where you need the extra strength.

The beauty of crab cakes is that they go together quickly (very handy when you need fast results!). Whisk together all your ingredients, except crab and frying oils, testing for flavor. Add salt and pepper. Gently fold in crabmeat, then cover and chill at least 1 hour. Fashion into patties (not too big—or they'll tend to fall apart, which would not help your symbolism!). Fry lightly in a half-and-half combination of butter and olive oil. Serve hot with hot mustard, a butter drizzle, or another favorite fish garnish.

Makes about 6 servings

Cultivation Oysters

Oysters represent an internal process, a time when we look within and cultivate our inner treasures so that we can grow and change. To that symbolism we bring the number twelve for completion, spinach for a strong will, and fennel to keep you safe until the transformation is complete.

½ cup thinly sliced onions
1 cup finely chopped fennel bulb
3 tablespoons butter
3 tablespoons vegetable oil
Kosher salt for seasoning and to taste

1 pound fresh spinach, washed
1 teaspoon fennel seeds
Pepper to taste
12 oysters, shucked (retain the bottom shells)

PREPARATIONS

Change is something that takes time, especially when dealing with the inner self. To help with the process, for the entire week before making this dish meditate for at least 5 minutes daily preferably when you first get up. Focus on the type of change you want to make. Think of this time like a spiritual daily vitamin to set a specific tone in your aura that helps with manifestation.

Preheat oven to 400 degrees F. Gently fry the onions and fennel bulb in 1 tablespoon of the butter and the oil until tender and brown. Sprinkle with a bit of salt and set aside. Next, boil the spinach with the fennel seeds until tender. Drain and press out any excess liquid. Puree the spinach with the remaining butter and season to a personally pleasing level with salt and pepper (I also like a bit of garlic). Mix into the puree.

Arrange the oysters in a symbolic manner if you wish over a base of salt. Pour the puree evenly over top and bake for about 13 minutes.

Makes 1–2 servings

Don't Clam Up!

In the language of dreams, clams speak of withdrawal or withholding. However, since we're going to open up these clam shells—you can likewise open yourself and liberate your words!

5 tablespoons rice vinegar	½ fresh jalapeño, minced
2 tablespoons peanut oil	¼ teaspoon salt
2 teaspoons sesame oil	⅛ teaspoon ground cumin
½ teaspoon peeled and finely grated fresh ginger	2½ pounds small littleneck clams
1 small white onion, thinly sliced	1 to 2 cups coarse salt

Preparations

Make yourself a cup of mint tea before you begin this recipe. Stir it clockwise and say in a loud, confident voice:

> *I will not swallow my words*
> *I will be heard!*

Also if it's a nice day—open a window in your cooking area. Communication is associated with the air element.

Preheat oven to 400 degrees F. Whisk together all the ingredients to make a sauce, except for the clams and salt. Open the clams (thinking of likewise opening your mouth), and reserve the juices and lower shell. Put the salt in a large baking dish, and arrange securely in it the bottom shells of the clams. Fill each shell with a clam and an equal portion of the juices. Bake the clams until the clam juice is boiling. Continue baking for another 4 minutes then serve with the sauce liberally available. Alternatively you can broil the clams about 5 inches away from the heat for about 2 minutes, until cooked through.

Makes 3–4 servings

Salt of the Sea Chowder

This is an all-time favorite at our house. In sea terms an "old salt" is someone who really knows his way around both boats and open waters. The abundant mix of seafood in this dish is ideal for helping you navigate your own turbulent seas and turn toward clear sailing.

1 clove elephant ear garlic, diced
1 teaspoon crushed garlic
1 teaspoon fresh basil
1 teaspoon thyme
1 bay leaf
Pinch of oregano
Salt and pepper to taste
1 tablespoon butter
1 tablespoon olive oil
2 stalks of celery
2 large carrots
½ red onion
1 cup shredded crabmeat
1 cup diced clams
1 cup shredded lobster meat
1 cup shredded whitefish fillet
½ pound shrimp, peeled and diced
2 potatoes, diced
½ cup cooked bacon, crumbled
8 cups chicken stock
2 cups heavy cream

PREPARATIONS

To get in the right frame of mind, think nautical! Get a toy sailboat (perhaps a children's bath toy) and sail it in your pantry sink. Put a symbol of your goal on the boat's sails or side and add a verbal component, such as:

Release the magic, bring good winds to the sails!
Meet this goal without fail!

 Lightly sauté garlic, basil, thyme, bay leaf, oregano, and salt and pepper in butter and olive oil. Meanwhile use a food processor to puree the celery, carrots, and red onion. Add the puree to the herb blend (adding more butter if needed). Cook until the puréed vegetables are tender and lightly browned.

Next, transfer the herbs to a stockpot. Add the seafood, potatoes, bacon, and stock. Cook over medium heat until it reduces by about 2 cups and the potatoes are tender. Add the heavy cream (to personal taste). Cook down again until the chowder reaches desired thickness. Test for seasoning and adjust if necessary. Serve with a pat of butter on top and garlic breadsticks.

Makes 8 ½-cup servings

GOOD VIBRATION: VEGETABLES, SALADS, AND SIDES

Do not dismiss the dish saying that it is just simply food. The blessed thing is an entire civilization in itself.

—ABDULHAK SINASI

Vegetarian fare is certainly not new. Historians have found evidence of vegetarian ideals in Egypt around 3200 B.C.E. In Hinduism meat was being eliminated from diets from the Vedic period onward. By 1000 B.C.E. the killing of cows was forbidden. Many Buddhists and Jains also practiced some form of vegetarian regime.

Greek philosopher and mathematician Pythagoras encouraged vegetarianism. Other notable figures from the region agreed with him, including Socrates, Plato, and Aristotle. What these ancients didn't quite realize was how longlasting their writings and ideas

Vegetable Visions

- Radishes have the rather unlikely name of "winter rose" in the French language. The word *radish* means "easily grown" as it is a very hearty vegetable, and grows rapidly. Egyptians grew radishes as part of the pyramid workers' diets to keep them healthy and strong.
- Napoleon was a spinach lover
- Lettuce has been grown by humans for about 2,500 years. Two famous early fans of this green were Aristotle and later Columbus, who brought lettuce seeds with him to the New World.
- The word *broccoli* comes from a Latin term meaning "strong branch." To the Romans broccoli was known as the five fingers of Jupiter.
- When carrots were first introduced to Europe, they weren't eaten. Rather English women wore the carrot tops in their hair.
- The word for cabbage comes from an old French term meaning "big head." Humans have grown cabbage for 4,000 years.
- Corn is one of the most important plants to the United States, where it is used in over 500 products, at least one of which is disposable diapers!
- Rhubarb is sometimes called the "pie plant" because it's almost always served in a pie. It originated in Siberia, coming to North America around the late 1700s.

would become. During the Middle Ages, for example, we find Saint Francis of Assisi focused on animal rights issues. During the 1700s great writers like Alexander Pope and philosophers like Voltaire advanced similar philosophies. And modern-day bookshelves include books wholly dedicated to a vegetarian lifestyle.

With more spiritually minded folk turning to this lifestyle partially or wholly, it's my hope that this chapter will help complete your magical menus. I am not a vegetarian, nor is every recipe in this chapter strictly vegetarian. You can, however, pretty easily eliminate any meat element(s) from the recipes here without harm to the overall dish.

Vegetables

Then a sentimental passion of a vegetable fashion
Must excite your languid spleen,
An attachment à la Plato for a bashful young potato,
Or a not-too-French French bean!

—Sir William Schwenck Gilbert

The word *vegetable* comes from a Latin term meaning to animate, be full of life, or invigorate, which may have had to do with animistic ideas about the spirits in plants. Now since we have an entire vegetable kingdom, the term has slowly transformed from signifying anything in that realm to meaning only edible items.

Camouflage Corn

Corn was the cornerstone of many Western cultures—so much so that the Encyclopedia Britannica *describes it as the "grain that built a hemisphere." Typically the symbolic value of corn is that of sustenance, but corn spirits were also protectors of tribes and villages. In this recipe the hot spices sustain that protective energy, especially when you're having troubled times.*

6 ears fresh sweet corn, in the husk	⅓ cup crumbled Mexican blend cheese
3 tablespoons unsalted butter, melted	1 tablespoon powdered chili (spice to your taste)
½ cup sour cream	

Preparations

Since the entire purpose behind this recipe is to reinforce your magical wards, take the time to create a semiformal sacred space around your grill. You can do this using the ideas in chapter 2, or by applying your own path's invocations.

About an hour before serving, place the ears of corn in a deep bowl, cover with cold water and weight with a plate to keep them submerged. Light a charcoal fire and let it burn until the bed of coals is medium-hot; adjust the grill 4 inches above the fire. Lay the corn (husks on) on the grill and roast for 15 to 20 minutes, turning frequently, until the outer leaves are blackened. Remove, let cool several minutes, then remove the husks and silk. About 10 minutes before serving brush the corn with melted butter, return to the grill and turn frequently until nicely browned. Serve right away, passing the cream, cheese, and powdered chili for garnish.

Makes 6 servings

Asparagus Aphrodisiac

Asparagus has been considered an aphrodisiac since Roman times. The garlic improves blood circulation and genital blood flow, and orange supports your mood with love.

Simply Asparagus

- Asparagus is actually a member of the lily family.
- In perfect growing conditions this vegetable has been known to grow as much as ten inches in one day.
- After sowing asparagus it's best to wait three years to begin harvesting it, to enable it to first develop a strong root system. However after the first harvest and if the plant is properly cared for it will continue to yield for fifteen years.

1 pound fresh asparagus ends,
     trimmed
1 tablespoon butter
1 tablespoon olive oil

1 tablespoon garlic
2 tablespoons orange zest
Mixed Italian cheeses for
     garnish

PREPARATIONS

Gather your ingredients together and bless them saying:

> *Asparagus bring passion and zest*
> *Orange yields to love's behest*
> *Garlic for fire and energy*
> *By my will, this spell is freed!*

You can use this incantation any time you feel like it throughout the cooking process.

Place the asparagus in a large frying pan with about ½ cup of water. Bring the water up to steaming and cover, cooking until the asparagus just begins to get tender. Drain off the water. Add the butter, oil, garlic, and orange zest, frying everything together until the asparagus is gently browned on two sides and fully cooked. Serve with a sprinkling of cheese shaped like a heart.

Makes 4 servings

Stable Potatoes

Before the discovery of the potato, parsnips were a staple in European diets. Additionally, both potatoes and parsnips, being root vegetables, offer tremendous grounding energy to this dish.

2 pounds parsnips, peeled and
     cut into 1-inch pieces
2 pounds russet (baking)
     potatoes, peeled and cut
     into 2-inch pieces
1 tablespoon plus ½ teaspoon
     salt

1 cup heavy cream
¼ cup (½ stick) unsalted butter
¼ teaspoon black pepper
Pinch of sugar

The Potato Patch

Although Spanish conquistadors didn't find the gold and silver for which they were looking in Mexico, they did learn of potatoes there in the mid-1500s. It wasn't long afterwards that potatoes were transported by ships as a durable food. Interestingly enough, sailors who ate them did not get scurvy.

It was likely closer to 1600 when the first potatoes started being grown in Europe. For a while people feared them because the potato is a member of the nightshade family (which has some very poisonous family members). Francis Drake also came home from the West Indies with a crop of potatoes that he gifted to Sir Walter Raleigh to cultivate on his lands, including those in Virginia.

Preparations

Peel off one of the potato's eyes and take it outside. Push it into the soil, saying:

> *In this potato magic's bound,*
> *Help me keep both feet on the ground!*

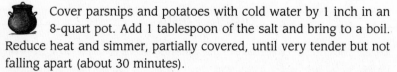 Cover parsnips and potatoes with cold water by 1 inch in an 8-quart pot. Add 1 tablespoon of the salt and bring to a boil. Reduce heat and simmer, partially covered, until very tender but not falling apart (about 30 minutes).

While that's cooking, simmer cream, butter, pepper, and remaining ½ teaspoon of the salt over moderate heat. Drain the vegetables completely and put them through a food processor or blender to cream them, adding the liquid and sugar you've had simmering on the stove. Serve hot.

OPTION

For those who enjoy a chunkier soup, cut the parsnips and potatoes into cubes before cooking, and then add them to the cream mixture instead of blending all the ingredients together.

Makes 6–8 servings

Lunar Lucky Onions

Cooked or raw, onions have long been considered good luck. Simply dreaming about them is said to bring good fortune. In the Middle Ages in Europe, it was a good luck charm to carry an onion in one's pocket, especially in the left pocket. I cannot help but wonder if this occurred due to the onion being linked with the moon and intuitive thinking.

By the way, you can easily adapt this recipe to suit vegetarian guests— simply eliminate the bacon (use olive oil instead of bacon fat for sautéing the vegetables) and substitute vegetable stock for the turkey stock.

3 pounds mixed large onions (if they add up to a lucky number, all the better)

1 pound sliced bacon, cut into 1-inch-wide pieces

3 celery ribs, cut into ½-inch-thick slices

1 teaspoon salt

1 teaspoon black pepper

3 garlic cloves, minced

1 pound baby spinach, trimmed and coarsely chopped

1¼ pound rye or wheat bread cut into ½-inch cubes, lightly toasted

2 cups salted roasted cashews, coarsely chopped

½ cup (1 stick) unsalted butter, melted

1¼ cups turkey or vegetable stock

PREPARATIONS

It's said if you wish to change your luck, turn a silver coin in the light of a full moon. With that in mind, why not wait for a full moon to prepare this dish, and turn the onions in its light. Turn them clockwise to keep good luck moving forward, or counterclockwise to negate bad luck; then make your meal!

Slice off ½ inch from the tops of all the onions, and trim just a bit from the bottom so they stand without falling over. Remove all but about three layers from the middle of each onion (a melon baller or small ice cream scoop works well for this). Reserve the onion.

Chop up enough of what you removed so that it measures 3 cups. Meanwhile cook the bacon until crisp and drain (reserve about ⅓ cup of fat for frying). Sauté the onion, celery, salt, pepper, and garlic, stirring regularly, until the vegetables soften. Put them into a bowl and toss with the spinach, bread, cashews, butter, and stock. Add cooked bacon. Cool.

Preheat oven to 425 degrees F. Arrange onion shells, open sides up, in a 13-by-9-by-2-inch baking pan, then add ½ cup water and cover the pan tightly with foil. Roast the onions in the middle of the oven until tender but not falling apart, 25 to 30 minutes. Remove them from the oven long enough to stuff the centers, reducing the oven temperature to 350 degrees F. If you have too much stuffing, the remainder can be baked in another dish. Bake for about 20–25 minutes more until spinach is limp. If you wish, you can garnish these with melted cheese (white cheese would maintain the lunar symbolism).

Makes 6 servings

Healthy Broccoli

Historically we really don't see much about this edible until the mid-1500s. It was still so little known as to be called sprout cauliflower or Italian asparagus in the early 1700s. More modernly, it's funny that people often joke about mothers saying "eat your broccoli." Apparently, however, recent advances in science show that broccoli is not only highly nutritious—it helps promote healing! So that's the energy this comforting soup is intended to create.

8 cups broccoli florets	3 tablespoons unsalted butter
2 cups chicken broth	Salt to taste
1 cup heavy cream	Ground white pepper to taste

Preparations

This is a very simple and nourishing dish to make even when you're feeling a little under the weather. Take the time before you begin to pamper yourself in small, meaningful ways—like taking a vitamin or drinking a full glass of juice to bolster energy levels.

Cook broccoli in large pot of boiling salted water until tender but still bright green, about 5 minutes. Drain. Combine broth and cream in heavy large saucepan and bring to boil. Carefully pour the hot mixture into a food processor or blender, add the broccoli, and puree. Return the mixture to the saucepan and season to taste with salt and white pepper. Drizzle with cream and an extra pat of butter.

Makes 8 one-cup servings

Strong-Hearted Pie

Besides the symbolism of strength, dream lore tells us that spinach represents the heart chakra. Since this dish is a circle, it's a great way to protect your emotions and stay true to your values.

1½ cups finely chopped onion	1½ cups chopped tomatoes
½ cup olive oil	3 teaspoons dried dill
1 pound frozen chopped spinach, well-drained	1 teaspoon garlic powder
2 cups grated feta cheese	10 pre-made phyllo cups

PREPARATIONS

Cut out a heart from a piece of paper. Fold it in on itself (as if closing it) while saying:

> Protect my heart; the magic starts
> To my emotions, strength impart

Put this in a food saver bag or some other place where it can be kept safe (even as you wish to keep your heart safe).

Preheat oven to 375 degrees F. Sauté the onion in ¼ cup of the oil over medium-low heat, stirring occasionally, until it is golden. Add the spinach, and cook the mixture, stirring, until well blended. Remove the skillet from the heat, stirring in the feta, tomatoes, dill, and garlic. Let this filling cool.

Meanwhile brush each phyllo cup with a bit of the remaining olive oil. Fill each one with a healthy portion of the spinach filling. Bake for about 25 minutes until golden brown.

Makes 10 servings

One Tough "Hill of Beans"

Beans were found in Anasazi ruins in the Southwest. Since these people disappeared a long time ago, the beans were very ancient indeed. In other words, beans are very tough and difficult to "kill." In fact, the beans found in the ruins actually germinated after centuries of storage. We'll be trusting in the durability of the beans for those times when you need to tough it out!

5 plum tomatoes, each cut
   into 4 slices
Salt and pepper
¼ pound French green beans
   (Note that you can use
   yellow beans if the color is
   better for its symbolic
   value.)

1 tablespoon balsamic vinegar
1 tablespoon olive oil
1 tablespoon brown sugar
1 teaspoon dried basil
½ teaspoon lemon zest
½ teaspoon Dijon mustard
1 teaspoon minced garlic
1 cup mixed baby salad greens

PREPARATIONS

Choose a stone that represents the area of your life where you need the energy of this dish applied. Carry it in your pocket (close to your center of gravity) while you're making the beans. Also hold it in your hand while you're consuming the meal. This will charge the crystal and make it into an effective charm to keep with you.

Season the tomatoes with a bit of salt and pepper then roast them for fifteen minutes at 450 degrees F. Cool. While they are roasting, boil the beans for about 3 minutes, until just crisp tender. Drain and cool. Whisk together the rest of the ingredients (except the greens) to make a vinaigrette. Place a mound of salad on each plate with a tomato and layer of beans on top. Drizzle with the vinaigrette, moving clockwise to engender positive energy.

Makes about 4 servings as a side dish

Salad and Salad Dressing

*To make a good salad is to be a brilliant
diplomatist—the problem is entirely the same in
both cases. To know exactly how much oil one must
put with one's vinegar.*

—OSCAR WILDE

Salad comes from a Latin term that means "salted," and which pertained to vegetables that were traditionally blended with salt, oil, and vinegar. By the Middle Ages salads were composed mostly of leafy vegetables and flowers, the exception being in England where fruits were also included. By the late 1600s and 1700s, however, salad (and dressings) closer to those we currently enjoy had become an art form.

And of course what would salad be without dressings and sauces? Soy sauce has been used to dress greens in China for 5,000 years, and Babylonians used vinaigrettes nearly 2,000 years ago. Even our Worcestershire sauce comes from a blend used since the days of the Caesars. The key difference is what each culture paired with what items. Romans liked simple salted salads; Egyptians liked vinegar, oil, and spices; and Mary, Queen of Scots, preferred a creamy mustard dressing for her celeryroot and lettuce concoctions.

A Side Salad

Caesar salad actually has nothing to do with the Roman emperor. Instead it honors restaurateur Caesar Cardini, who created the blend in 1924. The story goes that he was putting together a salad for guests with whatever he had handy. The original blend included garlic, croutons, boiled eggs, parmesan cheese, romaine lettuce, olive oil, and Worcestershire sauce. Many movie stars came to Mr. Cardini's restaurant to enjoy his salad, including Clark Gable, W. C. Fields, and Jean Harlow.

Cole slaw gets its name from a Dutch term meaning "cool," which is really rather odd since the original version of this blend in Dutch regions would have been served *hot*!

CABBAGE CUTS

- One acre of cabbage will yield more edible vegetables than any other plant because it matures in only three months.
- The largest cabbage ever grown weighed over 120 pounds.
- The emperor Claudius and his senate voted that no other dish was as tasty as corned beef and cabbage.
- Cabbage is the national food of Russia. In fact, Russian princes sometimes paid tributes with gardens that were filled with cabbage.
- Babe Ruth believed cabbage was lucky, and he wore it under his hat for every game.

Long Life Cabbage

While it might not come immediately to mind, cabbage is one of the most nutritious vegetables available today. Many people believe it has strong anti-aging and anti-cancer properties.

¼ cup seasoned rice vinegar
1 tablespoon peeled fresh
   ginger, minced
1 teaspoon sugar
½ to ¾ teaspoon dried hot red
   pepper flakes

1 pound cabbage (½ head),
   thinly shredded (mixing
   red and green is good
   symbolically—red for life
   and green for health)
1 scallion, thinly sliced (or red
   onion if you prefer)

PREPARATIONS

Two other items in your pantry that promote longevity are lemon and sage. Take a small pinch of sage and put it in a teacup with one-quarter of a whole lemon and pour in hot water to make a tea. Bless the tea by saying:

> *Good health, long life*
> *No worries or strife*
> *Through the magic of this meal and tea*
> *Bring me longevity!*

Boil vinegar, ginger, sugar, and red pepper flakes (to taste) in a small saucepan over moderate heat, stirring until the sugar is dissolved. Put the cabbage and scallion or onion into a bowl and toss it with the dressing still hot. Serve immediately, thinking healthy thoughts.

Makes 4 servings

Cauliflower Accord

The strong lunar nature of cauliflower combines with olives here to make a very peaceful, calming side dish suited to nearly any meal.

½ cup white vinegar

6 tablespoons stoneground mustard

1 cup olive oil

Salt and pepper to taste

6 cups cauliflower florets

2 cups pitted black olives, halved

1½ cups chopped celery

1 bunch green onions, chopped

¼ cup chopped fresh Italian parsley

16 cups arugula

Preparations

Accord is all about balance and equity. In cooking, the stirring is part of what brings your components into harmony. So while you're stirring your ingredients for this dish, breathe deeply and focus on thoughts of peace. Visualize the white light of peace saturating every ingredient.

Whisk together the vinegar, mustard, and oil, seasoning to taste with salt and pepper. Combine cauliflower, olives, and celery in large bowl. Add ¾ cup of the dressing; toss to coat. Marinate overnight, reserving the rest of the dressing for serving. Arrange the arugula on a large platter topped with the cauliflower and drizzled with the remaining dressing.

Makes 6 one-cup servings

Multi-Tasking Squash

Squash comes in a huge variety of colors and sizes, and some of these can grow to exceed 240 pounds and produce hundreds of seeds. These characteristics provide this vegetable with the symbolic value of slow, steady development that leads to substantial rewards.

2 cups olive oil
¼ cup balsamic vinegar
1 tablespoon chopped fresh
    oregano
1 teaspoon thyme
Salt and pepper to taste
1 pound large white
    mushrooms, caps only

4 medium zucchini, cut in
    ½-inch-thick slices
4 baby yellow squash, cut in
    ½-inch-thick slices
1 large red bell pepper, cut in
    2-inch squares

PREPARATIONS

Multi-tasking typically means that you're on the go. So, take out your keys (or something else that's usually with you wherever you're working) and bring them into your sacred pantry. Let them absorb the magic created by this dish, and perhaps rub a bit of the herbs into them to charge the metal more thoroughly with high-intensity energy.

Whisk together the oil, vinegar, and herbs, seasoning the mixture with salt and pepper. Put 1 cup of this dressing into a large bowl, and add all the vegetables. Toss and let sit while your broiler preheats. Spread the vegetables out evenly on the broiler pan. Cook about 3 minutes per side. This is an excellent opportunity to add a verbal component if you wish . . . something like:

> *Veggies cooked beneath the fire*
> *Raise the energy ever higher!*
> *Bring me growth, and rewards*
> *In this meal my magic's stored!*

Turn the vegetables out onto a platter and pour the remaining dressing on top, seasoning with fresh ground salt and pepper.

Makes 6 servings

Secret Sesame Noodles

The peanut is a symbol of mystery and anticipation (hidden treasure), so make this dish when you're trying to uncover the truth or discover your inner treasures.

3 tablespoons soy sauce

2 tablespoons rice vinegar

½ teaspoon dried hot red pepper flakes

2 tablespoons brown sugar, firmly packed

½ cup natural crunchy peanut butter

1 tablespoon toasted sesame oil

1 teaspoon grated peeled fresh ginger

½ cup chicken broth

1 pound lo mein noodles

Chopped scallion and cucumber strips for garnish

Preparations

If you have an unshelled peanut it makes the perfect talisman for not only enhancing this dish, but something portable that you can keep with you (only opening it when you need the magic to manifest quickly). You can energize the peanut with an incantation like:

The truth be told, the truth can't hide
Bring it to my seeking eyes

Place everything but the noodles and garnish in a saucepan and simmer the ingredients until smooth and thick. Let cool slightly while you cook the noodles (al dente). Drain the noodles thoroughly and rinse under cold water. Drain them again, and put in a large bowl. Toss the noodles with the sauce so they're evenly coated. Garnish with the scallions and cucumbers.

Makes 4–6 servings

Fortification Salad

Watercress is thought to have originated in ancient Greece. According to legend the watercress that grew in the springs of Crete was eaten by the god Zeus to fortify himself against his murderous father Cronos. If it's good enough for Zeus—it's good enough for our magic!

DRESSING

- 2 tablespoons vegetable oil
- 1½ tablespoons sesame oil
- ¼ cup fresh lemon or lime juice
- 1 tablespoon fish sauce
- 2 tablespoons sugar
- 2 dashes Tabasco
- Black pepper to taste

SALAD

- ¾ pound watercress, coarse stems
- 1¾ cups thinly sliced red or green cabbage
- 1½ pound firm-ripe mango, peeled, pitted, and diced
- ½ cup coarsely grated carrot
- ¼ cup fresh cilantro leaves, minced
- ¼ cup fresh basil leaves, minced
- ¼ cup fresh mint leaves, minced

Preparations

While you're fortifying yourself, why not also fortify your sacred space. Bring a yellow candle (like Zeus's lightning bolts) into the kitchen. Put a small offering of almond, fig, and/or saffron nearby (all sacred to Zeus). Light the candle and welcome his energy into your space as you work.

 The beauty of this dish is its simplicity. Just put everything in a large bowl and mix it thoroughly. Serve just as is, or if you like with freshly grilled shrimp.

Makes 4–6 one-cup servings

Radical Red Dressing

The color of this dressing makes it a perfect, slightly sweet topping when you want zeal, energy, love, health, or power.

1 cup vegetable oil
⅔ cup red wine vinegar
⅔ cup ketchup
Bacon bits
2 tablespoons Worcestershire sauce
1 tablespoon soy sauce

1 teaspoon paprika
1 teaspoon salt
5–6 garlic cloves, peeled and finely minced
¼ cup sugar

Preparations

Wait for a bright shiny day and prepare this in direct sunlight to energize it further. (The sun also supports healthful qualities.)

 Place all ingredients together in a suitable container (one with a good, airtight cap) and shake thoroughly. Chill before serving (shaking again) and store in the refrigerator.

Makes about 2½ cups

Yin-Yang Dressing

The masculine symbolism of cucumber is balanced out with the cream and yogurt in this dish, making a lovely god–goddess blend.

½ cup sour cream
½ cup plain whole yogurt
1 cup finely chopped
    cucumbers
1 tablespoon extra-virgin olive
    oil
1 tablespoon fresh lemon juice

1 tablespoon minced garlic
1 tablespoon finely chopped
    chives
1 teaspoon sugar
1 teaspoon dill
¼ teaspoon salt

Preparations

Make a yin-yang symbol to glue on your storage bottle for this dressing. As you're drawing it call upon the god and goddess to mingle in harmony in the blend.

 As with the red dressing, this needs to be stored in an airtight container in the refrigerator after mixing. Chilling and shaking helps maintain the balance of energies and flavors.

Makes about 2 cups

Jumpin' Ginger

Akin to the Radical Red Dressing, this is very high energy thanks to the ginger. The citrus adds clarity, to direct your energy in the best possible way.

1 cup olive oil
½ cup wine vinegar
¼ cup balsamic vinegar
¼ cup cider vinegar
2 sprigs fresh dill
2 slices each fresh lemon and
    orange

1 garlic clove, minced
½-inch piece fresh ginger,
    peeled and diced
¼ teaspoon orange extract
¼ teaspoon lemon extract

Preparations

This makes a visually appealing dressing, so you may want to display it in a nice container (also, if you see it regularly, you'll be reminded of the magic it generates when used!).

Warm the oil and vinegars together. Place the remaining ingredients into the bottle in such a manner as to be eye-catching. Pour the warmed liquid over the top and cap tightly. Let this sit for at least 24 hours before use (it's even better after a week).

Makes 2 cups

Side Dishes

Anybody can make you enjoy the first bite of a dish,
but only a real chef can make you enjoy the last.

—Francois Minot

As the nineteenth century progressed, the form of eating was changing, especially in France. A similar variety of dishes appeared on the table, but now they appeared in a more "logical" order and grouping. The first course was an appetizer—often a variety of soups, all of which were set up along the side of the table to make room for future removes. That's where we got the term "side dish."

Affection Tomatoes

When the "love apple" was shipped to England under that name, the powerful and wealthy sought it as an aphrodisiac. History books say Sir Walter Raleigh gave Queen Elizabeth a big, juicy tomato as a gesture of affection.

TOMATO BY ANY PRONUNCIATION

- Tomatoes were originally grown by Aztecs and Incas. The fruit didn't arrive in Europe until the sixteenth century where the people of Italy and Spain were among the first to utilize them in cooking.
- Originally tomatoes were yellow. The Italians called them *pomo d'oro*, which means "golden apple."
- Tomatoes are the most popular vegetable in America, most shoppers buying them at least once a week.
- Tomatoes are good for you. They reduce the risk of colon and stomach cancers—if eaten once a day.

¼ pound sliced apple-cured bacon

6 tablespoons extra-virgin olive oil

6 slices firm white sandwich bread

Salt and pepper to season

¼ cup finely diced Spanish onion

3 tablespoons red-wine vinegar

4 assorted medium-firm tomatoes, cut into ⅓-inch-thick slices

30 small fresh basil leaves

1½ ounces blue cheese, crumbled, at room temperature

PREPARATIONS

Make sure to give your love a kiss before starting this dish, and bring an image of him or her into the kitchen with you so you can direct your energy more effectively.

Cook bacon until crisp, then drain. Pour off bacon fat reserving it. Put the olive oil in the same skillet and toast the bread until golden brown on both sides. Put these aside, seasoning with a pinch of salt and pepper on each.

Fry the onion in about 2 tablespoons of the bacon fat for dressing. Add vinegar and whisk until emulsified. Keep this warm. Put one slice of bread on each plate. Evenly divide the tomato slices among them, stacking them with basil and bacon between each slice. Top with the blue cheese and a spoonful of the warm bacon dressing.

Makes 6 servings

Cool as a Cucumber

Fresh cucumbers were once placed under a stricken woman's nose to help her recover from "the vapors." Magically they're associated with the water element, peace, and healing.

1 seedless cucumber,
  unpeeled, halved
  lengthwise, grated
1 tablespoon coarse salt
2 cups plain yogurt
½ cup sour cream
2 tablespoons fresh lemon
  juice

2 tablespoons minced fresh
  dill
1 garlic clove, minced
6 pita breads, cut in half, then
  cut into wedges
Olive oil

PREPARATIONS

Maintaining your composure is largely connected with vital breath. Before starting this dish, take three very deep, cleansing breaths in through your nose and breathe out through your mouth. Release tension and worries on the first breath. Release any lingering negativity on the second breath. And fortify your strength on the third.

Mix cucumber and salt in a small bowl; cover and chill 3 hours. Drain off any liquid you can from the yogurt, and put the drained yogurt in a bowl with the sour cream, lemon juice, dill, and garlic. Likewise squeeze excess liquid from the cucumber, then add it to the yogurt blend with a bit of pepper. Chill for 2 hours.

Preheat oven to 400 degrees F. Just before serving prepare your pita by brushing it with olive oil, and placing it on baking sheets. Bake for about 10 minutes (till crisp), and then serve with the cucumber dip. This is also very tasty with the addition of chopped shrimp or crab bits.

ALTERNATIVE

I like making this with sliced cucumber and serving it on a pita like a side salad.

Makes 6–12 servings (¹/₂ piece each)

Sacred Onion Soup

I call this Sacred Onion Soup because it contains five types of onions, one each for the five points of the pentagram. It's very rich in flavor and offers a tremendous amount of lunar energy to any meal.

1 large red onion, chopped
1 large white onion, chopped
1 Spanish onion, chopped
2 yellow onions, chopped
1 bundle green onions, chopped
2 tablespoons butter

Pinch of sugar
1 tablespoon minced garlic
8 cups beef broth
3 tablespoons Worcestershire sauce (or to taste)
Garlic croutons and crumbled cheese, for garnish

PREPARATIONS

Wear your pentagram while preparing this dish, or if you don't have one, draw one and put it on the refrigerator door with magnets (magnets attract the energy desired). Think about the symbolism it presents and what it means to you intimately. You'll internalize that meaning even more as you eat!

Sauté the onions in the butter with a pinch of sugar. Brown them well, but do not let them burn. Add the garlic, beef broth, and Worcestershire. Let this cook down by at least 1 cup and taste test. Adjust your spices, then serve with croutons and cheese on top.

Makes 8–10 servings

JUST DESSERTS:
SWEET SPIRITUAL TREATS

*It's nice to eat a good hunk of beef but you want
a light dessert, too.*

—ARTHUR FIEDLER

Everyone enjoys a treat now and again, and what could be more tantalizing, fun, and tempting than a sweet snack filled with clever, proactive magic? The root word for dessert is *deservier* (meaning—"remove dishes"), after which, of course, is when sweets would appear on the table. Early desserts were not so much meant to appease a sweet tooth as they were to impress. The more elaborate the presentation, the better. For our purposes, we'll substitute focused magic for flash and fanfare, and still make something delicious to share!

Cake

Page one is a diet. Page two is a chocolate cake.
It's a no-win situation!

—Kim Williams

The most primitive peoples in the world began making cakes shortly after they discovered flour. In medieval England, the cakes that were described in writings were not cakes in the conventional sense. They have been described as flour-based sweet foods as opposed to the description of breads, which had no sweetening. Yet the words for *bread* and cake were, for a while, somewhat interchangeable, and there are many examples of sweet breads.

Greek cake consisted of nut and honey in a rather flat form. Romans made cheesecakes on pastry but most of these were offered to the gods. Nonetheless it wouldn't be long before people would discover the pleasure of cake. By the eighteenth century cake pans had been developed, and by the nineteenth century cakes were an everyday feature in cookery for the middle class.

HAVING YOUR CAKE

There are four basic methods for mixing cake batters. The first is to whisk the ingredients. This is typically used for things like sponge cakes that require a mix of tiny bubbles. The second is creaming, which is the most common. This begins by thoroughly blending the sugar with butter, and then adding the other ingredients. The third technique is called "rubbing in." Here fat and flour get worked together before the other ingredients are added. Finally we come to the melting method. This is best suited for heavy cakes and muffins, and requires that the fat, sugar, and liquids be heated before adding anything else.

Fairy Cake

This cake honors the legend of Thomas the Rhymer (thirteenth century). The story goes that Thomas was set upon by a hag who took him to the land of the Fay. The old woman warned him not to eat of any of the trees he would see on the journey, no matter how hungry he got, or he would be trapped. Finally, just when he felt his hunger would overcome him, the woman offered him an apple from a perfect tree. She said this apple bore the gift of truth. Upon eating it, he saw that the woman was not old at all—but very young. They spent what seemed to be three days together feasting, only to discover that seven years had passed in the real world. At last when Thomas arrived home, he found himself to have the gifts of prophesy, poetry, and an enchanted harp. He became a wise ruler of his lands and in his elder years he was at last called back to Fairyland, where he remained.

3⅓ cups cake flour

2 teaspoons baking powder

1½ teaspoons baking soda

2 teaspoons ground cinnamon

1½ teaspoons ground allspice

1½ teaspoons ground nutmeg

1½ teaspoons ground ginger

½ teaspoon salt

3 extra-large eggs, room temperature

1⅔ cups packed dark brown sugar

1 tablespoon pure maple syrup

1 cup vegetable oil

1 tablespoon pure vanilla extract

2 cups unsweetened applesauce (can be flavored if you wish)

1½ cups honey roasted walnuts, coarsely chopped

PREPARATIONS

Sweet butter is supposed to attract fairy folk. So, while you butter the bottom and sides of your cake pan, add a little rhyme like:

> *From out the mists of space and time*
> *Hear the magic, heed the rhyme*
> *Open the path, open the way,*
> *Good fairy folk be welcome here today!*

Don't forget to put out a piece of the cake when it's done just for them!

 Preheat oven to 350 degrees F. Sprinkle 2 tablespoonfuls of flour into the baking pan, knocking out any excess.

Mix the flour, baking powder, baking soda, cinnamon, allspice, nutmeg, ginger, and salt. In a separate bowl break the eggs and add the brown sugar and syrup. Beat this on high for 5 minutes, scraping the sides as you go, then add oil and vanilla. Turn down the speed to low and beat until the mixture is smooth. Finally continue mixing, adding a bit of the applesauce and flour mixture alternately. Fold in the walnuts by hand, then pour into the pan. Bake for about 55 minutes until a toothpick inserted in the center comes out clean. Cool for at least 10 minutes in the pan before inverting onto a cake rack to cool completely. To make the fairies really happy, serve it with a dollop of sweet cream.

Makes 8–10 servings

Peachy Keen Longevity Cakes

Chinese legends speak of a peach tree that blossoms once every 3,000 years. Afterward it produces magical fruits that grant eternal life, youth, health, and vitality. It's a sacred plant in Taoist tradition, and its fruit is eaten in China on birthdays to symbolize a wish for longevity.

1 large egg
1 large egg yolk
½ teaspoon orange extract
½ cup granulated sugar
⅔ cup heavy cream, well-chilled
¾ cup cake flour
1 teaspoon double-acting baking powder

¼ teaspoon salt
Confectioners' sugar for dusting the cakes
Fresh peaches, peeled and sliced
Fresh raspberries for garnish

PREPARATIONS

Sometimes I think that a long life is not quite so important as one well lived. Nonetheless, we can apply the energy of this cake either to our health or to the longevity of a project that we hold dear. In either case, set up a spot in your kitchen to honor Shou-xing, the Chinese god of longevity, who is typically depicted carrying a peach. Put a slice of peach or a whole fruit here for him, and light a candle expressing your desire before you make the cake.

Preheat the oven to 350 degrees F. Beat together the egg, yolk, extract, and ¼ cup of the granulated sugar until the mixture is thick and pale in color. Separately beat the cream, adding the remaining ¼ cup granulated sugar, until the mixture peaks. Fold the beaten cream into the eggs. In another bowl sift together the flour, baking powder, and salt. Fold the flour mixture into the cream mixture. Divide the resulting batter among 6 buttered and floured ½-cup muffin tins. Bake for about 20 minutes until golden brown. When they're cool, serve with a dusting of confectioners' sugar, the peaches and berries on top.

Makes 6 small cakes

Tonic Cake

Blueberries were prominent in Russian folk medicine, used as a preventative measure and curative. The blueberry is still prized for its antioxidant health benefits and continues to be used in folk remedials. This means that the following dessert is not only good, but good for us (smile).

2¼ cups cake flour, sifted
1 teaspoon baking powder
1 teaspoon baking soda
½ teaspoon salt
1 cup buttermilk
Several drops blue food coloring
1 teaspoon distilled white vinegar
1 teaspoon vanilla extract
1½ cups sugar
½ cup (1 stick) unsalted butter, softened
2 large eggs

FROSTING

2 (8-ounce) packages cream
  cheese, softened
½ cup (1 stick) unsalted
  butter, softened

2 tablespoons vanilla extract
2½ cups powdered sugar
3 pints fresh blueberries

PREPARATIONS

Take three blueberries out of the pints, one each for your body, mind, and spirit. Bless them, saying:

> *Bless my spirit with a healthy path*
> *Bless my mind with positive perspectives*
> *Bless my body with wellness*
> *In these berries, and this dish*
> *Place my prayer, seal my wish!*

Eat the berries before you start cooking.

Preheat oven to 350 degrees F. Oil and flour two 9-inch cake pans (2-inch deep sides). Sift the flour, baking powder, baking soda, and salt into a medium bowl. Whisk the buttermilk, food coloring, vinegar, and vanilla into the dry ingredients. Using an electric mixer, beat the sugar and butter, adding the eggs one at a time and beating until well blended. Slowly add this to the other ingredients and beat until thoroughly mixed. Divide the batter between the prepared pans. Bake for 30 minutes. Cool before turning out the cake.

Meanwhile, beat cream cheese and butter in large bowl until smooth. Add the vanilla and powdered sugar. Beat until smooth. Use 1 cup of frosting on one layer of the cake, arranging half the blueberries on top of the frosting. Put the second layer on top, flat side down, and press gently. Decorate with the remaining frosting and blueberries evenly applied to the top and sides (if you want, you can pattern the berries in a symbolic way!).

Makes 6–8 servings

Pie

A good custard pie is eggs and milk and sugar
falling naturally into place and cooking up all tawny
and soft on top of a tender butter crust that cracks
clean like Georgia peanut brittle when you cut it.

—Elizabeth Sahatjian

Greeks originated pie pastry, and the Romans carried home recipes for it when they conquered Greece. Cato (a Roman statesman) helps us know this because he documented a period recipe for a very popular pie called *placenta*. And, of course from the hub of Rome the wonders of pie slowly spread throughout Europe, being adapted and tweaked to suit different cultures.

Normans began the custom of sending a pie to the king at Yule. Oddly that pie was made of something akin to eel! This delicacy was also very popular in the English court. The fish was cooked with syrup, which was later mixed with wine and spices and served with bread. So for quite a while in many settings the pie was nothing like the dessert we now know—it was merely a convenient way to cook meat and fish!

Come the fourteenth century pies took on a new form with *sotelties*, a decorative dessert meant to be entertaining to guests. The popularity of this art continued for the next two centuries, as evidenced by the nursery rhyme, "Sing a Song of Sixpence." Birds, however, were not the only thing set before the king. Frogs, turtles, rabbits, and other small animals also were surprise fillings, released when the top of the pie was opened.

When the Pilgrims came to America they, of course, brought along their favorite pie recipes. Upon arrival, these were adapted to the berries and other edibles they found in the New World. At that time pies were cooked in brick ovens; as the settlers moved west more regional pies appeared.

PIECE OF THE PIE

Pie à la mode was probably first served around 1890 in the Cambridge Hotel in New York. Here a professor regularly dined, ordering ice cream with his pie. An observant diner nearby asked him what this dessert was called. When he didn't know, she made up the name Pie à la Mode. The professor liked this designation so much, he ordered it by that name every time thereafter. In time, his insistence at various restaurants over this dessert's name resulted in the proper designation being added to menus!

Mincemeat pie, on the other hand, has a much longer history. It is a throwback to the time when pies were typically made of spiced meats. In fact, it wasn't until the seventeenth century that sweet ingredients like sugared nuts and dried fruit were added to this particular pie. No matter what, however, eating mince pie on each of the Twelve Days of Christmas is said to ensure good luck for the following year. Alternatively to refuse mincemeat pie would lead to bad luck.

The pasty is a type of pie that's meant for one person. The original ones weighed about two pounds and were literally "fast food" for early people. These pies were cooked with meat and vegetables inside. The top was then marked in such a way that a traveler could grab what they wanted and eat on the road.

From a magical perspective pies are a beautiful way to bake up magic because they're contained in a sacred circle that acts like a womb for your energy.

Nectar of the Gods Pie

You've probably heard the term "nectar of the gods." It was nectar made of the juice and pulp of the apricot, which was reputedly the drink of choice of the Greek and Roman gods. Adding to this symbolism, the apricot is known as "moon of the faithful," in the Far East, and ancient Persians referred to it as the "egg of the sun." This makes for a dessert that's very amenable to whichever pantry protector you desire to honor!

9-inch pie crust (uncooked)	6 tablespoons sugar
1 tablespoon egg white, lightly beaten	½ teaspoon almond extract
	2 tablespoons brandy
4 cups fresh apricots, halved and pitted	2 tablespoons cornstarch
	½ cup apricot preserves

PREPARATIONS

A lot here depends on for whom you're preparing this pie (as you can utilize it to better commune with him or her). One blessing I used (that you can adapt) goes like this:

> *Moon of the faithful, egg of the sun*
> *With my magic become as one*
> *I call upon Lady and Lord*
> *In this dish, your presence be poured!*

Preheat oven to 425 degrees F. Bake the pastry for about 20 minutes, then prick the bottom, and bake for an additional 5 minutes or until lightly golden. Cool so you can touch it, brushing the bottom and sides with the egg white.

While that sits, cut the apricots in half, pitting them. Stir these with the remaining ingredients, except for the preserves, until well coated. Before putting the apricot mixture in the baked shell, cover the edge of the crust with foil so that it won't burn. Arrange the apricot halves decoratively in the shell (perhaps so they look like a bright sun). Turn down the oven to 350 degrees F. and bake for 1 hour, until the mix is bubbling and the apricots are tender. Warm the preserves and brush them over the top of the pie before serving.

Makes 6–8 servings

Sun Spirit Pie

Some Native Americans believe the pecan tree to be representative of the Great Spirit. Similarly pumpkin represented life and abundance.

¾ cup canned solid-pack pumpkin

2 tablespoons light brown sugar, packed

1 large egg, lightly beaten

2 tablespoons sour cream

⅛ teaspoon cinnamon

⅛ teaspoon freshly grated nutmeg

Pinch salt

¾ cup light corn syrup

½ cup light brown sugar, packed

3 large eggs, lightly beaten

3 tablespoons unsalted butter, melted and cooled

2 teaspoons vanilla

¼ teaspoon finely grated fresh lemon zest

1½ teaspoons fresh lemon juice

¼ teaspoon salt

1⅓ cups pecans (5½ ounce), chopped

Precooked pie shell

Preparations

Since this honors the Sun Spirit, make the pie as close to noon as possible (when the sun is most powerful). Leave the components in the bright light for a few minutes to absorb supportive energy. You may also wish to light a yellow-gold candle in your kitchen for more fiery vibrations.

Preheat oven to 350 degrees F. Whisk together pumpkin, brown sugar, egg, sour cream, cinnamon, nutmeg, and a pinch of salt in a bowl until smooth. Separately, stir together corn syrup, brown sugar, eggs, butter, vanilla, lemon zest, lemon juice, salt, and pecans. Spread the pumpkin mixture evenly in the pie shell, and spoon the pecan mixture evenly over it. Bake the pie at 350 degrees F. until the crust is golden, about 35 minutes. (Note: Filling sets up more as it cools.) Cool and serve with whipped cream to which you've added a few drops of yellow food coloring for a lovely golden glow.

Makes 6–8 servings

Full Moon Tropical Pie

In northern India, coconut is the fruit born by the "Tree of Life." In Oceanic cultures, coconuts were kept by priests and given as fertility symbols to women who wished to conceive. In Sanskrit, the coconut palm is known as kalpa vriksha, *meaning "tree which gives all that is necessary for living." Magically speaking coconut is a lunar food and the white creamy texture of this pie makes it look like a full moon!*

CRUST

1 cup sweetened flaked coconut, packed

1 cup graham cracker crumbs

3 tablespoons butter, melted

1 large egg white

FILLING

1 (15-ounce) can cream of coconut

6 large egg yolks

2 tablespoons fresh lemon juice

2 cups chilled whipping cream

½ teaspoon imitation coconut extract

3 tablespoons coconut rum

1 cup plus 1 tablespoon sweetened flaked coconut

Preparations

This pie is best prepared on a waxing to full moon for a similar fullness of lunar energy. As with the solar pie, let the components for this bask in moonlight to charge them with the moon's energy. Light a white or silver candle instead of a yellow one to honor the Moon Spirit.

Preheat oven to 350 degrees F. Blend the first four ingredients in a food processor until sticky crumbs form. Press the crumbs onto the bottom and sides of 9-inch pie pan. Put this in the freezer for 10 minutes then bake it for 10 minutes. Refreeze the crust while you make your filling.

Whisk 1 cup of the cream of coconut, the egg yolks, and the lemon juice in a non-aluminum bowl. Put the mixture in a double boiler, whisking constantly until a candy thermometer registers 160 degrees F. Remove this from the heat and beat until cool (about 5 minutes).

By the power of the moon and my will
Within this pie my magic fulfill!

Combine the whipping cream, extract rum and remaining cream of coconut in another large bowl. Beat until soft peaks form. Fold cream mixture and 1 cup toasted coconut into egg mixture. Freeze until softly set, stirring occasionally, about 3 hours. Spoon the filling into the crust and then return to the freezer overnight. Sprinkle with coconut, and if you wish top with mango and banana slices before serving.

Makes 6 servings

Cookies

The essence of what makes life worth living—the small moments, the special family getaways, the cookies in the oven, the weekend drives, the long dreamlike summers

—Richard Louv

Throughout the world various countries have their own special word for cookies. In England and Australia they're called biscuits. The German word is *keks*, the Spanish term is *galletas*, and Italians have several names (depending on the type of cookie) including biscotti. Our word for cookie actually originates in the Dutch *koekie*, which roughly translates as tiny cake.

Originally cookies weren't really a snack item, but rather a means of testing out cakes. A cook would bake just a small amount of batter to check the oven temperature. Apparently around the seventh century C.E. in Persia, one cook discovered these bits weren't so bad eaten on their own, and began making cookie-cakes in a variety of sizes, especially for important functions. The Crusades then helped bring spices and cooking techniques to northern Europe. By the fourteenth century, cookies could be found in Paris. By the seventeenth century they were everywhere! We can thank the English, Dutch, and Scotch immigrants for bringing these treats to North America.

During the colonial period a favorite "tea cake" was a butter cookie that included rose water. For the longest time cookies didn't even have a section in cookbooks but were lumped in with cakes. But as was the case with other sweets, expansion gave cooks around the nation access to unique ingredients to try in their blends.

The thing I like about cookies is that dough allows for shaping and decorating on an individual level. If you wanted to, you could create a batch of magically neutral cookies and decorate each one so it created a specific type of energy! This allows you to put a lot of power in a handful of sweet, and it's the perfect way to have "cakes" for a coven meeting!

HAND IN THE COOKIE JAR

The origin of brownies is unclear to historians. Some think the first brownies resulted when someone added baking powder to a chocolate cake recipe, but that's a best guess. In 1897 Sears published the first known recipe for this favorite of modern cookies along with a mix that bakers could buy and make at home.

Meanwhile the beloved chocolate chip cookie came about in 1930 when Ruth Whitman (who ran the Toll House Restaurant) experimented with another cookie recipe. She added chopped semisweet chocolate to the recipe, and thus the Toll House cookie was born.

Students of history tell us that the original fortune cookie appeared in the twelfth century when Chinese soldiers put messages in moon cakes to keep information secret. An alternative origin may be attributed to a Chinese custom upon the birth of a child, when cake rolls with a birth announcement were sent to family members.

Fortune Finding

What kitchen witch is complete without at least one recipe for divinatory cookies (also known traditionally as fortune cookies)? The beauty of these treats is that you can write fortunes suited to nearly any gathering or magical focus.

¼ cup flour	¼ cup sugar
½ teaspoon Chinese five-spice powder	2 large egg whites

Preparations

Think about the function for these cookies, and then write out suitable fortunes on white paper in nontoxic ink. Get creative—you can make runic fortunes or use other symbols too!

Preheat oven to 400 degrees F. and butter two baking sheets. Sift the dry ingredients together, and whisk the egg whites in a separate bowl until they froth. Slowly integrate the eggs into the dry components until you have a smooth batter. Put 2 teaspoons of batter on one part of the first baking sheet and use a spoon to spread it into a 3- or 3½-inch dish. Continue to shape disks on the other sheets until you have no more room. Place the cookies in the oven for 5 minutes. When they come out of the oven you have to work quickly. Put one cookie at a time on a work surface using a spatula, put the fortune in the center, then fold the cookie in half. If you wish, you can then bend the cookie into the traditional crescent moon shape (which also accentuates divinatory energy). Put the shaped cookie on a piece of waxed paper to cool and continue with the rest of the cookies. Note that these are best consumed on the same day they're prepared.

Makes about 12 cookies

Enlightenment Rounds

In Muslim tradition, the fig tree is the most intelligent of all. Throughout Asia the fig often symbolizes knowledge and enlightenment, especially that which is nurtured by the mother aspect of the goddess.

Filling

1 cup packed soft dried figs (no stems)	1 teaspoon finely grated fresh lemon zest
¾ cup golden raisins	1 tablespoon cinnamon
¾ cup orange blossom honey	¼ teaspoon cloves
¼ cup orange brandy	¼ teaspoon nutmeg
1½ teaspoons finely grated fresh orange zest	¾ cup chopped almonds
	¾ cup chopped walnuts

DOUGH

4 cups all-purpose flour

1 cup plus 2 tablespoons sugar

1 tablespoon baking powder

1 teaspoon salt

1 cup (2 sticks) cold unsalted butter, cut into ½-inch cubes

2 large eggs, lightly beaten

½ cup whole milk

1 teaspoon vanilla

½ teaspoon orange extract

1 teaspoon finely grated fresh orange or lemon zest

Confectioners' sugar (dusting for garnish)

PREPARATIONS

They say that Buddha was awakened while meditating under a fig tree. In this case, we'll adapt the idea a bit by eating a pinch of the figs and meditating briefly before making the cookies. Visualize a pure white light pouring into your crown chakra to help connect you with your higher awareness while you bake.

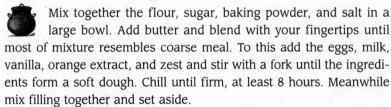 Mix together the flour, sugar, baking powder, and salt in a large bowl. Add butter and blend with your fingertips until most of mixture resembles coarse meal. To this add the eggs, milk, vanilla, orange extract, and zest and stir with a fork until the ingredients form a soft dough. Chill until firm, at least 8 hours. Meanwhile mix filling together and set aside.

After chilling the dough, preheat the oven to 350 degrees F. Drop balls of the dough onto a greased cookie sheet. Make an indentation with your thumb or the back of a spoon (this is like the "eye" of the cookie). Fill this eye with the energized filling. Bake for 17 minutes until golden around the edges. Sprinkle with confectioners' sugar while still warm.

Makes about 2 dozen cookies

Lasting Love Cookies

In the Far East and Pacific regions people believed that ginger aided with love magic because the heat provided warmth and passion. To this foundation, this recipe adds molasses so that once you find love, you stick with it!

COOKIES

1 cup shortening	2 teaspoons baking powder
1 cup sugar	1 teaspoon salt
½ cup molasses	1 tablespoon cinnamon
½ cup honey	2 teaspoons ground cloves
2 egg yolks	2 teaspoons ground ginger
4 cups all-purpose flour	1 teaspoon ground nutmeg
1 teaspoon baking soda	

FROSTING

1 cup confectioners' sugar	½ teaspoon vanilla extract
1 tablespoon melted butter	Red food coloring
1 tablespoon milk	Sprinkles

PREPARATIONS

These are ideal for Valentine's Day or romantic anniversary spells and rituals, so time them accordingly. When you frost the cookies you'll have the chance to decorate them with hearts, and spreading the frosting is like layering the energy you've created with extra sweetness and love. Keep that goal in mind.

Using a mixer, cream together the shortening, sugar, molasses, and honey. Add the egg yolks and mix well. Separately sift together the flour, baking soda, baking powder, salt, and spices. Stir this a little at a time into the shortening blend. Wrap the dough in plastic and chill for 2 hours.

Preheat oven to 350 degrees F. Roll out dough on a lightly floured surface to ¼-inch thickness. Cut out shapes with a heart-shaped cookie cutter. Place the cookies on a greased cookie sheet and bake for about 9 minutes. Cool before frosting.

To make the frosting, blend the sugar, butter, milk, vanilla, and a few drops of food coloring together until smooth. Spread this evenly over the cookies. Also cut out a small heart from a piece of cardboard. Hold this just slightly above the frosting on each cookie and use it to pattern your sprinkles into a heart.

Makes about 2 dozen cookies

Miscellany

Sweets to the Sweet.

—WILLIAM SHAKESPEARE

There seems to be no lack of creativity when it comes to sweets . . . no sugary confection that hasn't been attempted at least once. And while they might not always be "good for us," there's no denying sweets have a magic all their own without any tweaking by kitchen witches! Here are just a few more recipes that hopefully will inspire your own.

Gypsy Dew

When you want to break out of a rut and really kick up your heels, this recipe is ideal to turn around negativity and improve your outlook. The melon here protects you from falling into old habits, and the rosemary sauce inspires the conscious mind with fresh, exciting ideas.

½ cup water
½ cup white wine
½ cup sugar
1 (3-inch) strip of orange zest
1 tablespoon chopped fresh
rosemary leaves plus

rosemary sprigs for
garnish
¼ cup fresh orange juice
4 cups melon balls cut from a
honeydew melon, chilled

PREPARATIONS

When you're trying to change patterns, the traditional custom has been to turn something around. For example, gamblers would turn around their chairs and sit backward to reverse bad luck. To prepare for this recipe you can try something similar, like turning your shirt inside out before starting to make the dish. As you turn the item of clothing, add an incantation, like:

> *Turn and change, turn and change—old ways now rearrange!*

You can continue the incantation all the while you cook.

In a small saucepan stir together the water, wine, sugar, zest, and chopped rosemary. Boil the mixture, stirring counterclockwise to decrease the influence old habits have over you. Continue until the sugar is dissolved, and simmer it for 4 minutes longer. Strain the syrup through a fine sieve set over a bowl, pressing hard on the solids, and chill it, covered, until it is cold. Stir the orange juice into the syrup. In a serving bowl toss the melon balls with the syrup, and garnish the dessert with the rosemary sprigs.

FUN ADAPTATIONS

To make yourself more sociable and amenable to company, substitute pineapple juice for the orange juice. Likewise, to transform the way you behave in relationships, use strawberry juice.

Makes 4 servings

Honeymoon Hazelnut Pudding

You need not be on your honeymoon to enjoy this heart-pleasing pudding. Prepare it any time you want to bring more savvy into a bumpy relationship, or spice up a good one! European brides received hazelnuts on their wedding day so that they would be wise, sensitive, and insightful.

½ cup hazelnuts, toasted and husked	3 large eggs, separated
5 tablespoons sugar	5 tablespoons water
4 ounces semisweet chocolate, chopped	2 tablespoons brandy flavoring
	Pinch of salt
	½ cup chilled whipping cream

Preparations

Wear your mate's favorite outfit or minimally something in his or her favorite color while preparing this dish. Light a red candle in the kitchen to set the mood, and say:

> *With good intention, by my will*
> *With the power of love, this pudding—fill*
> *Nuts for wisdom and insight, sweet*
> *My magic fills this little treat!*

Grind hazelnuts with 1 tablespoon of the sugar in a food processor until the mixture forms a paste. Melt the chocolate in a small metal bowl set over a saucepan of simmering water, stirring until smooth. Remove from over the water, and as you do this, visualize any problems between you and your mate likewise melting away—leaving behind nothing but warm sweetness.

Whisk the egg yolks, 2 tablespoons of the water, flavoring, and 2 tablespoons of the sugar in large metal bowl to blend. Focus intently on your feelings and try to remember to always stir clockwise to keep that warm, welcoming energy moving forward.

Set the bowl over the same saucepan of simmering water and whisk constantly until thick ribbons form when whisk is lifted and thermometer inserted into mixture registers 160 degrees F, about 6 minutes. Cool mixture slightly. Fold in chocolate and hazelnut paste.

Using an electric mixer, beat the egg whites and salt in a large bowl until soft peaks form. Because of the upbeat energy created by the mixer, this is a good time to add an incantation, like:

> Higher and higher, our hearts fill with fire
> Passion and love, blessed from above.

Visualize the whites being filled with a sparkling pink light (pink being the color of gentle love).

Stir the remaining 2 tablespoons of sugar and 3 tablespoons of water in a very small saucepan over medium heat until the sugar dissolves. Increase the heat and boil until thermometer inserted into mixture registers 220 degrees F, about 4 minutes. Gradually add the hot syrup to the whites, beating until firm peaks form and whites are cool. Fold into chocolate mixture in two additions.

Beat the whipping cream in a medium bowl until soft peaks form. Fold this mixture into the pudding. Spoon the pudding into four goblets, dividing equally. Chill the pudding for at least an hour and up to a day. Garnish each serving with whipped cream and toasted hazelnuts.

Makes about 3 servings

Sweet Tree-t!

The Algonquins called maple syrup by a name that means "drawn from trees" and regarded it as the tree's blood (affirming a life-giving spirit in nature). The life force of the tree is said to become one with the person who eats of it. With that in mind, use this recipe when you want to connect more strongly to the earth, or when working tree-oriented magic.

1¾ cups all-purpose flour

1¾ teaspoons baking powder

½ teaspoon baking soda

½ teaspoon salt

¼ teaspoon freshly grated
    nutmeg

2 tablespoons cold butter, cut
    into bits

1 cup buttermilk

1 cup finely diced pears

2 cups pure maple syrup

2 cups water

Sweet cream for garnish

PREPARATIONS

Bring something of the natural world with you into your kitchen, a living plant being the best choice. Sit with the plant quietly for a few minutes and focus on its energies. Welcome the spirit of the plant, and all of nature into your sacred space. When you feel a shift in the vibrations in the room, begin the recipe.

 Sift the dry ingredients together. Crumble the butter into the dry components until the mixture feels like meal. Add the buttermilk, pears, and mix until evenly moist. Bring the syrup and water to a full rolling boil in a large pot (at least 4 quarts). Drop balls of the dough into the boiling water. Turn down the heat to moderate and cover until the dumplings are dry on top (20 minutes). Serve warm with a drizzle of sweet cream.

Makes about 12 servings

GATHERING GOODIES
AND PICNIC FARE

*That faint semblance of Eden, the picnic in the
greenwood*

—HERMAN MELVILLE

T he word *picnic* derives from the French and seems to have
come into public use around the 1700s. The verb *piquer*
means to nibble or peck at food. The addition of the *nic* comes
from an odd custom of rhyming words, which was quite popular
in that time. Overall it pertained to what we might now call a
potluck dinner. It took more than 200 years for the word to mean
an outdoor meal!

I believe such meals have been commonplace for much longer
than we might immediately think. Travelers taking their meals
alongside a road, merchants heading to new lands . . . even Jesus
with the loaves and fishes! But in the form we currently think of
them, we're looking at the early 1800s. For example, in Mrs.

Beeton's *Book of Household Management* we're told that the proper picnic must have at least thirty-five different dishes from which to choose. Ah, but don't panic. Today's gatherings and picnic fare need not be quite that complex.

The most important things for the kitchen witch to consider are the theme of the event, how many will be eating there, what limitations the setting places on the type of foods, and of course food safety. The theme helps in picking out a dish with the right components, namely ones that support the overall energies being created. Knowing your location helps you in determining whether you can offer a hot or cold dish.

In terms of safety, I can't stress this enough—especially for camping. Cooking and eating outdoors has some risks that can be neatly negated by following the safety tips provided in the sidebars in this chapter. After all, the concept of perfect love and trust means that folks *trust* they won't get food poisoning and that the people who feed them have handled their meals properly.

Full of Bologna

While we often use this phrase disparagingly, bologna actually has an interesting history. It takes its name from the Italian town where the meat's original form was that of mortadella, made with Italian spices. Bologna, being a major trading port, became famous for its mortadella, and the blend is still made in villages around the city. With this in mind, take this meat roll to a gathering when you're looking to make some good trades (perhaps even use your bologna for barter!).

1 whole all-beef bologna (5–6 pounds)	1 teaspoon onion powder (optional)
½ cup stoneground honey mustard	1 teaspoon garlic powder (optional)
1 cup brown sugar	

PREPARATIONS

Trade and barter are associated with the air element, which is connected to effective communication skills. So light a yellow candle in your kitchen before you begin to cook, saying:

> *To help with barter and trade, this meat is made*
> *Bring words sweet as honey*
> *So I can save money!*

Preheat oven to 250 degrees F. Line a roasting pan with aluminum foil. On a clean countertop lay out two large pieces of plastic food wrap and place the whole bologna on the wrap. Score the top of the meat about ¼-inch on all sides (you can do this as decoratively as you wish). Mix the coating ingredients together and press half this mixture into the bologna on all sides. Carefully turn it over so the coating is even, then wrap securely in the plastic, and wrap the whole roll with aluminum foil. Place this in the preheated oven for 2½ hours.

Leaving the oven on, unwrap the bologna (discard the wrappings) and coat it with the remaining mustard blend. Return this to cook unwrapped for another 2½ hours, turning it regularly so the bottom doesn't burn. Transport it to the event whole, slicing when you're ready to serve or haggle!

Makes 20–30 servings

FULL OF BALONEY

It is pretty well established that "baloney," meaning nonsense, originated with "bologna" the meat product. Bologna was historically regarded as a humble food whose ingredients are a bit dubious. So the new word became a metaphor for "junk" or "silliness." The term came into popular usage in the 1930s when one catchphrase was, "It's baloney no matter how thin you slice it."

Leg Up Turkey

There is something truly medieval about eating whole turkey legs. As picnic fare, they're a great finger food, they transport well, and they can be eaten cold. Symbolically we're using this part of the bird for those events where we could use a little extra assistance. The phrase "get a leg up" comes from equestrian circles where a helper creates a foothold to heft the rider upward.

8 turkey legs, rinsed and patted dry

2 tablespoons paprika

2 tablespoons kosher salt

2 tablespoons garlic powder

1 tablespoon black pepper

1 tablespoon onion powder

1 tablespoon oregano

1 tablespoon thyme

½ cup hot sauce

¼ cup Worcestershire sauce

2 tablespoons fresh lemon juice

Oil for deep frying

3 cups all-purpose flour

1 tablespoon salt

1 tablespoon freshly ground black pepper

1 tablespoon cayenne

2 teaspoons garlic powder

Ranch dressing (for dipping/garnish)

PREPARATIONS

Since you'll probably want to know that help will be on hand when you arrive, make a communication charm out of a bay leaf and put it under your phone. Bless the leaf by saying:

> *Magic be nimble, gods be kind*
> *Bring helping hands, the right people find*
> *Remove all barriers, bring down the wall*
> *Let those who will help, give me a call!*

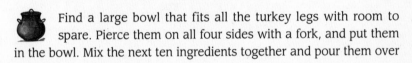 Find a large bowl that fits all the turkey legs with room to spare. Pierce them on all four sides with a fork, and put them in the bowl. Mix the next ten ingredients together and pour them over

the legs. Put in the refrigerator to marinate for at least an hour. Turn the legs to allow for even absorption of flavoring.

When you're ready to cook the legs, heat the deep-frying oil to 365 degrees F. Meanwhile combine flour, salt, pepper, cayenne, and garlic, and roll each turkey leg in the mixture. Slowly put each leg into the fryer, cooking two or three at a time. Fry for 5 minutes, until the skin is golden brown. Season as desired when they first come out of the oil (anything you apply to the skin sticks for more flavor). Wrap legs individually for transport.

Makes 8 servings

Pork of Plenty

Greeks mixed a bit of pork with their soil before sowing seed. Similarly, Egyptians had pigs run over freshly planted ground to push in the seeds. Both of these customs come from an ancient idea that pigs bring fertility to the earth, making this dish ideal to prepare for an Earth Day gathering.

3 pounds boneless pork butt	1 tablespoon brown sugar
¼ cup soy sauce	1 tablespoon minced garlic
2 tablespoons cooking sherry	2 teaspoons Chinese five-spice
1 tablespoon orange blossom	powder
honey	¼ cup honey

PREPARATIONS

Assuming that you're utilizing this dish for earth-oriented energy, save a little of the fat and mix it with some flower seeds. Go to some place where you can plant these two together, saying:

> *The fertility of the earth, be filled anew*
> *Let flowers grow, heal your lands*
> *Accept this magic from my hands*
> *So mote it be!*

Take that focus with you back into your kitchen.

Slice the entire pork butt into ¾-inch strips, and put the strips into a non-aluminum bowl, adding all ingredients but the honey as a marinade. Refrigerate overnight, stirring regularly.

The next day, in a preheated 350-degree F. oven, roast the pork on a rack inside a roasting pan with a little water in the bottom. (Watch during roasting time to make sure the water doesn't evaporate completely.) Roast for 1½ hours, brushing regularly with the honey during the last 15 minutes. Remove from the oven, and when the pork is cool, shred it as finely as you like. Serve with rolls and a side of honey barbecue sauce for dipping.

Makes 10-plus servings

Perfect Love "Cakes"

This Scottish quick bread called a scone very likely takes its name from the Stone of Destiny (or Scone), the place where Scottish kings were once crowned. The original triangular scone was made with oats and griddle-baked. Since this recipe includes cheese (a love food) make your scones round like the magic circle and serve them as "cakes" after any ritual gathering.

1¾ cups self-rising flour	¼ cup hard cheese, grated
½ cup (1 stick) butter, chilled and diced	⅓ cup buttermilk
	melted butter (optional)

PREPARATIONS

I like to chant while making these as it seems to raise energy even as the dough rises! Here's one example:

> *In perfect love, and perfect trust*
> *Go or stay; do as you must*
> *The flesh may be weary but the soul is free*
> *To love God within all, so mote it be!*

Preheat oven to 400 degrees F. Rub the flour and butter together in a bowl until it resembles coarse meal. Stir in the cheese and add enough buttermilk to make a soft, pliable dough. Transfer to a floured board, and knead the dough lightly. Roll and cut out scones in any shape you deem appropriate for the event. Bake for about 18 minutes. Brush with a little melted butter for a glossy finish. Cool on a wire rack.

Makes about 12 scones

Tempestuous Tomato Salad

Tomatoes are an all-time favorite love food in many settings because of their rich color. Now that tomatoes come in a variety of colors, they can represent all aspects of love, from passionate to the love between friends. This salad honors the spirit of love in all its forms. It's suitable for serving at a handfasting, reunion, or any gathering where you want to literally "share the love!"

1 pint red cherry tomatoes	3 stalks celery, chopped
1 pint orange cherry tomatoes	2 seedless cucumbers, sliced
1 pint yellow cherry tomatoes	1 cup Italian salad dressing
1 each red, yellow, orange, and green bell pepper, sliced	1 cup balsamic vinaigrette dressing
1 red onion, sliced	Blue cheese or feta, crumbled (optional garnish)
1 white onion, sliced	Bacon bits (optional garnish)

PREPARATIONS

Make this the night before the gathering so the components have time to soak up the mingling of energy. As you pour on the dressings and mix the salad, add an incantation like

> *Red for the heart of true love*
> *Yellow for friendship*

Orange for warmth
White for spirit and purity
By my will, this spell is freed!

I love food that's as easy to make as it is to serve. Just put all your ingredients in a large container with a secure lid. Shake the mixture periodically through the night so it stays well coated. If you wish, sprinkle the cheese and bacon bits on top just prior to serving.

Note: It's nice to serve with pita, or strips of marinated cooked chicken.

Makes 8–10 servings

Meet 'n' Greet Salad

In American history, the Puritans thought of fennel as a "meeting seed." Meeting seeds were the seeds of various herbs that parishioners chewed during church meetings to stay awake. And while staying awake isn't normally a problem at Circle, I think the symbolism is fun for gatherings where we often stay up way later than we would normally!

1 (¾-pound) fennel bulb
¼ cup fresh lemon juice
1½ tablespoons extra-virgin
   olive oil

Freshly ground black pepper
6–8 ounces tomato-basil feta
  (or to taste)

Preparations

What's your "waker-upper" when you're tired? For me it's good old coffee, so I use a handful of chocolate-covered espresso beans as part of a charm for alertness. If you'd like to make one for yourself, just put the beans in a bright-colored cloth (yellow is a good choice for conscious awareness) and tie it up with a string. Bless it by saying:

Let me be pleasant, for goodness' sake
Let me be alert, focused and awake!

When you need energy quickly, eat one bean, which you can later replenish. Always leave one bean in the bundle, however, to maintain the magic.

Trim away outer layer of fennel, reserving tender stalks and any feathery tops. Quarter the bulb lengthwise, and cut each quarter lengthwise into very thin slices. Cut reserved stalks crosswise into very thin slices. Rinse in cold water and chill for an hour.

Chop reserved fennel tops. Toss together the fennel slices, fennel tops, lemon juice, oil, and freshly ground black pepper to taste. Arrange on a platter and chill for 3 more hours before garnishing with the feta.

Makes 4 servings

FENNEL FACTS

- Greek mythology tells us that fennel was a gift from the gods that blessed us with knowledge.
- Romans believed that eating fennel helped keep a person slim.
- Medieval people used fennel to treat disease, bring good luck, and protect homes from wandering spirits.
- The Puritans agreed with the Romans and used fennel as an appetite suppressant.
- Fennel is an effective deterrent to fleas and flies.

May Day Chicken

This dish could also be used at Lammas celebrations or any other gathering during which the fairy-folk are thought to be active. Lore tells us that fairies love raspberries and often live inside of them for thousands of years!

1 tablespoon oil
4 sweet onions, cut into
    ¼-inch slices
¼ cup sugar
2 cup fresh or frozen
    raspberries
1 teaspoon orange zest
½ cup sugar

¼ cup water
1 teaspoon garlic powder
½ teaspoon chili powder
½ cup raspberry vinegar
4 boneless, skinless chicken
    breasts
2 tablespoons oil for grilling

Preparations

It's said that fairies are naturally attracted to fun-loving humans. So consider wearing playful clothing and putting on some really funky music while you make this dish. Put out some sweet cream or bread to welcome your devic guests.

 Place oil in a large pan over medium-high heat. Add onions. Cook until onions just begin to turn brown on the edges. Add sugar to onions and continue cooking, stirring frequently to prevent burning, until onions are fully caramelized.

Meanwhile in a separate pan put the berries, zest, sugar, water, spices, and vinegar. Heat to a simmer, and cook down until it thickens. Cool and puree. Add this to the onions and simmer for 30 minutes. Set aside.

Prepare your grill to a medium heat and spray the surface with nonstick spray. Grill the chicken about 2½ minutes on each side. After the first turn, put a layer of raspberry sauce on each side for the last 2½ minutes. Serve with additional sauce for dipping.

Makes 4 servings

Courage Kabobs

Medieval knights wore scarves embroidered with a bee hovering over a sprig of thyme as a symbol of courage. That makes this dish ideal for when you're feeling a little nervous about attending your first gathering or a new Circle where you're not overly familiar with the people or site.

2 pounds halibut fillets, cut
    into 1-inch cubes
Grated zest of one lemon
2 tablespoons fresh lemon
    juice
4 or 5 fresh thyme sprigs

1 teaspoon minced fresh
    thyme
½ teaspoon salt
½ teaspoon freshly ground
    black pepper
8 bamboo skewers, soaked in
    white wine for 30 minutes

PREPARATIONS

Since thyme is the key ingredient for the energy you're creating, focus on that component and energize it, saying:

> *Courage come quick, courage be mine*
> *Courage in this meal I bind!*

 Place the halibut in a bowl and add the lemon zest, lemon juice, thyme sprigs, minced thyme, salt, and pepper. Refrigerate for at least 2 hours turning regularly to marinate. Put the cubes

---

SWEET AS THYME

- Thyme has been used medicinally for about 5,000 years.
- Egyptians used thyme as part of the mummification process.
- Greeks considered thyme an aphrodisiac.
- Thyme is an excellent bee-attracting herb (which in turn makes a flavorful honey).
- English considered a bed of thyme to be a suitable home for fairies.

onto the skewers. Preheat the broiler and put the skewers about 5 inches from the heat. These will turn opaque after about 5 minutes per side.

Makes 4–6 servings

Life on the Road Carrots

Foil bundles for which this recipe calls are typically called hobo packs because they're easily portable, perfect for camping or carrying. The ginger-and-carrot blend inside provides you with good instincts so your path stays true.

6 large carrots, peeled and cut into 1-inch rounds
1 (2-inch) finger of fresh gingerroot, peeled and cut into matchsticks
6 scallions, white and green parts, thinly sliced

⅓ cup soy sauce
¼ cup olive oil
1 teaspoon brown sugar
Heavy-duty foil
Kosher salt and freshly ground pepper, to taste

PREPARATIONS

Carve the image of an eye into the carrots before slicing them, focusing on your goals.

Put all the ingredients into a large bowl, except salt and pepper and toss gently to combine. Tear off four sheets of heavy-duty foil, each about two feet long, arranging the vegetables in even proportions in the center of each. Season with salt and pepper, then fold the foil around the vegetables, making well-sealed packets. On site, place these packets to one side of hot coals for about 25 minutes until tender.

Makes 4 servings

Make It Count Beans

The term "bean counter" seems to have come about in very recent history as a synonym for someone who is very picky about details. It first appeared in a 1975 Forbes *magazine article that referred to accountants as "smart, tightfisted and austere bean counters." Now, while we don't need to be austere, I have always been of the opinion that our path need not be costly. Make this dish when you're on a tight gathering budget to help make ends meet.*

4 slices bacon, diced
½ cup chopped onion
1 tablespoon minced garlic
4½ cups cooked navy beans
1 tablespoon cider vinegar
2 tablespoons molasses
½ cup honey
½ cup ketchup

1 tablespoon prepared mustard
1 tablespoon Worcestershire sauce
1 teaspoon dry mustard
⅛ teaspoon cayenne pepper
¼ teaspoon salt

Preparations

You'll want to make yourself a charm that helps with frugality. One easy token for this is a penny (i.e., pinching pennies!). If you have one minted in the year of your birth, all the better. Bless it with a little rhyme, like:

A penny pinched, a penny found
In this coin and meal my magic's bound
A budget to keep when things are tight
Let my magic take to flight!

Sauté the bacon, onion, and garlic together. Drain off excess fat. Preheat oven to 350 degrees F. Combine bacon mixture with remaining ingredients and bake all in a 2-quart ovenproof dish for 30 minutes covered, and for another 45 minutes uncovered. Serve hot or cold.

Makes 4 ½-cup servings

Walk Toward the Light Cucumbers

In a Babylonian religion called Manicheanism, cucumbers were believed to contain a great deal of sacred light (goodness). The elect of this religion would eat cucumbers so that the gas produced would allow them to belch and share the light with other followers!

Large cucumbers (as many as you wish)

Per cucumber you need:

3 ounces cream cheese, softened

1 tablespoon blue cheese, crumbled

2 teaspoons fresh parsley, minced

1 teaspoon fresh dill, minced

1 teaspoon onion, grated

PREPARATIONS

In keeping with the light theme, wear yellow or golden clothing and work in a location where you're receiving plenty of sunlight or moon-light (cucumbers are traditionally associated with the moon).

Peel the cucumber and cut a 1-inch slice from each end. Slice in half. Remove the seeds and turn the cucumber over on paper towels to dry a bit. In the meantime combine the other ingredients and spread this mixture into the space left by the seed removal. Wrap with plastic wrap, chilling for 4 hours before serving in ½-inch slices.

Makes 2 servings per cucumber

Gypsy Squares

The key ingredient in this dish is the Loukanika, a spicy Greek sausage said to be loved by Gypsies or those with a Gypsy spirit (making this dish perfect for enjoying on the road!).

¾ pound Loukanika

2 medium eggs

½ cup flour

1 teaspoon baking powder

¾ teaspoon salt

3 cups reduced-fat mozzarella

1 ½ cups nonfat cottage
  cheese

PREPARATIONS

Infuse the sausage with extra energy using a verbal component, like:

> *Gypsy meat, Gypsy feet*
> *Infuse my magic into this treat!*

Brown sausage, and then drain it on a paper towel. Preheat oven to 350 degrees F. Beat eggs, flour, and baking powder in a large bowl. Fold in the remaining ingredients and turn into a 9 by 9 by 2-inch oiled pan. Bake for 40 minutes. Cool for 10 minutes before cutting into squares and wrapping for transport.

Makes 16 2-inch squares

Flexible Fruit Rollup

Drying fruit is one way of preserving the harvest, and also preserving the magical energy of the fruit. So, choose your fruit according to the energy you wish to create and carry with you to the gathering.

1 cup chopped fruit (berries
  work very well)

2 tablespoons honey

PREPARATIONS

The magical element in this dish is determined by the type of fruit you choose. However, one suggestion: A good time to add a verbal component is while the fruit is in the blender (whipping up your energy).

 Preheat the oven to about 140 degrees F. (no hotter). Lay a piece of plastic wrap on a cookie sheet to cover it. Put the fruit and honey in the blender, mixing until very smooth. If need be you can add a little water. Pour this onto the plastic wrap and spread it out evenly, using a spatula or the back of a spoon. This needs to heat slowly in the oven until dry (about 8 hours). Do not turn up the heat! Remove from the oven and cool completely, then roll this "fruit leather" in plastic wrap for transport.

Makes 1 large rollup

Godly Bananas

In Hawaii bananas were thought of as magical fruits due to their plentiful nature. The story of one wizard, Kukali, illustrates this. Kukali was traveling through the forests and up the mountains, carrying no food but for one special banana that his father had given him. When he grew hungry he carefully stripped back the skin, ate the banana, and then delicately folded the skin back together. In a little while the skin was filled again with fruit. So long as he never threw away the skin or lost it, he would never hunger. For our purposes banana is a good representation of the god aspect, and this particular treat is great for camping events.

1 banana per person, unpeeled	1 tablespoon brown sugar per banana
Semisweet chocolate chips	
Miniature marshmallows	Heavy-duty foil

PREPARATIONS

You need a good fire going for this dish, and fire is also a very strong masculine symbol, so it will naturally charge your fruit treats.

Slit each unpeeled banana lengthwise but not all the way (only one slit—just as in the story you need to be able to put the peel back around the banana). Carefully remove banana. Place 1 or 2 teaspoons each of the marshmallows and chocolate chips in the empty peel. Sprinkle the banana with the brown sugar and put back

---

BANANA-RAMA

- Banana is actually a berry grown on an herb.
- Banana trees are a relative of orchids and lilies.
- Alexander the Great discovered bananas on his conquest of India in 327 B.C.E.
- The first bananas in the New World came by way of a Spanish friar in the early 1500s.
- When missionaries arrived in Hawaii they discovered the Polynesian people there were raising about fifty varieties of bananas.
- Damp banana leaves make an excellent wrapping in which to grill various foods like fish.
- Pounded banana peels can be used to make poultices.
- On average a person in the United States eats thirty pounds of bananas annually.

---

into the peel carefully. Wrap with foil and put it over the coals (seam side up). Heat each packet about 7 minutes.

Corn Mother

Despite the shape of an ear of corn, it has long been associated with the mother aspect of the goddess because of the nurturing and nourishing nature of corn. It was so sacred that to waste corn meant poverty.

| 1 ear of corn per person | Salt, pepper, and garlic |
| Soft butter | to taste |

PREPARATIONS

Peel back the corn husks carefully, leaving them attached to the bottom of the corn. As you do think about those things that stand between you and the Mother goddess, and likewise peel those away in your mind's eye.

 Once the husks are pulled back, remove all the corn silk. Rub the soft butter onto the corn and sprinkle it with the salt, pepper, and garlic powder. Push the husks back up to surround the corn. Using a spray bottle, soak the outer husks with water. Wrap the ears with foil and put them on the coals of your campfire for about 15 to 20 minutes, turning regularly, until tender.

Bounty Bread

For many of my friends, making fry bread at gatherings (especially camping events) has become a well-beloved tradition where we come together, cook, and celebrate the bounty of our friendship. However, this is a good recipe for any type of providence working.

4 cups all-purpose flour	1 teaspoon allspice
2 tablespoons baking powder	1 ½ tablespoons melted butter
1 ¼ teaspoons salt	2 cups milk
1 teaspoon cinnamon	1 cup flour
1 teaspoon ginger	Oil for frying

PREPARATIONS

As you're presifting the ingredients it's a perfect time to bless and energize them. You could use an incantation, like:

> *Bountiful bread*
> *Let all be fed*
> *Bountiful bread*
> *Only loving words said*
> *Bountiful bread*
> *Let the magic be staid*

At home, sift together the dry ingredients and put them in an airtight container to take with you. At the campsite, place the presifted ingredients in a large bowl. Melt the butter, mixing it with the milk, and stirring both into the dry ingredients a little at a time. Beat until the dough becomes stiff.

Sprinkle the cup of plain flour on a surface and knead the dough until the flour is worked in. Separate the dough into whatever size breads you want, making the pieces no thicker than about ⅛-inch. Heat 3 to 4 tablespoons of oil in a large skillet. When the oil is hot, fry each bread until crisp and light brown on both sides. If you wish, sprinkle with powdered sugar or cinnamon sugar.

Makes 12–16 servings

Symmetry Slaw

One of the most important things to maintain at any gathering or festival is simple balance. With all the different energies and activities that surround, having your center sure helps keep you from getting off-kilter. The sweet-sour symmetry of this dish provides that balanced energy.

1 head green cabbage, shredded
½ small head red cabbage, shredded
1 green bell pepper, finely chopped
½ red bell pepper, finely chopped
1 bundle green onions, finely chopped
1 small red onion, finely chopped
½ large carrot, peeled and grated
1 cup mayonnaise
1 tablespoon prepared mustard
1 tablespoon sugar
2 tablespoons wine vinegar
1 teaspoon pepper
1 teaspoon dried cilantro
1 teaspoon basil
1 teaspoon parsley

Food Safety Tips

- Never reuse marinades that have been left at room temperature, and do not put cooked food into an unwashed container that contained marinade.
- If you cannot keep food properly chilled, when in doubt, throw it out!
- Use a separate cooler for drinks, so the one containing perishable food won't be constantly opened and closed.
- For safety, hamburgers and ribs should be cooked to an internal temperature of 160 degrees F. or until the juices run clear (not pink). Cook ground poultry to 165 degrees F. and poultry parts to 180 degrees F.
- Cleanliness is of utmost importance. Wash your hands and work areas with antibacterial soap if possible. Also make sure all your cooking utensils are clean.
- Discard foods left out for more than one hour.
- Reheat precooked meats until steaming hot.
- Pack foods in the cooler in the order opposite of when you'll be using them.
- Freeze the items that will be used later in your trip (again putting those toward the bottom of the cooler).
- Precook as many items as possible.
- Pack foods in well-sealed containers so they don't get soggy.

Preparations

Using your knife, carve a symbol that represents balance to you into the cabbage before shredding it (that way the energy of the symbol is evenly distributed as you cut!).

Combine the vegetables in one large bowl. In a separate container mix the remaining ingredients into the dressing. Toss the cabbage with the dressing so that it's evenly coated. Cover and refrigerate overnight, stir, and transfer to a suitable container for transport.

Makes 4–6 servings

Cleansing Ade

The ancients felt that one should not go into a sacred space without ritual purification, be it a bath, fasting, or some other rite. In keeping with that idea, we're creating a very refreshing, cleansing beverage that anyone at a gathering can enjoy. It's thirst quenching and helps cleanse your aura of any unwanted energies.

HELPFUL HINTS

- Use evaporated milk, as it lasts longer than regular milk. Mix it half with water and use it in anything requiring milk.
- Mix your meats with marinade and freeze them that way. As the meat defrosts it will naturally improve in flavor.
- To make cleanup easier, coat the outside of your cooking pots with bar soap before putting them on the fire.
- Pack your cooler tightly. The tighter you pack, the less the temperature of the contents will vary.
- Use a cooler to keep things hot too. Just line it completely with aluminum foil!
- Remember to bring along some foods that can be prepared without heating (in case of rain).
- If you're in a wilderness area, do not leave food scraps behind. They attract bears and other wildlife.

4-inch piece fresh gingerroot	Zest of 1 lemon
6 cups water	Zest of 1 lime
½ cup honey	½ cup fresh lemon juice
½ cup sugar	½ cup fresh lime juice

PREPARATIONS

In keeping with the theme of this beverage, spritz yourself with some spring water containing a drop each of lemon and lime juice. This helps remove impurities from your aura.

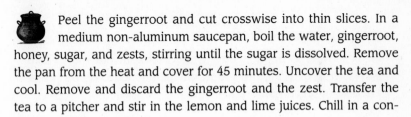 Peel the gingerroot and cut crosswise into thin slices. In a medium non-aluminum saucepan, boil the water, gingerroot, honey, sugar, and zests, stirring until the sugar is dissolved. Remove the pan from the heat and cover for 45 minutes. Uncover the tea and cool. Remove and discard the gingerroot and the zest. Transfer the tea to a pitcher and stir in the lemon and lime juices. Chill in a container suitable for travel.

Aqua Vitae

Numerous recipes have been given over the years for tonics that would promote life, health, and happiness. This punch comes by that energy because of its rich red color, which represents vivacity.

1 cup water	1 cup sparking water or ginger ale
1 cup sugar	
½ cup lime juice	1 lime, thinly sliced
½ cup lemon juice	1 lemon, thinly sliced
1½ cups orange juice	1 orange, thinly sliced
3½ cups red wine	1 cup maraschino cherries
2 ounces brandy	Fresh mint sprigs

PREPARATIONS

Health and vitality is often a matter of ongoing maintenance. With that in mind, make sure you get plenty of rest before that special event and before making this beverage. Also consider serving it in red cups to support the imagery.

 Bring water and sugar to a low-rolling boil until it forms a clear syrup (about 10 minutes). Meanwhile put the lime and lemon juices into a large portable container. Add the syrup and remaining ingredients. Chill before serving, garnishing with mint.

Makes 8 one-cup servings

THE VICTORIAN PICNIC

Picnics were so popular during the Victorian era that whole books were dedicated to proper picnic etiquette. Here's just a brief list of practices:

- Food for the guests was delivered ahead of the guests.
- Not more than two or three servants would come (as picnics were meant to be "casual").
- Gentlemen were to provide for the ladies first in everything.
- The site for the picnic was carefully chosen for its visual appeal.
- No ant hills allowed.
- Shade had to be available for the comfort of the ladies.
- Once eating began, gentlemen with musical abilities were encouraged to perform.
- Afterward all manner of games, including tag and croquet, were enjoyed by participants. Also simple but pleasant activities like collecting flowers might take place.
- No matter where a lady sat, a gentleman had to be invited to sit nearby.
- Before going home, all the picknickers were to enjoy tea together.

Appendix: Isn't It Divine?—Food Fit for Gods and Goddesses

Let's carve him as a dish fit for the gods

—William Shakespeare

For those readers who have chosen a kitchen god or goddess, or those who would like some creative ways to honor deity in their culinary adventures, this chapter should be really fun. While the power of our pantry patron or patroness certainly doesn't end at the kitchen threshold, it's nice from time to time to make something that reminds us of that being's importance in our lives. It's also nice to remember to thank him or her for blessings.

How exactly do you go about doing this? Well one easy way is to prepare a culturally accurate dish, especially if it's one with an ingredient that your deity favors. And failing that, how about preparing a dish that emulates all the attributes of your deity in its ingredients? Both methods are completely appropriate and functional, so go with what's practical and what works for you.

Now, I'm sure some readers are wondering what happens *after* the cooking's done. That will depend a lot on your perspective. Some people might leave the dish before a visage of the god or goddess for a set amount of time then return the remains to nature. This frugal witch isn't much for that idea especially since our ancestor priests and priestesses very often consumed a food offering after the ritualistic work was done. This was actually a way to commune with deity and accept those attributes into the human body of the participant. In modern vernacular doing this also honors the spark of the divine within *you*—THOU ART GOD/DESS! So, these recipes are written with your consumption in mind, but trust your instincts either way.

Finally, since there is no way I could provide recipes for every potential pantry protect/ress I have tried to provide a few diversified examples. You will likely find that many of the recipes could be applied in another suitable setting (in that an ingredient or two are often sacred to other beings too). Minimally all of them can be used solely for their metaphysical value. My hope is to give you functional examples from which to derive more ideas of your own when worshipping and thanking your personal deities.

Freyja's and Odin's Kitchen (Norse)

In Teutonic tradition, Freyja's name means "well-beloved," an indicator of what a valuable wife partner she was to Odin. Freyja protected marriages and fertility while her partner Odin presided over matters like skill, magical arts, and poetry, making for a very romantic pair! Thus the recipe I chose for them was equally romantic, as mead was a beverage often given to couples on their honeymoon.

Strawberries are among the sacred fruits of Freyja; they represent earth's bounty and inspire gentle love with their pink-red hue. The honey in the mead is perfect for inspiring the muse when you wish to speak to your beloved with sweet words.

MEAD

1 pound frozen strawberries in juice

1 (16-ounce) can frozen strawberry daiquiri juice concentrate

1 gallon water

1 quart heather honey (or orange blossom, which inspires devotion)

1 orange, sliced

1 orange-flavored tea bag

½ package champagne yeast

Preparations

Consider making this blend when the moon is in the waxing to full phase so the mead ages properly, and so your love "waxes" likewise full! Also while you're stirring and skimming the blend, chant:

> *Freyja, goddess of love so sweet*
> *Aid my quest—make love complete*
> *A kiss 'pon my lips warm, with gentle words*
> *Let this prayer and need be heard*

 Place all the ingredients except the yeast in a non-aluminum pan over medium heat. Allow the mixture to come to a low-rolling boil. As it does, some scum from the honey will rise to the top. Skim this off.

Let it boil for an hour, skimming as necessary; then let the mixture cool to lukewarm. Meanwhile, place the yeast in ¼ cup of warm (*not* hot) water and stir. Let this set until the heated mixture has cooled properly. Strain out the berries, teabag, and orange, then blend the yeast mixture into the strained liquid. Cover the pot with a heavy towel to work for 1 week (you'll know all is well if bubbles have formed on the surface within 24 hours).

Strain again, pouring the clearest liquid into bottles. Lightly cork and keep in a cool, dark room for 2 months. After this you can pour off the clearest liquid one last time, and bottle with tight-fitting corks. Allow the mead to age for a full year and a day before serving. Share this at weddings, anniversaries, engagements, or during romantic interludes for warm results. Especially effective if served from one common cup to symbolize unity of mind and heart.

Makes about one gallon

Amorous Aphrodite's and Adonis's Kitchen (Greece)

What a better duo for stirring up sexual prowess, passion, and fertility? Greek language implies that true passion embodies love in a broad sense—the overwhelming human need for companionship and a sense of belonging. This recipe therefore combines elements representing Aphrodite's playful and sensuous nature with elements representing the animal magnetism of Adonis. The result is some powerful fare for heating up your love life!

This recipe originates in Greco-Roman tradition, where it was considered simple fare. We derive the symbolic value of the dish from the red peppers that provide zest, and from the traditional regional symbolism for borage—namely courage, strength of character, and improved outlooks. In relationships, apply this energy when you're trying something new in the bedroom or when you're feeling ethically uncertain about a passionate situation.

3 cups water
1½ cups white rice
2 teaspoons dried borage
1 red pepper, cored, seeded, and sliced thin

½ green pepper, cored, seeded, and sliced thin
1 tablespoon olive oil

Preparations

As you move the ingredients around the pan while preparing this recipe, visualize a reddish pink light filling them and incant:

Adonis's strength and energy in every bite
Give me the Passion of Aphrodite!

Place the water, rice, and borage in a pot and bring it to a low-rolling boil. While this is warming, sauté the pepper slices gently in oil. When the rice is boiling, cover and simmer until cooked (about 20 minutes). Top the rice with the sautéed pepper and enjoy. By the way, if you'd like to add some happiness to the equation, decrease the borage by a teaspoon and replace it with one teaspoon of marjoram.

Makes 6 ½-cup servings

About Rice

In Japan, rice is more than just a staple. It is also a symbol of prosperity, health, and well-being. The traditional name *gohan* translates as "meal." Rice is the core of Chinese and Japanese cuisine, in which it is used in everything from main dishes to desserts.

In Bali, mythology tells us the Lord Vishnu caused the Earth to give birth to rice. Indra then taught humankind how to sow and reap it. Even in modern times rice continues to be treated respectfully and often is used in regional rituals.

In China the story is a little different. Animals gifted humans with rice. Apparently after the flood people returned to the land to find food scarce. When all appeared lost, a dog was seen running through a field, and on its tail hung a bunch of long yellow seeds. The people planted these seeds, which grew rice. It is considered the most important of the five sacred grains.

According to Shinto custom, the emperor of Japan is the living embodiment of Ninigo-no-mikoto, the god of fully mature rice. While this role is today perhaps only mythic, it is interesting to note the parallels in the importance of rice in the East and corn in the West.

Pantry Prosperity: Lakshmi's and Uma's Kitchen (India)

Abundance in all things, with a little luck as a side dish! Lakshmi embodies wealth in both temporal and spiritual things. Uma compliments this energy by bringing earth's bounty to our tables and our lives.

In India, chutney is a favorite food that mingles the earth's bounty together so it inspires our own. The sweetness in this recipe makes your prosperity likewise sweet once it arrives.

3 cups wine vinegar

½ tablespoon lemon peel, finely ground

½ tablespoon orange peel, finely ground

¼ cup diced candied ginger

1 fresh chili pepper, minced

1 garlic clove, chopped

1 teaspoon salt

1½ cups brown sugar

3 cups mixed fresh berries

⅕ cup almonds or other nuts, chopped

PREPARATIONS

Begin by lighting a candle to Lakshmi (gold is one good choice of colors). Also, burn some lotus or lily incense to honor her. This is an excellent time to say a prayer that indicates your needs. Leave the candle and incense burning while you prepare the recipe.

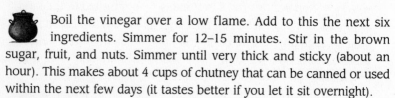 Boil the vinegar over a low flame. Add to this the next six ingredients. Simmer for 12–15 minutes. Stir in the brown sugar, fruit, and nuts. Simmer until very thick and sticky (about an hour). This makes about 4 cups of chutney that can be canned or used within the next few days (it tastes better if you let it sit overnight).

Makes 4 servings

Ceridwen and Dagda's Pantry Inspiration (Celtic)

Ceridwen is the Welsh mother goddess in whose care is the great cauldron of inspiration and knowledge. The Dagda presides over the arts, knowledge, magic, music, prophecy, prosperity, and regeneration. Known as the "Good God" and "Lord of the Heavens," he, too, has a cauldron, filled in this case with an inexhaustible supply of food.

This recipe celebrates these two because pork is among the foods of paradise in Celtic tradition (which gives a whole new meaning to "hamming it up"). When combined here with one of the preferred beverages of these people (ale), you're guaranteed to be filled with the muse for a dramatic opening or social occasion. Make a real entrance!

1 (2–3 pound) pre-cooked boneless ham	2 tablespoons butter
1 cup pineapple juice	2 apples, peeled, diced
1 cup maple syrup	5 cloves
	1 teaspoon cinnamon

Preparations

Put on some Celtic music and take out whatever ovenproof dish you plan to use for this recipe. Bless it, saying:

> Creativity's cooking in my pot
> Creativity flowing—that's what I've got!
> By Ceridwen and Dagda—my words refine
> Let my talents rise and shine!

Peheat oven to 350 degrees F. Place the ham in an ovenproof dish that can be covered. In a small saucepan, warm the pineapple juice, syrup, butter, apples, cloves, and cinnamon. Stir gently until the apples are slightly browned. Pour this mixture over the ham and roast for 1 hour, basting every 15 minutes. If you have a meat injector, inject some of the cooking liquid into the meat in order to saturate it with more of the magical energy you've created.

Makes 3–4 servings per pound

Hearthside Happiness:
Recipes from Kwan Yin and Uzume's Kitchen

Uzume is the Japanese goddess of laughter and merriment, while Kwan Yin is a protectress of the home and family. What greater combination to bring joy and peace into your home? In that spirit, this recipe for pot stickers is ideal. They're traditionally called dim sum, or heart's desire!

5 ounces ground pork

1 teaspoon soy sauce

½ teaspoon salt

2 garlic cloves, grated

1 teaspoon grated ginger

2 tablespoons chopped garlic chives

Pinch of sugar

Wonton wraps

4 tablespoons sesame oil for frying

Yoshida's Classic Sauce (or any Sweet Soy)

Stoneground mustard

PREPARATIONS

This dish is doubly symbolic if you make it on New Year's, which is when it's often eaten in the Far East. If you'd like to add other special foods to serve alongside the dim sum, consider egg rolls (for wealth and prosperity), fish (for abundance), duck (for fidelity), or chicken (for happy marriage).

 Mix together the first seven ingredients and let them sit in the refrigerator for at least an hour. Then lightly sauté these until the pork is cooked through. Drain of excess fat and cool.

Place a single wonton wrapper in your hand, and a spoonful of the pork mixture in the center. Dampen the edges and fold over to seal. Pleat the top two or three times. Repeat with each wrapper until you run out of filling.

Heat 1 tablespoon of the oil in a large skillet over medium heat. Place about 20 dumplings at a time in the pan. Cook until the bottoms are golden brown, then add a cup of warm water to the skillet. Cover and steam for about 8 minutes until the water evaporates completely and the wraps are translucent. Repeat with the remaining dumplings, refreshing the pan each time with oil. Serve hot with sauce and mustard for dipping.

Makes about 40 dumplings

Suggested Reading List

If you're interested in learning more about kitchen magic and the history and lore of all kinds of foods and beverages, the following books are a good place to begin:

Ainsworth-Davis, James Richard. *Cooking through the Centuries*. London: J.M. Dent and Sons, 1931.

Andrews, Tamra. *Nectar and Ambrosia*. Oxford, England: ABC-Clio, 2000.

Arnold, John P. *The Origin and History of Beer and Brewing*. Chicago: Wahl-Henius Institute of Fermentology, 1913.

Beyerl, Paul. *Herbal Magick*. Custer, Wash.: Phoenix Publishing, 1998.

Cunningham, Scott. *The Magic in Food*. St Paul, Minn.: Llewellyn Publications, 1991.

Davidson, Alan. *The Oxford Companion to Food*. New York: Oxford University Press, 1999.

De Cleene, Marcel, and, Marie Lejeune. *A Compendium of Symbolic and Ritual Plants in Europe*. Ghent, Belgium: Man and Culture Publications, 2004.

Gordon, Leslie. *Green Magic*. New York: Viking Press, 1977.

Hale, William. *Horizon Cookbook and Illustrated History of Eating and Drinking through the Ages*. New York: American Heritage Publications, 1968.

Hechtlinger, Adelaide. *The Seasonal Hearth*. New York: Overlook Press, 1986.

Hylton, William H., and Claire Kowalchik, eds.; *Rodale's Illustrated Encyclopedia of Herbs*. Emmaus, Penn.: Rodale Press, 1987.

McNicol, Mary. *Flower Cookery*. New York: Fleet Press, 1967.

Roberts, Annie Lise. *Cornucopia: The Lore of Fruits and Vegetables*. New York: Knickerbocker Press, 1998.

Tannahill, Reay. *Food in History*. New York: Three Rivers Press, 1973.

Telesco, Patricia. *The Herbal Arts*. Seacaucus, N.J.: Carol Publishing Group, 1998.

———. *A Kitchen Witch's Cookbook*. St. Paul, Minn.: Llewellyn Publications, 1992.

———. *A Witch's Beverages and Brews*. Franklin Lakes, N.J.: New Page Books, 2001.

Visser, Margaret. *Much Depends upon Dinner*. New York: Grove Press 1986.

———. *The Rituals of Dinner*. New York: Grove Weidenfeld, 1991.

Wolf, Burt. *Gatherings and Celebrations*. New York, NY: Doubleday Books, 1996.

Worwood, Valerie Ann. *The Fragrant Mind: Aromatherapy for Personality, Mind, Mood, and Emotion*. New World Library, 1996.

Index